THE
GENEVA
CONVENTION

THE HIDDEN ORIGINS
OF THE RED CROSS

ANGELA BENNETT

SUTTON PUBLISHING

Sutton Publishing Limited
Phoenix Mill · Thrupp · Stroud
Gloucestershire · GL5 2BU

First published 2005

British Library Cataloguing in Publication Data
A catalogue for this book is available from the British Library.

ISBN 0-7509-4147-2

Endpapers front: the first and last pages of the Geneva Convention of 22 August
1864. *(© Photothèque CICR); back*: Signing the Geneva Convention, 22 August
1864, in a painting by Armand Dumaresq. *(© Photothèque CICR (DR))*

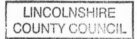
Typeset in 11/14.5pt Sabon
Typesetting and origination by
Sutton Publishing Limited.
Printed and bound in England by
J.H. Haynes & Co. Ltd, Sparkford.

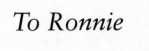

To Ronnie

. . . we have only one wish to express, namely that the literature of the Red Cross . . . be enriched by books intended for the public. Although the meaning of the Red Cross (*Geneva Convention*) may be universally known, its past and its organization do not enjoy the same privilege . . . except in critical times, its work makes too little noise to attract much attention.

. . . we know from experience that a narrative . . . not too long to frighten busy people – in other words, the majority – but written in such a manner as not to weary the reader, would meet a very general wish and would consequently supply a great need.

Gustave Moynier, *La Croix-Rouge, Son Passé et Son Avenir*

Contents

Acknowledgements

I would like to thank the following for their invaluable help and support: THE INTERNATIONAL COMMITTEE OF THE RED CROSS for kindly allowing me to reproduce the photographs featured in the plate section of this book; and particularly JOËLLE ALBRECHT-GLAISEN of the Picture Library; ANNE JUNOD of the University Library, Geneva, for locating the articles by Charles Dickens; M. MAURICE AUBERT, former Vice-President of the International Committee of the Red Cross; M. LAURENT MARTI, former Director of the International Red Cross and Red Crescent Museum in Geneva; SUSANNA SWANN, a Head of Operations at the International Committee of the Red Cross, for so kindly affording me so much of her time for a fascinating interview; M. JEAN-FRANÇOIS QUÉGUINER, Legal Adviser at the International Committee of the Red Cross; all the invariably helpful staff in the ICRC library; and finally BERTIE, my long-suffering rabbit, for his patient presence and observation during the gestation of this book.

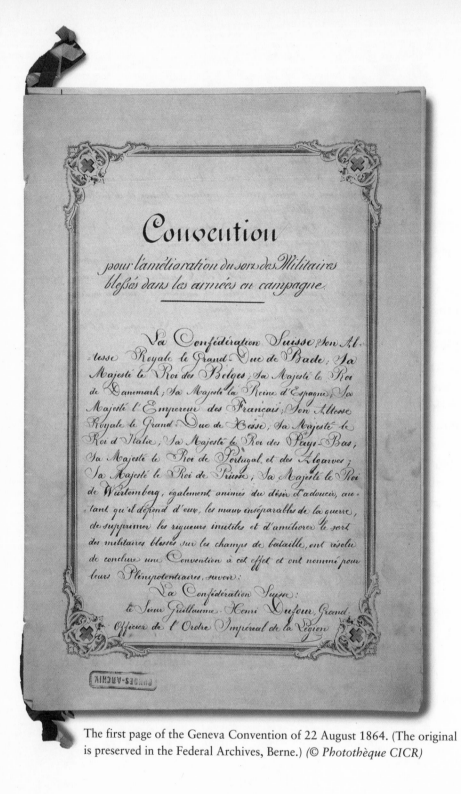

The first page of the Geneva Convention of 22 August 1864. (The original is preserved in the Federal Archives, Berne.) *(© Photothèque CICR)*

Introduction

Armed conflicts, civil and international wars, are the cruellest realities of modern life. The total numbers of dead, wounded and suffering are terrifying. Despite all efforts to replace war by peaceful settlements, there have been over one hundred and seventy armed combats in the past fifty years and in the past twenty years, most horrifying of all, 90 per cent of the victims have been civilians.

Obviously, prevention of armed conflict should be the first aim, particularly since modern weapons inflict increasingly violent and lethal injuries. International humanitarian law has as its objective the protection of civilians and those no longer able to protect themselves, in the name of the principles of humanity and the dignity of the human being.

In the beginning, there was no law for war and only one rule – survival of the strongest. '*Vae victis*', alas for the conquered. True, more than two thousand years ago, Philip II of Macedonia decreed that any prisoner taken in war who could recite Homer should be released, and the Crusades produced the Knights Hospitallers and clemency towards prisoners, exercised by the mighty Saladin. In the seventeenth century, on the other hand, Hugo Grotius, a Dutch theologian, inspired as he was by the Christian faith, didn't hesitate to write in his *De jure belli ac pacis* (Of the law of war and peace) that the massacre of women and children was included in the law of war! In all fairness to him, it should be added that he also said 'War should always be waged with a view to peace'.

It was not until the Age of Enlightenment that glimmerings of humanitarian law began to see the light of day, stating that war should be limited to the military and that civilians should be spared. Jean-Jacques Rousseau in *Le Contrat Social* of 1762 stated the basic principle on which the Geneva Conventions are founded: soldiers who lay down their arms cease to be enemies. They again become mere men, and one is no longer entitled to take their lives.

International humanitarian law can truly be said to have been born on the battlefield of Solferino during the Italian campaign of the Franco-Austrian War in 1859 when Henry Dunant was shocked to his core by the suffering of 40,000 wounded men, left to die without food, water, shelter or medical aid of any kind. His book *Un Souvenir de Solferino* appealed for the setting up of voluntary relief societies in each country in peacetime and the ratification of an international and sacrosanct treaty ensuring legal protection for medical personnel.

On 22 August 1864, the first Geneva Convention was signed in Geneva by representatives of twelve states. It was the first instrument of international humanitarian law and eventually led to the creation of the Red Cross as we know it today.

Some people may be surprised to learn that although the original Convention was signed in 1864, today's Geneva Convention actually consists of four conventions drafted on 12 August 1949 and their additional protocols of 8 June 1977. Some three hundred pages in all. At the end of this book, you will find a chronology and summary of the Conventions in what, I hope, is a reasonably digestible form.

Here's how the International Committee of the Red Cross sums it all up:

> In time of war, certain humanitarian rules must be observed, even with regard to the enemy . . . The Geneva Conventions are founded on the idea of respect for the individual and his dignity. Persons not directly taking part in hostilities and those put out of action through sickness, injury, captivity or any other cause must be respected and protected against the effects of war; those who suffer must be aided and cared for without discrimination. . . .

And here's how it works in practice in today's increasingly dangerous world:

In November last year, White House Counsel Alberto Gonzales was nominated new Attorney General, replacing John Ashcroft. A religious Texan, Gonzales urged Bush to ignore the Geneva Conventions when setting up the concentration camp in Guantanamo Bay in Cuba, where the US administration says that they don't apply. In a memo, Gonzales allegedly denigrated certain legal protections enshrined in the Geneva Convention for people captured during military hostilities. 'The Geneva Convention? It's quaint,' he has said on various occasions. 'Quaint', an adjective that conjures up pictures of cuddly grannies in knitted shawls. Nothing very cuddly about Mr Gonzales. He also said that the Geneva Convention was not applicable post Twin Towers.

The American administration of George Bush is obviously an easy target when it comes to discussing non-observance of the Geneva Convention. But it's by no means alone. Israel. Iraq. Sudan. North Korea. The list is, dismally, almost endless. Why is all this heedless violence escalating at such a crazy, sickening pace? The answer to that would fill endless tomes, if there is time for them to be written before the entire world is reduced to rubble.

Who would have thought that the world's first treaty on human rights, which pioneered international law, could have been founded by two young men, diametric opposites who cordially loathed each other, yet were outstandingly complementary?

Henry Dunant, a young businessman, was so horrified by the appalling conditions of the wounded on a battlefield he visited quite by mistake that he wrote a book about it. Reading this, Gustave Moynier, a self-effacing lawyer in Geneva, was so impressed that he decided to help him do something about it.

These two young men drew up a code of practice for the treatment of war wounded in battle. But it was necessary to enlist the support of the influential rulers all over the 'civilised' world to make this a practical reality. Dunant's epic crusade across Europe resulted in impressive attendance at the first international conference where, despite sometimes tumultuous debate, the Convention was approved. In 1864. Just over a hundred and forty years ago.

But hardly was the ink dry on the Convention than Dunant was accused and convicted of defrauding a bank and forced to flee the country. Evidence shows that he was in fact framed by his 'respectable' colleagues to protect their reputations. Even today, the powers that be in Geneva are reluctant to discuss the subject. Hounded by his creditors, he was condemned to live out the rest of his life in poverty-stricken exile until at last, rehabilitated in old age, he was awarded the first Nobel Prize!

Few people know what the Geneva Convention really stands for, and fewer still that it gave birth to the Red Cross, of which it is an integral part. This book brings to light the genius of Moynier, almost completely forgotten today, and gives a clear insight into the philosophy and workings of the Geneva Convention and the Red Cross, that extraordinary movement which for more than a century has successfully ignored all accepted rules of organisational structure.

But now welcome to the nineteenth century. The elegant salons, the suffering and horror of the battlefield, the frustrations and tortuous complications which nearly destroyed the Geneva Convention and the Red Cross in their early years. This is no boring history lesson. This is the story of something acutely, devastatingly topical, the story of the Geneva Convention.

ONE

Henry Dunant is Shocked

In a tranquil and thyme-scented setting a few miles south of lovely Lake Garda, on a hot June morning in 1859, the golden Italian dawn came up on a scene of idyllic innocence. Butterflies and bees hovered thoughtfully over clouds of gently undulating harebells before plunging into honeyed depths. Skylarks sung as they soared in the still air and a cuckoo called from the woods nearby. A rabbit washing its ears beside a bramble bush hesitated, paws poised in surprise, ears erect.

It was so faint it could have been pure imagination. But wait – there it was again. So distant as to be almost imperceptible to human senses. But the rabbit thumped, thumped again, turned tail and ran swiftly for cover.

Now the sound confirmed its presence. Far away, too far for anything to be visible to the naked eye, there was a faint but un-mistakable beat, more like a vibration transmitting itself through the ground. Now it grew stronger and, straining the eyes, a long, dark moving mass could just be seen outlined against the horizon. Nearer and nearer it came. Gradually the mass resolved itself into hundreds of thousands of men. As they drew closer, they became recognisable as French dragoons, mounted musketeers on sleek chestnut chargers, followed at a brisk trot by lancers and hussars. Beside them, the Guards and cuirassiers in their gleaming armour flowed forward like a broad, glistening river across the Lombardy plain. Slightly further back and to their left, the Sardinians advanced under the command of King Victor Emmanuel.

They had been seen by their enemy too. In the Austrian camp, the alarm rang out. The long line of low hills suddenly came alive with

1

regiments of what, from a distance, looked like toy soldiers taking up position, moving gun carriages into place, loading cannon, busying for battle. Now, on all sides bugles sounded the charge and drums rolled ominously.

Coming up from the east to meet the Franco-Sardinian army, as if for a joyous midsummer's day parade, highlighted by the rising sun, the Austrian infantry advanced, their black and yellow battle flags emblazoned with the imperial eagle fluttering above the massed ranks of white-coats. They had been torn from their sleep after only two hours and breakfasted on nothing more substantial than double rations of schnapps.

By six in the morning, these two great armies had clashed and the battle was fully joined. Along a front extending 15 miles between the Mincio and Chiese rivers, 400,000 men started killing each other in an orgy of almost unimaginable savagery.

The freedom of Italy was at stake in this war being waged against Emperor Franz Josef of Austria. To this end, the Prime Minister of Sardinia-Piedmont enlisted the aid of Napoleon III and, throughout May and June 1859, the French and Sardinian armies won a series of brilliant victories, marched triumphantly into Milan and pursued the Austrians ever further east. The next crucial stage in the campaign was to capture the key site of Solferino.

Neither side had accurate information of their enemies' positions. Unknown to the French, the Austrians had doubled back and recrossed the River Mincio and were therefore much nearer, and more numerous, than their adversaries imagined, having reinforced their armies with troops from their garrisons in Verona and Mantua. The Austrians themselves believed that only a small part of the Franco-Sardinian armies were in the immediate vicinity and were rudely awakened by their large-scale attack at dawn.

Although lacking the military genius of his illustrious uncle, Napoleon III had nevertheless wisely realised that the next day would be one of stifling heat and so decided to attack early. Putting on his socks at five on the morning of 24 June, he was surprised to hear cannon fire and to be told that the Austrians had already occupied Solferino. Hastily, the Emperor rejoined the imperial

2

Guard, accompanied by his faithful but totally incompetent chief-of-staff, the seventy-year-old Marshal Vaillant.

Heavy artillery fire from the Austrians, entrenched among the cypress trees on the commanding heights of Solferino and Cavriana, mowed down wave after wave of the hot-blooded French infantry, who flung themselves up the rocky slopes under a steady stream of shells and grapeshot that thundered into the ground, raising dense clouds of soil and dust that mingled with the fumes of belching guns.

The raging battle grew ever more furious in the blistering heat of the noonday sun. French regiments fell upon the Austrians who advanced without a pause in mass formation, as menacing and impregnable as iron walls. Whole divisions threw aside their knapsacks and leapt at the enemy with fixed bayonets. Each foot of ground, each mound, each rocky promontory was the scene of frenzied fighting. The bodies of men and horses lay heaped at the foot of the hills and in the valleys.

Swearing by Allah to avenge their fallen colonel, the Algerians dipped their hands in the blood of the dead and smeared their faces before rushing into the enemy ranks with bestial roars and hideous shrieks, killing all in their path without quarter or mercy. The horrified Austrian captain, scarcely able to believe what he was witnessing, yelled 'The law of nations! This is no way to fight.' But he yelled in vain.

In hand-to-hand fighting, Austrians and French trampled on each other, slaughtering their adversaries over piles of bleeding corpses, smashing in skulls, disembowelling with sabre and bayonet. When muskets were broken and ammunition exhausted, the men fought with fists or stones, or seized their enemies by the throat and tore at them with their teeth.

The carnage was made all the more hideous by squadrons of cavalry galloping past, crushing the dead and dying beneath their hooves. Following the cavalry came the artillery at full speed, its guns crashing over the corpses, breaking and mutilating limbs beyond all recognition. Blood spurted out under the wheels, the earth was soaked with gore and the field littered with human remains.

Eventually, the French reached the hills and their artillery fire, its range far superior to that of the Austrians, spattered the ground with dead and wounded over whom went the cavalry of the final assault. Horses, maddened by the excitement of battle, sprang at the enemy horses, gnashing and biting, while their riders hacked each other down with sabres. In the fury of the onslaught, the Croats, ignoring their officers' attempts to restrain such savagery, massacred every man in sight, killing off the wounded with the butts of their rifles.

The Austrians gave ground but rallied again and again, only to be scattered once more, gradually being forced to abandon, one by one, the positions they had so staunchly defended. The French infantry swarmed up the slopes of Solferino where the Austrians were entrenched in the chateau and a cemetery surrounded by thick walls. Another French division advancing on the heights seized the cemetery and dashed into the village, the infantrymen and riflemen of the Imperial Guard carrying the chateau by storm. On the summit of the hill, the French colonel hoisted his handkerchief on the point of his sword to signal victory.

At about four in the afternoon, after thirteen hours' fighting, the Austrian commander gave the order to retreat, although in some places the battle went on until late into the night. Some of the Austrian officers killed themselves rather than survive this fatal defeat while their broken-hearted Emperor, Franz Josef, wept in despair as he flung himself into the path of his fleeing men, only finally consenting to retreat to Valeggio on the east bank of the Mincio.

At about five, a violent storm broke out. The sky grew black, a tempest-force wind sprung up, raising whirlwinds of blinding dust, breaking branches off the trees and hurling them about the battlefield. Thunder rumbled round the nearby mountains and icy rain and hailstones drenched and bombarded the fleeing Austrians. The battlefield was shrouded in darkness, effectively bringing all fighting to a halt.

In the meantime, Marshal Vaillant seemed totally oblivious to the battle or the cries of the wounded writhing in agony all around him, having been busily engaged in alternately consulting his watch and observing the gathering storm clouds. At the first clap of thunder, he calmly proceeded to compose a meteorological report which he later sent to the Académie des Sciences in Paris where it was acclaimed and awarded a prize for its outstanding accuracy and interest.

As the rain ceased and the sun reappeared at around six that evening, it revealed a scene of utter desolation. In the order of 6,000 dead and 42,000 wounded lay all around, in some places heaped pell-mell together. Their piteous cries for help arose on every side. There was scarcely any water for them, or the horses. As for food, whole battalions had been without rations all day and the knapsacks they had laid aside in the heat of the fighting had been plundered by the 'hyenas of the battlefield'. Exhausted soldiers and officers were reduced to drinking at muddy pools of water red with blood. Then, as the daylight faded, overcome with hunger and fatigue, they flung themselves down among the carnage and tried to sleep. As darkness fell, furtive figures stole among the dead and wounded, many of whom were found lying absolutely naked the following day.

After one of the bloodiest battles of the nineteenth century, over 40,000 wounded men lay dying in agony under a blazing sun in stifling heat with no water, food, medical attention, shelter, help or comfort of any kind. But out of this terrible tragedy, this appalling suffering and seemingly pointless carnage, emerged two events of immense importance. First, Lombardy was won back from long years of Austrian oppression, the initial step towards achieving a free, united Italy. And, second, a certain Swiss gentleman by the name of Henry Dunant was horrified. The first changed the path of a nation. The second changed the conduct of war throughout the world and led to the creation of a movement that is known and actively supported as no other movement, political belief or religion has ever been supported before or since. The Red Cross.

For that same evening, unknown to the generals and statesmen of the day, or indeed to anyone who fought in that terrible battle, a coach rattled into the little town of Castiglione driven at breakneck speed. The passenger who alighted was dressed elegantly, if somewhat incongruously for the surroundings, in impeccably tailored tropical white. Outside his native Geneva, his name was then virtually unknown. Although his work has since saved the lives of millions and mitigated the suffering of countless billions of others, it is still known by surprisingly few to this day.

High of forehead and determined of chin, with limpid brown eyes and drooping moustaches married to luxuriant dark reddish sideburns, Henry Dunant was at this time thirty-one years old. Born on 8 May 1828 in a wide and handsome house in the best part of Geneva, he was the eldest of five children in a family that was both pious and patrician. His father, a descendant of Archbishop Jean XI de Nant and a member of the State Council, was a successful and highly respected businessman who also engaged in voluntary work for the welfare of minors and prisoners. His mother, a Colladon – one of Geneva's proud families – was the daughter of the director of Geneva Hospital, a highly intelligent and charitable lady, much taken up with 'her poor'.

Like his mother, the young Henry was sensitive, imaginative and warm-hearted, almost excessively so. He burst into floods of tears when she told him the fable of the wolf eating the lamb while, on a family expedition to Marseilles, the sight of a gang of convicts shackled together gave him nightmares for months.

Growing up in a world of pious wealth, a Geneva that was undergoing a 'revival' of its Calvinist beliefs following the preaching of the Scot Robert Haldane, Dunant early developed religious convictions and high moral principles. From the age of eighteen, all his spare time was devoted to visiting the sick and needy and lending his ardour to various charitable causes. He was the leading figure in the development of the Young Men's Christian Association of Geneva and it was largely due to his extraordinary drive and energy that the movement rapidly extended and the World Alliance of YMCAs was formed as early as 1855.

Such devotion to good works at that age was exceptional even in those days, even in pious Geneva. One of Dunant's co-workers,

Max Perrot, later recalled taking part in spirited discussions of theological matters and being amazed at his companion's zeal and apostolic fire. Not everyone was so favourably impressed, however. Louise Dubois, for instance, that provocative, dark-haired friend of his sister's who laughingly taunted him for being such a goody-goody.

Louise Dubois . . . the very mention of her name brought Dunant out in a cold sweat at the memory of that awful afternoon. He and his parents had been lunching at the Dubois residence one Sunday and he was just leaving for his weekly Bible-reading visit to the prison when Louise unexpectedly intercepted him in the hall and drew him into a small salon on the pretext of asking him some urgent advice.

With the door safely closed behind them, Louise wasted little time or subtlety in revealing her intentions to the naively innocent but handsome young man who seemed so tantalisingly immune to her charms. Pushing him playfully down on to a low settee, she purposefully set about seducing him. Dunant had never even been alone in the same room with a girl before in his life, and this sudden and blatantly explicit introduction to sexuality terrified him out of his wits. Violently pushing the astonished girl away from him and stumbling to his feet, he rushed scarlet-faced from the room and somehow found his way out of the house. For hours he wandered through the streets in a daze of shocked disbelief, her parting words flung after him going round and round in his horrified mind, 'You and your lofty ideals . . . they're just a cover-up . . . You're not a real man at all.'

His mother, in whom he later confided the nightmare events of the afternoon, did her best to comfort and reassure her shaken son, but the trauma lingered on, fed by real or imagined whisperings and the venomed insinuations of the furious Louise who had never before suffered such a humiliating rebuff and determined to take her revenge. It was probably an enormous relief to Dunant when the bank to which he was apprenticed temporarily appointed him general manager of its Algerian subsidiary and he could escape from the city that had been the scene of his shame.

The warmth and glamour of Algeria dazzled Dunant and he promptly succumbed to colonial fever. An unfortunate encounter with an unscrupulous local who vaunted the fabulous profits to be made there led to his acquiring a concession of 19 acres at Mons-Djemila, and forming a company to exploit it. Obviously he would not get very far with 19 acres so he applied to the colonial authorities for a further 1,100 acres, in the meantime raising enough capital to build a first corn mill and obtaining authorisation to use a waterfall to turn it. But the profits were slow in coming, as were the desired concessions. His 'partner' suggested buying livestock to make up the shortfall. When that scheme failed, money was borrowed to invest in copper-bearing mines, then forests . . . One fiasco followed another and soon Dunant was up to his ears in debt while his distinguished shareholders back in Geneva calmly and confidently awaited their promised 10 per cent return on their investment.

Dunant was an eternal optimist. If only he had the concessions he needed, he was convinced the situation could be reversed to brilliant success. But repeated applications to ministers in Paris and the Governor-General in Algeria mysteriously but systematically came up against a brick wall. He now introduced a new piece on to the board.

From his earliest years, when he attended Sunday school and listened spellbound to Pastor Gaussen's colourful explanations of Daniel's interpretations of the dreams of Nebuchadnezzar, Dunant had developed an obsession with Napoleon Bonaparte. For it was Gaussen's unshakable belief that Napoleon III was predestined to become head of a restored Holy Roman Empire. All through his youth, Dunant followed Napoleon's exciting exploits with passionate interest. Now, it seemed, the Emperor might hold the key to his present predicament. Some time ago, he had written an unashamedly flattering treatise entitled 'The Reconstitution of the Holy Roman Empire by His Majesty the Emperor Napoleon III', substantiating his theory with obscure historical arguments and his own analysis of the prophet's interpretation, he now set about having this lavishly printed and adorned with the imperial arms.

Napoleon III was known to be susceptible to such blandishments and, who knows, such an offering might spark his generosity.

Undeterred by the fact that Napoleon was currently engaged in a major war, Dunant packed his bags and left for Italy, little imagining the delays, discomforts and traumas that lay ahead. After crossing the Alps, he had great difficulty finding out where the Allied armies actually were. Arriving in Pontremoli, he was directed to Brescia. Seized with impatience, he spent the whole night in his diligence, bumping over the countryside devastated by the retreating Austrian army, crossing rivers with water sloshing in through the carriage windows. Eventually he reached Brescia, only to be told the Emperor had already left. The town was full of troops and normal activities were at a standstill. But luck was on his side. Finding a cabriolet and a driver who thankfully knew his way, he arrived at last in Castiglione.

On 25 June, Dunant awoke to a nightmare landscape. On the plain below Castiglione, corpses of men and horses were thickly strewn as far as the eye could see – over the battlefield, the road, the ditches, the fields. Crops were flattened and devastated, vines and orchards ruined, villages deserted, walls broken down, houses shattered and riddled with holes. The few inhabitants who had crouched terrified in the darkness of their cellars without food for nearly twenty hours were beginning to creep out and survey the horror of the scene. The approaches to Solferino were choked with the dead and wounded and all around the village the ground was littered with broken helmets, weapons, spent cartridges and blood-stained remnants of clothing.

Dunant was gripped with horrified fascination. Picking his way through the piles of bloody debris, he could hear faint cries from those still living and saw abject misery and unspeakable suffering at every step. Some of the wounded being picked up were in the last stages of exhaustion with haggard, vacant and uncomprehending eyes. Others had fits of shaking while still others whose gaping wounds had already turned septic, with chips of bone or earth or scraps of clothing aggravating their frightful injuries, writhed in agony and pleaded for release. In some cases, the dead and even the

9

wounded had been plundered by marauders. Desperate for boots, the Lombardy peasants had wrenched them from the swollen feet of corpses. Dunant noticed that some of the dead wore peaceful expressions: those that had been killed outright. But most of the faces he saw were contorted in agony with staring eyes, paralytic grins baring clenched teeth, hands clawing the earth.

It took three days and nights to bury the dead in shallow, mass graves. As for the wounded, there were large hospitals in Brescia, Bergamo and Milan that could easily have accommodated them, but there was scarcely any transport to take them there. So they were crowded into the nearest town or village where every house, church, square and street had been turned into a temporary hospital. Because it was the nearest, the greatest number were taken to Castiglione where Dunant saw them arrive, some in army wagons, others on mules going at a trot, causing the wounded they carried to cry out in excruciating pain. Altogether, over nine thousand wounded men – mainly French and some Austrians – were brought in to Castiglione between 25 and 30 June, some of them having waited six days without any water, food, shade or help of any kind before they were picked up where they had fallen. For a town of 5,000 inhabitants such an influx caused indescribable congestion. The wounded lay everywhere, in the streets, squares and courtyards, sheltered from the sun by improvised awnings of sail cloth. Thick clouds of black flies settled on the town and the stench of putre-faction was all-pervasive. Some of the men were suffering from tetanus, others undergoing torture from over-tight bandages that had not been changed since the field dressing. Wounds were covered with flies and the wretched sufferers haunted by the fear of being devoured by worms. Dunant moved between the packed lines, moistening parched lips, loosening bandages, bathing wounds, washing faces, giving whatever help and comfort he could.

The French army medical services were quite inadequate to respond to this enormous flood of suffering. There were pathetically few doctors: ten to start with, four of whom were called away to duty in Cavriana the next day, and the small number of nurses constantly dwindled as they stayed behind to look after their wounded while the army moved on. Doctors and nurses achieved miracles, working throughout the night, but supplies and equipment were also in lamentably short supply. The Emperor, on hearing of the shortage of dressings, immediately ordered all his personal linen, sheets and tablecloths to be cut up for use as bandages.

In one of the churches in Castiglione, the Chiesa Maggiore, Dunant found almost five hundred soldiers lying on the floor, while another hundred lay outside on straw with strips of canvas for shade, all of them apparently forgotten. He decided this should be his special responsibility, his centre of operations. Busily he set to work, gathering together a number of women to help in looking after the wounded.

Many of his helpers were beautiful young girls, whose tender ministrations enormously improved the patients' morale. They went down the lines of men, giving them fresh water to drink and washing their wounds while the local boys ran to and fro between the church and nearby fountains filling buckets and canteens. Soup and beef tea were provided by the quartermaster's services but all other provisions and necessities were almost totally lacking. Dunant sent his driver into Brescia on a shopping expedition and he came back laden with camomile, oranges and lemons, shirts, sponges, bandages, cigars and tobacco. An ex-naval officer and several English tourists were recruited to help as well as an Italian priest, a journalist from Paris and a few officers who had been ordered to stand by in Castiglione. Some of these helpers soon left, however, overwhelmed by the sheer horror and the stench. A Neuchâtel businessman (who later turned out to be Philippe Suchard, the chocolate manufacturer) spent two days dressing wounds and writing letters to their families for dying men while a Belgian became so over-excited while he worked that he had to be restrained for fear that he might develop a high fever.

Some of the wounded would cry out 'Don't let me die!' and seize Dunant's hand with extraordinary vigour in a last access of strength before dying. An old sergeant remarked bitterly, 'If I had received attention sooner I would have survived, but now I shall be dead by nightfall.' And that very evening he died. Dunant came upon an African infantryman lying motionless near the altar. He had had nothing to eat for three days and a bullet was still lodged in his body. After they had washed his wounds and given him a little soup, he took Dunant's hand and carried it to his lips in mute and inexpressible gratitude. Another poor wretch had had nose, lips and chin sliced off by a sabre. Unable to speak, he lay uttering guttural sounds and making heart-rending signs with his hands. Another, with his skull gaping open, was dying, his brains seeping out onto the floor. His companions kicked him out of their way but Dunant managed to shelter him for his last few moments. Overcome by horror and compassion at what he saw, he went tirelessly from one to the other, his craving to help creating a feverish energy.

The Austrians, he found, were deeply suspicious of their conquerors, some refusing medical attention and tearing off their bandages. A Croat serving with the Austrian forces even snatched the bullet which had just been removed from his wound and flung it in the surgeon's face. The Austrians might well have been apprehensive of the Milanese who loathed them, but Dunant made no distinction between ally and enemy wounded. 'Tutti fratelli' (we are all brothers) he would say and, with great difficulty at first, made his faithful helpers at Castiglione follow his example. One Austrian prisoner, only nineteen years old and shaking with fever, was noticed by all. His hair had turned white on the battlefield, a fact confirmed by his comrades.

Dunant was touched by the uncomplaining resignation and calm acceptance of the men as they lay quietly under their blankets after their wounds had been washed and they had been given soup. Wherever he went, they followed him with their eyes, all heads turning to the right if he went right, all swivelling left when he went left. And all of them wanted to claim him as coming from their own region. 'Ah,' said some, 'he's obviously Parisian.' 'No,' said others, 'he looks to me more like a Southerner.' 'Surely you're from Bordeaux, aren't you, Sir?' enquired a third.

Worn out but unable to sleep, Dunant felt the need to get away from the horror and gloomy scenes surrounding him at Castiglione.

On the evening of the 27th, he called for his carriage and, with the same driver who had brought him there, set off to find Marshal MacMahon whom he had met in Algeria, with a view to seeking an audience with the Emperor. On the way, he was told that MacMahon was stationed at Borghetto, quite close to the Austrian army, but this news threw his wretched driver – who had fled Mantua to avoid serving with the Austrians – into such a panic that he could scarcely hold the reins and almost tumbled off his seat at the sight of a large, open umbrella riddled with gunshots stuck at the side of the road.

At Borghetto, Dunant was warmly received by MacMahon and took the opportunity of requesting that the Austrian doctors captured by the French should be allowed to practise, at least to look after their own wounded. It seemed both intolerable and absurd to keep such men inactive, together with other prisoners of war, when there was such a desperate shortage of medical staff. MacMahon promised to see this was done and also gave Dunant a pass for the Emperor's headquarters in Cavriana. Proceeding there, Dunant failed to get an audience with Napoleon but at least delivered his volume on the Roman Empire to his personal secretary.

Back on duty in Castiglione the next day, Dunant was touched to see how the wounded in the Chiesa Maggiore who had not yet been moved were clearly overjoyed at the return of their 'man in white'. Once again, he found himself in the midst of the nightmare world of screams and suffering, pools of blood on makeshift operating tables where terrible amputations were performed without anaesthetics by harassed surgeons, sometimes on the enemy wounded who were unable to understand or communicate in a language not their own. At least he could help here by acting as an interpreter and persuading the voluntary helpers to make no distinction between friend and foe. 'Tutti fratelli', he would repeat time and time again and gradually others echoed it.

Perhaps it was the renewed impact of the terrible suffering he witnessed and his despairing awareness of the scarcity of human and material resources to alleviate it that prompted Dunant to send an impassioned appeal to the *comtesse* de Gasparin in Geneva who had

13

organised the despatch of tobacco to the fighting men in the Crimea. 'Every fifteen minutes for the last three days,' he wrote, 'I have seen a human being die in unimaginable agonies. A glass of water, a cigar, a friendly smile – and they become changed natures and calmly and peacefully await their hour of death.' The *comtesse* lost no time in having extracts from this letter published in the *Journal de Genève* and *L'Illustration* in France and the people of Geneva instantly responded.

Tired and dispirited, Dunant began to think of making tracks for home. On his way, he spent three days visiting the hospitals in Brescia where he found the doctors, medical students and entire population unstinting in their efforts to help the wounded. But here again, the health services were sadly inadequate to cope with the situation. Busily, he set about organising voluntary aid committees and collections of bedding, clothing and provisions, as well as distributing tobacco, pipes and cigars in the churches and hospitals.

In Milan too, the wounded were being cared for with the greatest devotion by society ladies in their own magnificent houses, who would spend months like guardian angels beside the beds of the sick. As he watched them nursing the wounded so kindly and efficiently, the thought occurred to him that such service should always be kept ready. Then he reflected that these were the lucky ones, the less seriously wounded, and he remembered how, in the overcrowded hospitals with their shortage of nurses, medicines and dressings, the hopeless cases were simply left to die untended, without food or medical assistance, all available resources being reserved for those thought to have some chance of recovery.

Exhausted and sickened by the traumatic experiences of the past few days, Dunant headed for home. Although they had been pushed to the furthest recesses of his mind by the recent horrors, his Algerian business worries could no longer be ignored or postponed. He was cast into even deeper despondency by a note he received from the Emperor's private secretary, thanking him for his volume on the Roman Empire but declining the dedication and requesting him to suspend publication. As he wearily recrossed the Alps, it seemed to Dunant that his Italian mission had been entirely in vain.

TWO

Enter Gustave Moynier and Friends

Gustave Moynier was not easily excited. In fact he could not remember having ever been roused to any appreciable level of enthusiasm about anyone or anything in his life. His equilibrium was rarely ruffled. But as he sat at his desk that November morning with the mist blanketing the lake outside his window, he had to admit that he was deeply moved by the book he had just laid down. It was an account of the battle of Solferino and its aftermath by a man as yet unknown to him in all but name. And not only was he moved but he was also experiencing something very akin to excitement at the realisation that the appeal it contained seemed to be addressed personally to him. Here was exactly the kind of challenge he had been looking for to satisfy his thirst for bolder projects and wider horizons than his present relatively small-scale and somewhat parochial activities offered.

Anyone meeting Moynier for the first time would have been struck by his singularly stern expression and sober appearance, his hypnotic and unblinking gaze. Thin of lip and nose, his moustache drawn straight across his face like a bolt, everything about him seemed rigid and unbending. Although only in his mid-thirties, he had more the air of an uncompromising High Court judge than the philanthropist and organiser of local charities which in fact he was. Perhaps in some ways he was the product of the Geneva of his day.

Geneva in the middle of the nineteenth century was very different and yet in many ways much the same as it is today. The cruel 'bise' regularly blasted its icy way through the Grand Rue and paddle steamers even then glided serenely over the calm surface of the lake. Its stocky, eminently sensible and ever-serious citizens still find it

15

difficult and usually unnecessary to raise their sights above the Alps, away from the calm and comfortable security within their borders. Their buildings have always reflected the importance they attach to strength and durability, the overall effect relieved by sturdy window boxes of resolutely cheerful geraniums. Hospitality and efficiency are endemic to Switzerland and, even a century and a half ago, hotel guests were assured they would find 'horses available at the arrival of every train'.

Of course, the pace of life was slower then, the architecture less glassy and geometric, the only traffic on the roads horse-drawn and the international organisations, now so inextricably part of the city's life, quite undreamed of. Even the word 'international' was almost unknown and only really came into use with the setting up of the Workers' International in 1862 and the drafting of its statutes by Karl Marx in 1864. Railways were new and the annual report of the Chemin de Fer Central Suisse in 1859 proudly claimed to have just completed laying 205 kilometres of line. The telegraph, too, had just come into being with the first electric cable laid from Calais to Dover in 1851, the telegraph thereafter being regarded in much the same way as the microchip today, in other words it soon became the normal means of relaying urgent news, although it was still regarded by more conservative or mature sections of the community with a certain suspicion and reserve.

Geneva in those days was very much under the influence of two men, both long since dead. The Genevans were justly proud to have produced Jean-Jacques Rousseau in 1712, who spent part of his childhood in a house which is now the site of the popular department store, La Placette, and from whom they inherited their strong beliefs in the rights and dignity of ordinary men. His theories on conduct and government as expressed in *Le Contrat Social* stimulated the movement leading to the French Revolution. Another revolutionary element in his work at that time was the statement that 'war is not a relationship between men, but rather a relationship between States, whereby the individuals involved only happen to be enemies, not as men or even as citizens, but as soldiers', a sentiment which was to have great significance for this story.

16

The second man was John Calvin, the intellectual leader of the Reformation in the sixteenth century, who spent the last twenty-three years of his life in Geneva. His harsh but logical beliefs included the theory that it was God's command to labour industriously and, while it was virtuous to be thrifty, financial success might be taken as a sign of His favour. The Genevans then as now seem to have adopted Calvin's precepts. Ardent followers of the 'Reveil', the new evangelism that had taken hold in the 1830s, they were devout, hard working and genuinely eager to better the lot of those less fortunate than themselves.

For even in Geneva there were pockets of poverty, breeding grounds for crime and disease, and there were many societies and associations devoted to helping the wayward, sick and poor improve their way of life. One of the most prominent and active of these was the Geneva Society for Public Welfare, a private institution with some hundred and eighty members, administered by a central committee and presided over by Gustave Moynier.

In fact, Moynier was engaged in a vast range of philanthropic activities, including help in combating alcoholism, assistance to orphans, a school for the deaf and dumb and the founding of the Swiss Statistical Society. His methods of practising charity were revealing. Little warmth and spontaneity were involved. Instead, there was a great deal of research into root causes, intensive study into identifying the problem, statistics drawn up and exhaustive lists of possible solutions painstakingly compiled.

A highly efficient organiser, a clear-thinker whose ideas were always well marshalled, it might be wondered why a man of such calibre should be content to devote all his energies or, as some would say, waste his talents on charitable work. There were two reasons, the first being quite simply that he was a man of private means who had no need to earn money, the second being a little more complex. Gustave Moynier had in fact studied law in Paris and graduated with the highest honour, 'four white balls'. In due course he was called to the bar, his thesis for the occasion entitled 'Prohibition under Roman Law' receiving wide acclaim. But the bar brought him little satisfaction only the uncomfortable realisation that he had chosen a vocation quite unsuited to his temperament. Painfully shy and lacking in self-confidence, he was also a pitiless self-critic and felt himself quite unequal to the task of practising his profession. Looking around for a less demanding occupation, he joined the Society for Public Welfare and devoted himself to social reform.

Nevertheless, however unsympathetic and cold a fish he may have appeared, there was little doubt as to Moynier's efficiency, and his colleagues at the Society for Public Welfare entrusted him with representing the Society at various international humanitarian congresses, participation in which seems to have widened his horizons. By the time he was thirty, he had gained considerable stature and more than a modicum of self-assurance and was called on by his colleagues to assume the chairmanship of the Society.

Until quite recently, the subject uppermost in people's minds and the favourite topic of conversation in the fashionable salons of Geneva had been the Italian campaign. Public opinion, which had at first sided with Napoleon and the Italians, gradually and imperceptibly shifted over to the losing side as the Austrians retreated ever further east. The *Journal de Genève*, roughly equivalent if anything ever could be to *The Times* of London, published extensive reports on the war in Italy, reproducing telegrams from *Le Moniteur* in France as well as reports from the paper's own correspondents in Italy, the 'Sardinian States' and Lombardy itself. On 25 June, the day after the battle of Solferino, there was great excitement when the paper published a map of the theatre of war in Upper Italy, together with an 'electric telegraph' sent from Napoleon to his Empress at 7 a.m. on the 25th, reading simply but eloquently: 'Great battle – great victory'.

Although he had dutifully digested his daily ration of dispatches from the Italian front, Moynier failed to feel fired with any particular enthusiasm or excitement over these military matters (for although the fuel was being fed in, the spark was yet to come). His legally trained mind was far more intrigued by a report concerning the damages awarded to relatives of victims in the *Helvetia* steamboat catastrophe which had occurred during the national holiday on 1 August the previous year. The list of damages seemed to him preposterously high, ranging from 250 francs for a widow to 34,000 francs for certain particularly privileged parents. He was also wryly amused at the amount of front-page space devoted to the 'Tir Federal', the annual shooting display which lasted three days and included banquets, prize-giving, processions, gymnastic and jumping displays. The editorials particularly deplored the lack of splendid corsages, silk skirts and elaborate hairstyles which had so embellished the previous year's festivities in Berne.

But Moynier's numerous charitable activities left him little leisure to ponder such trivialities and he was, besides, busily occupied with various literary undertakings. In 1858 he produced a study on 'Employee participation in the profits of the Orleans Railway' and the following year he completed a 'Biblical Biography of the Apostle Paul' for whom he felt a certain affinity as well as boundless admiration.

One day in July, an item in the *Journal de Genève* caught his eye and held his attention. 'We have been asked to insert the following extract of a letter from Solferino in our columns, together with the note that accompanied it.' Unaware that he was being slowly drawn towards his destiny, Moynier read an emotional and heart-rending account of the wounded and dying at Castiglione with passing interest. The letter ended with an appeal for tobacco and cigars to alleviate the suffering of the wounded men since, according to the unnamed writer, the local varieties were perfectly execrable.

This was by no means the first account that Moynier had read or heard concerning the fate of the wounded in the Italian war. One of his colleagues in the Society for Public Welfare, the elegant, handsome and brilliant Dr Louis Appia of Piedmont origin, who had been successfully practising medicine in Geneva for the past ten years, had been busily involved in collecting cloth and lint for dressings following an urgent appeal in the *Journal de Genève* from his brother living near Turin who had witnessed the appalling condition of the wounded. This appeal harvested an amazingly generous response and Appia was able to despatch twenty-six crates to the various Italian hospitals, totalling over 2 tons.

Louis Appia was in fact itching to go to Italy himself and see what was happening at first hand. He had already tended the wounded during the revolutionary troubles of 1848 in Germany and this experience had led him to make war surgery his speciality. At the start of the Italian war he was writing a book entitled 'The Ambulance Doctor or Practical Studies on Wounds Inflicted by Firearms' and had also recently devised an ingenious new kind of stretcher to immobilise fractured limbs which he was anxious to get armies in the field to adopt. Whether it was his desire to help the wounded that was uppermost in his mind, or that of seeking experience and material for his book, or whether it seemed a good testing ground for his new invention, Louis Appia wasted no time in analysing his motives but set off for Lombardy in July 1859. There, armed with his stretcher, he busily toured the military hospitals in Turin, Milan and Brescia, finding ample scope for his professional services.

From Lombardy he wrote many enthusiastic letters to his friend in Geneva, Dr Maunoir. A charming, highly intelligent man with a delightful sense of humour, Théodore Maunoir was then in his mid-fifties. His career had been somewhat encumbered by numerous children from his own two marriages as well as those of his wife's. He was nevertheless a brilliant and highly esteemed diagnostician and surgeon whose interest in war surgery was heightened by the letters he received from his friend Dr Appia in Lombardy. Appia described in gruesome detail various enthralling clinical observations he had made, such as a bullet's trajectory through the human body, the latest amputation techniques, the incidence of tetanus, the effect of the new drugs and the use of chloroform. He remarked on the inadequacies of the medical services but seemed inclined to accept them as an inevitable corollary of war and certainly of less absorbing interest than his professional findings. Appia also succeeded in getting his invention successfully tested in a hospital in Milan and extracted a promise from the chief army physician that it would be brought to the attention of the Minister of War.

In a highly buoyant and cheerful frame of mind, warmed by the knowledge that his Italian findings would add substance to his treatise on practical studies into firearm wounds, Appia returned to Geneva in early August. His exuberant mood was in striking contrast to that of his fellow citizen, Henry Dunant, who was in Lombardy at about the same time as himself. Dunant was down in the dumps. In his own mind at least, he had achieved lamentably less successful results. All he had accomplished in the course of his travels was to ruin his health and furnish his already almost morbidly sensitive and susceptible mind with nightmare visions that refused to go away.

Dunant arrived back in Geneva on the same day that Napoleon III and the Austrian Emperor met on the friendliest of terms at Villafranca and signed a peace treaty that ceded Lombardy to Piedmont but left Austria in possession of Venetia. Although Napoleon's alleged aim in entering the war was to further the cause of Italian independence, he had backtracked on his promises and deserted his Sardinian allies at the critical moment. King Victor Emmanuel was not even invited to take part in the discussions, merely adding his signature of approval to the armistice document.

Drained of all his usual vitality, optimism and enthusiasm by the horrors he had witnessed, physically and emotionally spent, Dunant was in no mood to contend with the eager welcome of his friends and acquaintances in Geneva who had been roused to a fever pitch of crusading fervour by dispatches from the front describing the plight of the wounded, as well as by Appia's appeal and his own which had appeared in the *Journal de Genève* and in *L'Illustration*. Feeling only a desperate need for peace and forgetfulness, he recoiled from all the excitement and agitation and, in his unbalanced state, even launched a fierce attack on *comtesse* Gasparin, reproaching her bitterly for having published his letter. His mother, horrified to hear about this, quickly made him see reason and persuaded him to write to the *comtesse*, begging her forgiveness for having temporarily taken leave of his senses. Then, realising that her son had never been physically or mentally robust and needed rest and time to recover from his ordeal, she arranged to borrow a friend's chalet in the mountains above Montreux and took him there for a month.

The golden autumn weather and the peaceful jangling of Alpine cowbells, together with his mother's cheerful and soothing presence, were just what Dunant needed to recharge his batteries and make those ever-present spectres of the agonies of mutilated men recede at least temporarily from his tormented mind. Gradually he recovered enough energy and resilience to contemplate returning to the battle-field of his long-neglected business affairs and to start once again planning how to win the concessions he so desperately needed to put his Mons-Djemila venture on to a sound footing. Deciding that his best chance was to go to Paris and again press for an audience with the Emperor, he enlisted the help of General Dufour, a shareholder in the company.

General Dufour was one of Geneva's most famous and highly respected citizens, a distinguished soldier who, in 1847, had been in command of the Federal troops during Switzerland's civil war between Catholics and Protestants – a conflict that was practically free of bloodshed thanks to his admirable instructions to the army on the conduct of troops in the field, notably that enemy wounded should receive the same care as their own men. After defeating the secessionist Catholic forces, he restored peace and union between the cantons, thereby becoming the saviour of Switzerland and a national hero.

Earlier in his career, Dufour had taken an active part in organising the Swiss army and was responsible for setting up a training academy for officers at Thun where he made the acquaintance of an officer trainee by the name of Prince Louis Napoleon Bonaparte. Having been a great admirer of Napoleon I, Dufour rapidly developed a lasting friendship with the future Napoleon III – an all-important connection so far as Dunant was concerned.

The kindly General Dufour, then in his seventies and nearing the end of a brilliant career, gave Dunant a letter of introduction to the Emperor's aide-de-camp and, shrewdly aware of Dunant's propensity to get carried away by his own zeal and enthusiasm to the point where both he and his audience completely lost the thread of his argument, begged Dunant to be as clear and concise as possible and to ensure that the aide-de-camp understood that the Emperor was already aware of the aims of the Mons-Djemila company with which a number of high-ranking people were already actively associated. He also urged Dunant to tell the Emperor that there would appear to be shady work afoot in Algerian administrative circles, with subordinates deliberately ignoring instructions and sabotaging the decisions of their superiors who themselves tended to lose track of the whole affair in the general confusion.

Dunant had no qualms about aiming so high. His birth and background had made him conscious from an early age of belonging to the social élite. Comfortably aware that he could boast of a more ancient and aristocratic family than most, he had never experienced any difficulty in gaining access to people in the highest echelons of society and felt perfectly at ease in their midst. However, this did not prevent him being distinctly put out when he proudly introduced his mother to 'my colleague' General Dufour, only to find that she had known him as a young girl! Arriving in Paris in the autumn of 1859, he therefore felt confident that with the war over and life returned to its normal round, he would surely succeed in reaching the Emperor.

But this was not to be. Despite all his best efforts and preparations, including a sumptuously printed memorandum on the subject of the Mons-Djemila Milling Company intended to impress the Emperor, endless hours spent hanging around in antechambers and lobbying ministers, cornering and cajoling members of high society, he failed to gain an audience with Napoleon III. With his usual extraordinary optimism, Dunant then decided to try at least to enlist the interest and, if possible, the financial support of the beau monde in Paris and – why not? – treat himself to a little light relief at the same time.

Towards the end of 1859, Dunant turned up everywhere, going from one stylish salon to the next, basking in the glitter and glamour, the light-hearted social sophistication of Paris that was such a welcome contrast to the cold austerity of Geneva where he never really felt at ease. He was especially in his element in the company of older and middle-aged ladies who seemed to delight in taking him under their wing. Perhaps lacking in emotional security, Dunant found in them a reflection of the comfort and support he had always received from his mother. He seemed actively to avoid women of his own age. On the rare occasions he was seen in conversation with a young lady, he looked ill at ease and sought the earliest possible opportunity to escape. It was almost as if any young feminine face brought back to mind the sneering expression and scornful words of Louise Dubois.

As he flitted from salon to salon, lively conversationalist that he was, Dunant easily engaged many willing listeners, regaling them with tales of Algeria and Mons-Djemila and the wonderful opportunities for rich rewards for anyone who could help in securing the concessions he needed for his enterprises. Mistaking politeness for genuine interest, he eagerly talked on, invariably drifting off into a monologue on the murderous battle he had witnessed that summer and the part he had played in its aftermath, cataloguing all its horrors and striving passionately to arouse in his audience even a faint echo of his own indignation. But blood and tears were neither amusing nor welcome topics in the fashionable salons of Paris, any more than were his struggling business ventures and people gradually began to avoid that tiresome man from Geneva who was rapidly gaining the reputation of a crashing bore.

Reluctantly he had to return to Geneva, empty-handed once again, to face his anxious and long-suffering shareholders who had been persuaded the previous year to increase the share capital to 1 million francs. At least they were receiving a steady 10 per cent on their investment, a ruinous drain on Dunant's resources. Despite numerous approaches to such influential people as the Minister for Algeria and General MacMahon, the Commander-in-Chief in Algeria, made on his behalf by General Dufour and General de Beaufort, both shareholders, there were still no concessions, the wheels of his mill still lay idle while the livestock he had bought to graze his land were dying for lack of water and attention, the Arabs he had entrusted with looking after his interests apparently finding better things to do. As for his associate, he was too far away and too busy on his own account to supervise an agricultural venture of this kind. All Dunant's appeals to the provincial authorities had been to no avail, all his plans and documents and elaborately prepared statistics lay where he had left them on the Governor's table in Constantine three years ago, neglected, fly-blown, gathering dust. The prospects looked bleak indeed, such failure seeming doubly disgraceful in Geneva, a city synonymous with wealth and success.

Throughout 1860, Dunant tried desperately to raise money to inject life into his ailing Algerian ventures but, try as he might, his heart was not in it. Round and round in his mind went the nightmare images of Solferino and the Chiesa Maggiore in all their frightful detail and gruesome horror, to torture him without respite. Desperately he struggled to drive them away, grimly they refused to set him free. At last, after weeks of hesitation, he decided that his only chance of exorcising the spectres that haunted him was to set down on paper all that he had witnessed. He set about the task with brisk efficiency, renting a room close to the cathedral where he isolated himself for an entire year, much to his mother's anxiety. First of all, he carefully and methodically assembled his material – official reports of the campaign by the French, Italian and Austrian commanders, a map of the battlefield showing the disposition of the troops confronting each other between the Mincio and the Chiese, lists of army strengths and casualties.

Dunant sat down at his desk, intending to write a short account of the battle and its terrible aftermath. But as he got under way and warmed to his subject, describing the mounting fury of the combatants and the deadly struggles of the battlefield, he felt himself caught up by a strange external force that drove him on and powered his pen with a passion and eloquence he never knew he possessed. Even as an old man, Dunant vividly recalled this experience:

In writing the Souvenir de Solferino I was, as it were, lifted out of myself, compelled by some higher power and inspired by the breath of God. In this state of pent-up emotion which filled my heart, I was aware of an intuition, vague and yet profound, that my work was an instrument of His Will; it seemed to me that I had to accomplish it as a sacred duty and that it was destined to have fruits of infinite consequence for mankind. This presentiment drove me on and I had the sensation of being urged by a force beyond myself . . . the power certainly came from above for, in truth, I had no thought of myself. This recollection had to be set down; I cannot explain it any other way. It was inescapable: the poignant and grievous emotion experienced at Solferino had to be told in a brief and faithful account of what my eyes had witnessed. And I had so to plant it in the hearts of my fellows that the humane concept possessing my heart might bear fruit and develop by virtue of its own force.

Un Souvenir de Solferino was a brilliant, accurate and compelling reconstruction of the battle, followed by a detailed and harrowing description of the suffering and horrors it caused. The picture is drawn with such unerring skill, such sincerity and realism that the reader feels himself drawn on beside Dunant as he moves among the injured, witnessing in all their hideous horror the unspeakable wounds and mutilations, enduring the nauseating stench with the pitiful shrieks and cries of pain, the low moans and curses of the wounded wretches ringing in his ears. He feels the same anguish, the same repulsion, the same overriding compassion and burning desire to help, and experiences the same shocked indignation that such suffering should be allowed to continue. Certain passages are too painfully explicit to bear, making the reader recoil in horror and disgust and hastily turn the page. It was Dunant's intention to open people's eyes to the full horrors of war and in this he certainly achieved his goal. Moreover, there is a quality in his writing that is infinitely touching and goes straight to the heart, expressing such feeling and extreme sensitivity that even the most matter-of-fact of mortals can scarcely fail to be moved.

His aim was not only to shock his audience but also to awaken them to the true nature of war which has always been depicted in glorious colours, in terms of courageous deeds and triumphal marches, glamourised with splendid uniforms and exalted by the beat of martial music and the stirring blare of trumpets. As Dunant grimly noted, 'It is in the hospitals that one can see the monstrous price men pay for what is so grandiloquently called Glory.'

Then he went on to the aspect of the subject about which he felt the strongest – his indignation at the army's callousness and complete disregard for human suffering which he had witnessed at first hand; the way that soldiers who had fought heroically and risked their lives were abandoned, once wounded and their usefulness at an end, and simply left to their fate, however terrible that might be. The most important part of his book followed, the practical solution which apparently only began to take shape in his mind as he wrote. It took the form of an appeal to his audience. 'Would it not be possible in time of peace to form relief societies with the aim of providing care for the wounded in time of war, by zealous volunteers properly qualified for such work?' This, of course, was the idea that eventually led to the creation of the Red Cross.

In September 1862 the manuscript was finished and Dunant had 1,600 copies beautifully printed on handsome paper, paying the printer out of his own pocket. In November, he himself sent out copies to crowned heads and princes, ministers of war and foreign affairs, politicians, military men, philanthropists, writers, and all the important and influential men he knew. His instinct for propaganda was unerring.

The impact his words made was immediate and colossal, sending shock waves reverberating through Europe, arousing instant acclaim from Paris to St Petersburg. Copies of the book were passed from hand to hand and a second edition had to be printed as early as December. The press was unanimous in its praise and hundreds of letters and messages came pouring in, including one from Victor Hugo and another from Charles Dickens, then at the height of his fame. In January, Dunant received a letter from the Emperor's secretary, thanking him for both *Un Souvenir de Solferino* and his 'Reconstitution of the Holy Roman Empire by His Majesty the Emperor Napoleon III', which Dunant had taken the opportunity to slip in for the second time in yet another attempt at flattery.

But not all the reaction was favourable. Those whose profession was war regarded the book with a distinctly jaundiced eye. In Paris, Marshal Randon, the Minister for War, was positively hostile, declaring 'that book was written against France', while Marshal

Vaillant, Napoleon's aide-de-camp during the Italian campaign, expressed regret after reading it that captured cities were no longer burned and their garrisons slaughtered to a man. And there was a surprisingly cool, even negative reaction from Florence Nightingale who considered Dunant's proposal objectionable because 'such a society would take upon itself duties which ought to be performed by the government of each country and so would relieve them of responsibilities which really belong to them and which only they can properly discharge and being relieved of which would make war more easy'. In any case, she pointed out, such a medical organisation already existed in England.

Miss Nightingale made her reservations about the Committee even more explicit in a letter to Sir Thomas Longmore, Deputy Inspector of Hospitals. 'I need hardly say,' she wrote, 'that I think its views most absurd . . . 'just such as would originate in a little State, like Geneva, which never can see war.'

Even General Dufour, a sensitive and humane man who deplored the misery and suffering caused by war, and who unreservedly sympathised with the sentiments of *Un Souvenir*, expressed doubts over Dunant's proposal and considered that such a society would be difficult to set up and could hardly be anything but temporary and local. But he approved of the aims and suggested 'one should not despair of success'.

Dunant was not unduly discouraged by these objections which were, in any case, so heavily outweighed by praise. A further 3,000 copies of the book soon had to be printed to satisfy popular demand. Translations were made into English, German, Italian and Swedish. Charles Dickens lent his patronage both to Dunant's work and his book by publishing a summary of the story, in weekly instalments, in his journal *All the Year Round*. He dubbed Dunant 'the man in white' because of the tropical white suit he wore during the Lombardy campaign, and also because this was how the wounded at Castiglione had referred to him.

Un Souvenir de Solferino was enthusiastically reviewed in various periodicals and thus brought to the attention of many distinguished readers in Europe, including Queen Augusta of Prussia who was destined to become one of the staunchest supporters of the cause. Proudly, Dunant drew up a list of all the illustrious names who had written to him: the King of Württemberg, the King and Queen of Saxony, the Dowager Empress of Russia – his chest visibly swelling as the list grew longer every day.

Apart from his Algerian business affairs which had been temporarily eclipsed from his attention, there was only one cloud on his horizon, not even yet a cloud, more an irrational but uneasy presentiment. It concerned a visit he had received shortly after his book had appeared, a visit from a man who was destined to loom like a threatening storm cloud over his future and, in time to come, break over him with a fury of disapproval, sending him scurrying for cover.

For as he finished his enthralled reading of *Un Souvenir de Solferino*, Gustave Moynier had picked up his pen, intending to write a letter of congratulation to the man who had produced such a brilliant idea. Then, uncharacteristically changing his mind, he laid it down, rose from his desk and picked up his hat and walking cane instead. He would go and call on Dunant in person, and there was no time like the present.

THREE

Dunant Goes on Tour

Dunant was slightly taken aback when his manservant ushered in his distinguished visitor, known to him only by reputation as the chairman of the Society for Public Welfare of which he himself had recently become a member, as well as the the author of an impressive tome on the Apostle Paul. Moynier advanced into the room, grasped Dunant warmly by the hand and exclaimed: 'Mr Dunant, I have just finished reading your excellent book and I had to come and tell you at once. You have had a very fine inspiration. I congratulate you!'

Dunant was naturally flattered by such praise but there was something in Moynier's gaze and bearing that sent an unaccountable chill through his heart. It was as if his animal instincts sensed in advance the bitter antagonism that would develop between them and the disastrous results to which it would lead. As he listened to his visitor talking in glowing terms about his appeal and enquiring whether he had yet considered how best it might be implemented, Dunant felt an irrational diffidence and mounting unease. No, he replied, he did not yet have any precise ideas on how such a project could be put into practice.

Moynier was probably extremely surprised by this admission but he was also secretly delighted. Here was a golden opportunity for him to build an organisation on virgin ground, to exercise his brilliant talents as an organiser where they would obviously be so vitally needed and where, apparently, they would encounter little opposition. Straightaway, he proposed raising the matter at the next meeting of the Geneva Society for Public Welfare on 9 February and Dunant, slightly reluctantly, agreed. The time for exhortations, eloquence and abstract dreams, for basking in the warmth and limelight of public acclaim, was coming to an end. The time for actually getting down to work and turning the dream into practical reality had arrived.

On the agenda of the meeting of the Society for Public Welfare was the following item: 'Proposal (as set out in *Un Souvenir de Solferino*) for the formation of permanent relief societies for aid to men wounded in action.' It met with an unenthusiastic response from those present, whose initial reaction was annoyance at being thus distracted from their local charitable activities. Moynier had anticipated this. He fully realised how ambitious it was to expect a small association dealing with local issues in a small country, and with strictly limited resources, to launch out into a vast international undertaking of this kind. However, Dr Louis Appia, renowned for his skill and experience in field surgery, spoke strongly in its favour. Indeed, so eloquent did he wax on the subject that when he touched on his own invention, one member was heard to murmur, 'If only he could be strapped to his blasted stretcher, we might get away to lunch!' His friend, Dr Maunoir also rallied to the cause, declaring that medical services in the field were still highly inadequate and that voluntary nurses would indeed be a godsend before and after a battle.

On the strength of these endorsements the proposal was adopted and a committee of five set up with the aim of preparing a report which Moynier intended to present to the International Welfare Congress due to take place in Berlin in September. The members of this committee were Moynier, for having presented the proposal, Dunant for the original inspiration, Dr Appia and Dr Maunoir for their medical knowledge and because they had spoken in support, and General Dufour to add stature and because he actually knew something about warfare. So ended this seemingly unimportant meeting of 9 February 1863, destined to go down in history as marking the beginning of the Red Cross.

The Committee of Five met for the first time a week later, General Dufour being appointed Chairman, Moynier Vice-Chairman and

Dunant Secretary. Moynier pointed out that although the best way to achieve their aims was to bring them to the attention of an international congress, it was probably unrealistic to expect that such a congress, with so many other subjects of urgent business on its agenda, could deal with all the ramifications of such a far-ranging and long-term project. With Dunant's support, he therefore moved that the committee should constitute itself a 'permanent international committee' which would continue to work towards its goal of providing relief for the wounded beyond the mandate given it by the Society for Public Welfare. Unwittingly, Moynier thus made history. His proposal was adopted and the Committee of Five became the International Committee for Relief to Wounded Soldiers or what is now known as the International Red Cross.

The chief business of this meeting was to chart their plan of action and explore the various ways it might be implemented. Here the essential differences in the approach of the two leading figures began to become apparent. Moynier, the administrator, pinned his faith on international conferences where the different issues could be rationally debated and agreements eventually reached. Dunant, the visionary, was all for seeking the patronage of royalty and fashionable society. He also insisted they should go much further than simply sending voluntary nurses to the battlefield.

'We must provide better methods of transporting the wounded', he proclaimed. 'We must improve the standard of hospital treatment, send supplies of all kinds, get customs duties waived, create a museum of exhibits, get recognition by all civilised powers of an international and inviolable principle to be guaranteed by a kind of Covenant. We must . . .'. At this point, he became so carried away by the tide of his own zeal and enthusiasm that he lost all track of his argument. Rushing to recapture it from another angle, he interspersed his impassioned declarations with quotations from the Bible and was finally forced to a halt from sheer exhaustion.

The worldly-wise old General Dufour was inclined to agree with Dunant, at least as far as patronage was concerned; he certainly recognised the value of his visionary fire in kindling the necessary interest and impetus. Foreseeing possible opposition from the military authorities, he also suggested that the volunteers they were proposing should place themselves at the disposal of army commanders and that they should adopt a distinctive sign or uniform that would be universally recognised. Dr Maunoir also backed Dunant, declaring, 'We must get up an agitation. We must get our point of view recognised throughout the world among high and low, we must gain the support of the sovereigns of Europe as well as the masses.'

The meeting ended with Dunant being given the task of preparing a memorandum for the Berlin Congress. Pleased with the outcome, he left almost immediately for Paris, a Paris that since the publication of *Un Souvenir* had once again become a friendly and welcoming city where he was recognised and even lionised as a man of letters. Several years earlier, he had acquired French citizenship and a French passport without having to surrender his Swiss papers, a move that was to stand him and many others in good stead in later life. Apart from being a place where he could relax and bask in the warmth of public approval, Paris was also where Napoleon was and Dunant still harboured hopes of eventually winning imperial patronage to rescue his rapidly sinking Algerian affairs. Taking with him Dr Appia's work on military surgery, he again applied for an audience with his hero, and again he was refused.

There was probably nothing personal in this refusal. Napoleon at that time was fully occupied writing his life of Julius Caesar, as well as in hatching various ambitious military and imperialistic plans. Dunant's disappointment was mitigated by meeting a fellow Genevan, Colonel Huber-Saladin, who introduced him to a whole string of wealthy and aristocratic folk, distinguished dukes and elegant countesses. With their encouragement and promises of support, he returned to Geneva to attend another meeting of the Committee of Five. While he had been away, messages of sympathy and support had been received from many quarters, notably from the Grand Duke of Baden, Prince Alexander of Hesse and the King and Queen of Holland.

At the August meeting of the Committee of Five, Moynier reported that the Berlin Congress due to take place that month, and at which he had planned to present the committee's memorandum, had unexpectedly been cancelled. There was general consternation and dismay. But Moynier swiftly and somewhat surprisingly came up with a bold and ingenious suggestion: they themselves would convene an international conference in Geneva. His proposal was applauded and warmly approved by Dunant and the other three.

As well as the now redundant memorandum he had drawn up for the Berlin Congress, Dunant had also prepared ten articles of a draft convention which the committee now proceeded to study and revise. Openly critical of the army medical services, this document proposed the setting up of national committees to compensate for existing inadequacies. Other articles concerned the formation of local sections, the work of these committees and sections in peacetime to introduce improvements in the military medical services, the role of the Geneva Committee as an intermediary for the exchange of communications, and the responsibility of the national committees in wartime to supply relief to their respective armies and especially to take charge of the training and organisation of a corps of voluntary nurses who would wear an identical uniform or distinctive sign.

Remembering the adverse reception of *Un Souvenir* by certain military men, the committee realised that, in its present provocative and aggressive form, the draft convention stood no chance of universal acceptance. So, guided no doubt by the wisdom and experience of General Dufour, they reworded much of it to make it more palatable to the military, without whose support it could achieve nothing. It was carefully stipulated that the corps of voluntary nurses should follow the armies, being neither a hindrance to them nor occasioning any expenditure, and were to be placed at the disposal of army commanders to be used only when deemed necessary.

Within three days of the committee's meeting, Moynier and Dunant had organised the printing of a handsome sixteen-page brochure containing the carefully revised draft convention, together with an invitation to the Geneva Conference on 23 October. This was despatched throughout Europe to governments and heads of state, as well as to many military and medical men and various famous writers and philanthropists.

At the committee meeting, Dunant had announced his intention of going to Berlin to attend a statistical conference from 6 to 12 September. If he could get the participants interested in their cause, they could use their influence to have delegates sent to the Geneva Conference. In any case, he had a friend and ardent ally among the statistical delegates, a Dutch doctor in the service of the Netherlands army who passionately deplored the loss of life and the suffering caused by war and had long been seeking ways to reduce it. Fired with enthusiasm after reading *Un Souvenir de Solferino*, Dr Basting had immediately translated it into Dutch and had written several admiring letters to Dunant, suggesting he join him at the congress in Berlin where one of the commissions would be studying health and sickness statistics of civilian and military populations, during which he was planning to introduce the subject close to both their hearts.

Early in September, Dunant set off for Berlin and what turned out to be a marathon and epoch-making tour of the European capitals and royal palaces. Berlin in 1863 was gradually adjusting itself to a new king, William I, who had succeeded his brother Frederick IV in 1861 and, even more importantly, to the advent of a dynamic new Minister-President, Bismarck, the man destined to win Prussia a leading position in Germany and make her the dominating power in Europe for decades to come. William I was a firm believer in the military destiny of his country, but his plans to reorganise the army had been thwarted by his parliament's refusal to appropriate the necessary funds. Called in to help, Bismarck swept away such trifling obstructions, maintaining that army affairs were under the prerogative of the throne. Prussia's army was vastly strengthened and Bismarck's hand with it. Nothing seemed to stand in the way of him leading Prussia from conquest to conquest except for a very determined woman whose ideals and convictions were diametrically opposed to his own. As he admitted in years to come, his most daunting opponent was none other than Queen Augusta of Prussia, who did not share her husband's enthusiasm for military expansion. This formidable lady, possessing many of the less endearing qualities of Queen Victoria, was to become one of the most active proponents of the Red Cross.

However, the Prussian Queen was not in the forefront of Dunant's mind as he arrived in Berlin. He joined Dr and Mrs Basting in the Hotel Töpfer and they began planning how to persuade the unsuspecting statisticians to back the principle of neutrality for the sick and wounded and for medical personnel. This concept was way ahead of the proposed aims of the Geneva Committee's draft convention but it had long been germinating in Dunant's mind while Dr Basting considered it a vital and essential part of their plans without which the teams of voluntary nurses could work neither efficiently nor safely.

Eagerly, Dunant drafted a speech that Dr Basting would present the following day. Mrs Basting quickly translated it into German for her husband and they worked all night at polishing and improving the text. In the morning, still arguing the finer points, the two friends jumped into an open carriage and set out for the Herrenhaus where the congress was being held. With the papers spread out on the seat in front of them, Dr Basting was loudly declaiming his speech as the cab rattled over the bridge spanning the River Spree. A sudden gust of wind swept the papers into the air and blew them towards the parapet of the bridge. Dunant and Basting immediately leapt from the cab while it was still moving and rushed after the precious manuscript. Luckily, an old beggar who was passing by managed to catch the papers just before they flew over the parapet and into the rushing river below, thus saving the day, and perhaps the Geneva Convention as well.

Dr Basting's speech was so well received by the commission that he was invited to address the plenary session four days later. Here he gave full rein to his evangelical fervour, waxing eloquent on behalf of Dunant's cause and the principle of neutrality. In conclusion, he extended a formal invitation to the assembled delegates to attend the Geneva Conference the following month. Although the chairman pointed out that it would not be in order to put such a proposal to the vote and that the congress must content itself with offering its good wishes for the success of the forthcoming conference in 'lessening the sacrifices of health and of life that war entails', Dunant read into the chairman's cool words a resounding signal of support for their cause and left the Herrenhaus with tears of joy and triumph in his eyes.

With the congress over, Dunant and Basting proceeded to dip happily into the social life and hospitality of the Prussian capital, attending all the glittering functions and dinners organised in honour of the delegates. Both Dr Böger, the court physician, and Dr Loeffler, the chief medical officer of the army, told him of the great interest Queen Augusta had expressed in his aims after reading *Un Souvenir de Solferino* and how she proposed to support his efforts in every way she could. He had the honour of being presented to the King during a party at Potsdam, where he also had a long conversation with Crown Prince Frederick, who urged him to stick to his guns with his idea of neutrality for the wounded and those tending them.

Intoxicated by all this royal warmth and encouragement, coming on top of what he interpreted as keen interest on the part of the military men attending the congress, and fuelled by the passionate discussions in which he and Dr Basting had been almost continually engaged during the past few days, Dunant began to feel his hitherto only vaguely formulated ideas taking shape and crystallising. Neutrality shone out as the obvious answer to all the difficulties which the voluntary nursing corps they were advocating would otherwise surely encounter. How else could they possibly dress wounds and operate if they were continually in danger either of being wounded themselves or taken prisoner? Indeed, to institute voluntary nursing help without combining it with neutrality now seemed to him a positively dangerous step inasmuch as it could not possibly succeed.

With only a month to go before the conference in Geneva convened, there was no time to lose. Too late to change the original draft convention which had been sent out with the invitations. There was nothing for it but to send another. But what about the Committee of Five? Dunant boldly – and, in hindsight, wisely – decided to sidestep them. Well aware of the cautious nature of his countrymen and the influence which the meticulously minded Moynier must be exercising over the rest of the committee in his absence, he felt certain that, if approached, they would turn down his idea as foolhardy, impracticable, or just too late. He simply could not afford to risk a refusal. 'Why wait?' he reasoned to himself. 'Why create difficulties for ourselves by delaying when every hour that passes is critical to the success of our plans?' In any case, he intuitively felt he was taking the right decision. In fact, he had not the shadow of a doubt about it. As he had when he wrote *Un Souvenir de Solferino*, he clearly experienced the same bidding from above.

After feverish consultation, Dunant and Basting rushed round to von Decker, the court printer, and prevailed on him to lay all other business aside. The printer's men worked through the night to produce an elegantly styled new circular, which was actually nothing less than a fresh declaration of the committee's aims. It was dated 15 September and daringly signed by Dunant in the name of the Geneva Committee. This circular stated that in view of the highly favourable reception given to its plans by the Statistical Conference, the Geneva Committee now submitted further proposals in addition to the draft convention already despatched. In essence, these proposals recommended that each government in Europe should give its patronage and protection to its national committee; that governments should confer neutral status on military medical personnel and members of recognised voluntary aid detachments; and in wartime, they should provide facilities for the despatch of medical and other supplies for medical personnel.

This document was promptly circulated to all the delegates still in Berlin and despatched to all those who had received the original invitation to the Geneva Conference. The first statesman to express his approval was the Prussian Minister of War, Count von Roon. When he was asked to go and see him at the Ministry, Dunant reported that his aide-de-camp kept repeating, 'The Minister is very excited by your idea!', 'The Minister is absolutely carried away by your idea.' Be that as it may, von Roon was certainly a supporter of the concept of neutrality from the start and contributed a great deal in helping the Convention come into being. He even promised to back Dunant's idea for a uniform international flag denoting neutral status.

Rather nervously, Dunant wrote back to Moynier reporting on his latest move, carefully sweetening the pill with an enthusiastic account of all the illustrious names he had already garnered to form the nucleus of the national committee in Berlin, and flattering remarks on the Vice-Chairman's wisdom in having selected Berlin as the springboard for their operations. Punctilious Moynier was not so easily appeased, not deigning to reply and merely storing up in his immaculately organised mental filing cabinet this latest instance of what he considered appallingly rash and ill-considered conduct.

With an easier conscience and renewed zest, Dunant plunged back into the social life of the Prussian capital, attending a banquet given by the Minister of the Interior for some twenty of the most illustrious foreign delegates to the congress. To his delight, he found himself seated between Count of Ripalda, a Spanish senator and distinguished philanthropist, and Professor von Hermann, a Bavarian Councillor of State, while facing him was Baron von Weber, the son of the famous composer. During the dinner he pleaded his cause with great eloquence and considerable effect, particularly interesting his table companions in his idea for an international agreement to be concluded between the European sovereigns regarding neutrality of the wounded and military personnel and the universal adoption of a uniform ambulance flag to be used by all armies. He particularly stressed how vital it was for governments to send official representatives to take part in the Geneva Conference. Those sitting nearby took an active part in the conversation and each of them promised to lay the matter personally before their respective sovereigns: the Queen of Spain, King Maxmilian of Bavaria and King John of Saxony.

Dunant set the seal on his evening's work by sending copies of *Un Souvenir de Solferino*, together with the committee's brochure and his new circular, to each of his new friends at their hotels. Such zeal brought its own rewards. The very same day that he returned to Spain, Count de Ripalda requested an audience with Queen Isabella who not only granted her patronage but also instructed him to form a permanent Spanish committee for relief of the wounded. And, only a few days after the banquet, he received a message from Baron von

Weber that the King of Saxony would give him an audience. This proved to be one of the most memorable highlights of Dunant's life.

Hurrying to Dresden, Dunant booked in to the Hotel de France in readiness for his appointment at 10.30 a.m. the following day. Arriving at the royal palace – rather intriguingly known as La Chatouille Royale or 'The Royal Tickle' – Dunant was escorted by a waiting servant to the kindly old chamberlain, who took him by the hand and led him through a labyrinth of corridors in the old castle to a humble and sparsely furnished small room where there was not even a chair to sit on. The chamberlain left him with the advice that the King would enter by the door facing him and that Dunant should bow three times and wait for the King to speak. In due course, the old King appeared and benevolently enquired, 'What can I do for you?' Dunant briefly explained his mission and concluded with an impassioned plea for royal patronage and for a delegate to be sent to the conference in Geneva.

The King could not help smiling at such earnestness but kindly assured him of his patronage. As for sending a delegate, however, he would need to consult his parliament. Dunant suavely suggested that for such a cause, parliament would surely endorse whatever it was the King's pleasure to command. At this, the King smiled again and, after asking various questions relating to the matter of neutrality, concluded with these remarkable words: 'I shall certainly do all that I can, for without a doubt a nation that does not support this humane work will incur the censure of European public opinion.'

As soon as the venerable King withdrew, the old chamberlain reappeared and anxiously enquired whether Dunant was satisfied with the outcome of the audience. Then, again taking him by the hand, he led him back through the same chambers and passages and up the same staircase and delivered him into the charge of the same servant who had met him on his arrival, most kindly bidding him farewell and warmly wishing him bon voyage and success in his ventures, for all the world as if he were a favourite nephew.

Just as Dunant was getting into his carriage, Baron von Weber rushed up, all agog to hear how the audience had gone. As can be imagined, Dunant was in a state of wild excitement and launched into an emotional outburst of amazed gratitude at the excellence of the King and the kindness and extreme courtesy of His Majesty and his attendants. Not only had he gained the patronage of one of Europe's most venerated sovereigns but he had listened to a royal prophet.

Back at his hotel, Dunant immediately sat down and spent the rest of the day and the whole night composing letters to all his contacts in the European capitals, reporting on the success of his audience with King John and the keen interest he had shown in their humanitarian mission, reminding them once again of the importance of sending official delegates to the conference and being careful to emphasise the King's statement that any country not supporting the cause would incur public condemnation. As Dunant shrewdly recognised, this argument was a powerful tool, for the King in Dresden was one of Europe's most revered figures and his words were heeded by all who heard them. Official delegates to the Geneva Conference mushroomed as if by magic, no state wishing to assume the role of a pariah.

Despite his triumph in Germany, the need to get through to Napoleon had not been forgotten. He wrote a careful letter to Baron Darricau, one of the Emperor's key men whom he had met a few months earlier in Paris, asking him to find some way of acquainting the Emperor with his audience in Dresden, as well as of the great importance Prussia attached to the matter of neutrality, reminding him of Napoleon's own order after the battle of Montebello in 1859 unconditionally to release all wounded Austrian prisoners of war.

By one of those strokes of luck in which destiny seems to play so large a hand, Darricau received this letter just as he was setting out for the Tuileries. Reading it in his carriage, he was so won over by its contents that he handed it to the Emperor as soon as he arrived. With a wry smile of resignation, Napoleon, who had already received a letter in the same vein from General Dufour in Geneva, conceded defeat and authorised Darricau himself to represent France at the Geneva Conference. At long last, Dunant had scored a hit with the French Emperor.

Thus, despite fierce initial opposition from the French Ministry of War and Marshal Randon's thundering condemnation of *Un Souvenir de Solferino* ('that book was written against France'), France was unexpectedly won over to the cause. Not altogether unexpectedly to Dunant, whose negotiating talents should not be underestimated or overlooked. From Berlin the week before, he had written confidentially to General Dufour, indicating the favourable lie of the land in Prussia and advising him to write directly to Napoleon on this subject, suggesting he send Baron Darricau to the conference, being the man best qualified to deal with the question of the proposed neutrality.

From Dresden, Dunant sped to Vienna and requested an audience with Emperor Franz Josef. Unfortunately, the Emperor was away at his hunting lodge in Ischl at the time, but it was arranged for him to see the Archduke Rainier at the palace the following day. After launching into a long explanation concerning neutrality, his idea for a universal flag and, finally, what Dunant glowingly described as 'a truce of God', the Archduke's increasingly glazed expression turned to a beam of approval and relief as Dunant drew at last to a close and the Archduke emphatically declared, 'What a magnificent idea!' What a magnificent idea!' Adding, after a moment's deep reflection, 'What a magnificent idea.' He promised that Austria would send a representative to the conference.

Pressing his luck, Dunant went on to Munich to see the friend he had made at the Berlin banquet. But the Bavarian had drawn a blank with King Maxmilian, who refused Dunant an audience and referred him to General Frankh, his Minister of War. This proved a difficult interview with the General being openly hostile. 'Really, Sir!' he expostulated. 'Do you seriously mean to say that you are asking me to send a delegate from Bavaria to Geneva to attend a conference convened by yourself and other individuals whom I do not even know?' Refusing to be intimidated by such bluster, Dunant boldly replied that he was asking for nothing and merely felt it his duty to inform the Minister of the work in Geneva, which was very much in the interests of Bavaria, as it was of all other countries, and indeed of humanity itself, and which had already gained support from the highest quarters. With the Minister visibly wavering, he played his trump card of international ostracism – and victory was his. Bavaria would send a delegate to the conference.

Before returning to Geneva, Dunant found time to visit Darmstadt, Stuttgart and Karlsruhe where he received warm encouragement and elicited many promises to attend the coming conference from princely, ambassadorial and ministerial circles. Wherever he went, he produced what had now become the King of Saxony's famous phrase, which worked like a talisman, as it had done when he mentioned it in a letter he wrote from Dresden to Lord Grey, the Minister of War in London, who promptly appointed as delegate to the conference Dr Rutherford, the General Inspector of Hospitals.

Having managed to postpone his return to Switzerland until almost the last possible moment, he braced himself with the thought of all his royal trophies and recent triumphs and prepared to face his stern and sobersided colleagues on the International Committee.

Arriving somewhat apprehensively in Geneva, he was aghast to learn that the committee – uncertain, apart from two Swiss army doctors, a professor from Neuchâtel and a member of the Lausanne Welfare Society, as to who else if anyone would attend – had made virtually no preparations for the conference due to open only a few days hence. No official reception had been planned, no entertainments laid on. Not even a room had been booked to hold it in!

FOUR

A Question of Mules

Three days to go. Half the crowned heads of Europe or their representatives on their way to Geneva, and hardly any arrangements made to receive them! The next morning, 20 October, the committee met for the fourth time.

Having received only a handful of firm acceptances in response to the numerous invitations they had sent out, the committee had probably felt it unnecessary to make any elaborate preparations. As for Dunant's exuberant despatches from Germany, they had been taken with a generous pinch of salt by his colleagues who found it hard to believe that their appeal could have elicited such a dramatic response and suspected that he was once again being carried away by his own enthusiasm. In any case, the whole of Geneva was in a ferment of excitement over the Federal elections in five days' time, in comparison to which their little conference seemed slightly pathetic to all eyes but their own.

Even when Dunant eventually managed to convince his colleagues that dignitaries from all over Europe were coming to the conference, there was a distinct chilliness in their attitude. Shrewdly guessing the reason, he grasped the bull by the horns and asked, 'What did you think when you read my circular from Berlin on the subject of neutrality?' His words were met by an embarrassed silence. General Dufour looked straight and fixedly ahead as if on parade while Dr Maunoir suddenly found a dusty tome on the bookshelf of absorbing interest. Brushing invisible dust from his cuffs with offended fingers, the dapper Appia looked up abstractedly. 'Neutrality,' he murmured, 'an interesting question . . . .' Before he could continue, Moynier cut in. 'We thought quite simply that you were asking the impossible,' he said icily. Then, aiming his long, thin nose at Dunant with a hostile glare, he added, 'However, now that you have sent it, in the name of the committee, without even deeming it necessary to consult your colleagues, we shall just have to see what comes of it.'

Naturally, Dunant was quite prepared for the cool disapproval of his colleagues, although he was glad to note that General Dufour still seemed to be on his side – perhaps because his position had often brought him into contact with royalty and the aristocracy. Try as he might to appease them with an amazing account of his victorious tour of the European capitals on their behalf, they were not impressed. Such tactics were so completely foreign to their cautious and industrious mentality that the idea of getting far-reaching support by royal decree instead of months of hard, painstaking endeavour was impossible for them to conceive or concede. Moynier in particular seemed to harbour a deeper resentment, grudging him his success. His manner clearly indicated that in his opinion Dunant had merely been on a jaunt.

But with only two days left before the conference opened, there were more urgent things to do than worry about internal politics and small-minded jealousies. Busily, Dunant canvassed the various consulates in Geneva of the countries he had not visited and succeeded in convincing most of them of the need to send representatives to the conference.

Before the committee meeting, he had gone to make final arrangements with his friend Madame Eynard, who had kindly suggested that the conference could be held in the elegant Palais de l'Athènée which had recently been built in memory of her late husband, a famous Philhellenist. Had she not been recently widowed, 'la belle Eynard', as she was known, might well have been too young and beautiful for Dunant's comfort, reawakening in him what had become – ever since the episode with Louise Dubois – almost a phobia about young women. As it was, Madame Eynard was reassuringly brisk and efficient and came to the rescue over the matter of entertainments. Enquiring among her aristocratic friends – most of whom were still away in the country – she eventually managed to find a cousin who agreed to come back to Geneva and throw a party for the delegates on the eve of the conference.

As the morning of the fateful meeting dawned, signs of nerves began to show. Would the hall resound to the speeches of illustrious men, or would it rattle to the meaningless platitudes of a few well-meaning wafflers? Moynier was the first to arrive, striding purposefully from his carriage, his black moustache defying anyone to guess at his inward anxiety. He was joined within minutes by his four colleagues. They scarcely had time to exchange a brief word of greeting when the door opened and in came Prince Henry XIII of Reuss, representing the Grand Master of the Order of St John of Jerusalem. A fine start which was to set the tone of the assembly. The committee's apprehension rapidly turned to relief and delight as other distinguished delegates followed. Altogether, apart from the five committee members, there were thirty-one people present, representing sixteen states and four philanthropic societies. The states represented were Austria, Bavaria, Baden, France, Great Britain, Hanover, Hesse-Darmstadt, Italy, the Netherlands, Norway, Prussia, the Kingdom of Saxony, Spain, Sweden, Switzerland and Württemberg.

One by one, Dunant watched these eminent soldiers and physicians file in and take their places, feeling pride that it was he who had made this happen and, at the same time, understandable awe at the enormity of what he had set in motion, now that it was no longer just a dream but actually taking place. It all seemed strangely far removed from his recollections of Solferino and the Chiesa Maggiore, and yet that was, of course, precisely what this was all about, as General Dufour soon made clear as he rose to open the conference.

Tall and distinguished in his black frock-coat, with the rosette of the Légion d'Honneur, and his sparse hair swept fearlessly back from his bony brow, nobody could have been better qualified for this task than that noble old soldier. Not only was he one of the most highly esteemed men of his time, but in the course of his career he had also had ample occasion to form his own opinion of army medical services. Wounded and badly burned in action in 1813, he

47

had been rescued and taken prisoner by the English and spent ten days in the hands of an assistant surgeon and an incompetent nurse who administered at one time the entire dose of opium that should have been spread over several days, and made him drink a whole glass of oil. He was poisoned and, for ten days, feared he would go blind. Having formally welcomed the delegates, he began:

> As you are aware, gentlemen, the field medical services of the regular armies can provide only limited aid to the wounded on the battlefield. Their very considerable inadequacies . . . are evident to all of us, they have been described with almost frightening accuracy in a work by my compatriot, Mr Dunant. Gentlemen, we are now gathered to see if the philanthropic idea contained in this work can be put into practice. We are not sufficiently aware of the situation of the unfortunate ordinary soldier who, after enduring all manner of hardships, arrives on the battlefield and fights with courage and devotion for his country, only to be rewarded with excruciating pain, with nobody near to relieve his suffering and with the awful fear that he has been simply abandoned to his fate.

There would always be wars, the General acknowledged, it was unrealistic to hope otherwise. Instead of pursuing the illusory ideal of perpetual peace, humanity would be better served by at least making an attempt to render the consequences of war less terrible, by providing the manpower which was lacking, and in such a way as not to cause difficulties for those in command of armies in the field. After this admirably practical and succinct summary of the problem confronting the assembly, the General handed over the chairmanship of the conference to Gustave Moynier.

As for Dunant, so eloquent in private conversation, his fiery style combined with a rather unexpected diffidence in large gatherings were unsuited to public speaking, and he wisely contented himself with a back seat and the inconspicuous role of Secretary. At least he had the pleasant duty of reading out the resonant names and distinguished titles of the delegates. Various illustrious figures such as Florence Nightingale, Charles Dickens, Lord Shaftesbury, as well as the Kings of Belgium, Denmark and Portugal, ministers, generals and others had written expressing interest and support for the work of the conference.

Proud in the knowledge that he was the cause of all these messages, many of which were addressed to him personally – a fact he modestly forebore to mention – Dunant warmed to his task, oblivious to the fact that he was rapidly losing the interest of his audience who had come to discuss with those present, not to hear interminably from those who were not. At last he came to a suggestion from a certain Dr Twining, a member of the Social Science Association in London, who proposed a simple solution to the problem: the wounded should be put out of their pain 'so that they should not die with a fevered brain and blasphemy on their lips'. History does not record whether Twining was a doctor of medicine, divinity or even, perhaps, a vet!

Moynier took advantage of the ensuing laughter to move the conference on to the next order of business. In his opening address, he had already outlined the project before the assembly: committees to be set up in each European capital with the patronage and backing of their respective governments; the organisation and training by each committee in wartime of volunteer units to follow the army at a sufficient distance to avoid hampering troop movements, yet near enough to provide rapid assistance to the wounded in an engagement; the placing of such units at the disposal of army commanders; and the adoption of an identical uniform or distinctive sign enabling the easy and instant recognition of all medical personnel. Now he read out the committee's draft convention, after which he prayed for divine benediction on the work of the conference and the deliberations began.

Seated in the front row, Dr Loeffler, the Prussian delegate, warmly subscribed to the main points of the proposal. Appia smiled and nodded his satisfaction, for he was already acquainted with Dr Loeffler. The other German-speaking delegates, while following his lead and agreeing with the basic principles, were less enthusiastic. Opposition came from the Spanish and British contingents. Both declared that their medical services had already been greatly improved and whereas Spain, after denouncing the use of conical bullets as unnecessarily cruel, considered that charitable individuals wishing to help had only to join the army, Britain thought they had solved the problem by removing the medical services from the quartermaster's control and making them autonomous. Neither saw the need for the proposed societies, Britain failing even to mention them, clearly regarding such entities as quite superfluous.

So the arguments swayed back and forth, followed by the ever watchful eye of Gustave Moynier from the chair. The final assault came from the French. Baron Darricau had unfortunately been unable to attend and, despite the Emperor's positive response to Dunant's appeal, Marshal Randon had sent two men of his own persuasion who did their best to shoot the committee's proposals down. Deputy commissioner Préval opened fire by declaring that it was inadmissible for a group of civilians to meddle with the army medical services. He then pointed to the difficulties that volunteer relief helpers would cause by their inability to provide their own food and transport during a war. Since one of the most urgent needs was for adequate personnel to transport the wounded, he suggested solving the problem with mules. In his opinion, 1,500 mules were worth at least 15,000 men. Let the armies acquire such animals and that would be the end of the matter.

His colleague, Dr Boudier, was equally destructive. He waded in with a blistering attack on the calibre of the proposed voluntary workers. They would be mainly illiterate and incapable of caring for the wounded, he claimed, and would prove a burden to the officially recruited medical personnel. He saw them in tatters, with no means of transport, paralysed by the sight of blood, starving, dying, and, worst of all, incapable of fending for themselves as ordinary soldiers could, by plundering. This was too much for the British delegate who, ever keen to disagree with the French, was on his feet in a flash. 'The British experience has shown volunteers to be intelligent and dedicated. Nobody could call Florence Nightingale an illiterate vagabond.' There was a murmur of agreement round the room. 'Why otherwise would they volunteer?' he went on. 'If they wanted

to plunder, they have apparently only to join the French army.'
Moynier hastily intervened to avert a conflagration before their very
eyes and the incensed Boudier, now thrown entirely off his stride,
fell back on his colleague's argument for mules.

This broadside by Europe's leading military power, coming on top
of the somewhat disparaging and dismissive comments of previous
speakers, clearly swayed the delegates and might have had a disastrous effect on the outcome of the conference had not Dr Maunoir
stepped into the breach with his usual light touch and inimitable
sense of humour. Recoiling from the earlier suggestion that the
wounded be put down like dogs, he now bridled at the prospect of
the unfortunates being tended by donkeys. 'Our honourable
colleague, Dr Boudier,' he said, 'has painted an excessively gloomy
picture and, if he were absolutely right on all points, the only thing
left for us to do would be to buy mules.'

His witty remarks raised laughs all round and relieved the tension.
Dr Maunoir proceeded to demolish most of the French objections
with a skilful defence of voluntary nursing units. Of course the
proposed volunteers would have a rough time in the field, nobody
had thought of it as a holiday. But just as staff in the medical
services were obliged to be courageous in difficult circumstances,
those that voluntarily placed themselves in a similar situation might
reasonably be expected to display the same courage and resourceful-
ness.

With the conference steered safely back on course, the delegates
proceeded to review the draft convention article by article, and to
draw up a series of resolutions. One of the most important issues to
be debated was that of a distinctive emblem for voluntary medical
personnel. Dr Appia suggested that this should take the form of a
white armband to be worn on the left arm, thinking perhaps that a
nurse or doctor would always have white cloth at hand. In order to
avoid any possible confusion with the universally recognised flag of
truce, General Dufour proposed the addition of a red cross.
Although the minutes of the meeting make no mention of it, the
General may well have thought that this inverted Swiss flag would
be a suitable tribute to the country that had initiated the idea.

A distinctive emblem was also needed for military medical services since, at that time, each country designated its field hospitals and medical facilities by a different coloured flag – white in the case of Austria, red for France, yellow for America and Spain – and this led to endless confusion. However, this was a matter for states themselves to decide and the delegates could only express a recommendation that a single distinctive sign be adopted for the hospitals and medical services of all armies.

The conference was quietly discussing a point of relatively minor importance when Dr Basting, Dunant's old friend from Holland, suggested that this could be taken up later during examination of Article 3 of the Berlin circular. Moynier coolly replied that the Geneva Committee was not intending to submit the Berlin proposals for discussion by the conference. Dr Basting was immediately up in arms and protested furiously, declaring that the Geneva Committee could not have understood why the delegates had come to the conference in the first place. He had been personally informed by the Prussian Minister of War that neutrality – the nub of the Berlin proposals – was precisely the point of greatest interest to himself and to the King of Prussia.

Moynier's heart sank. He had in fact been carefully trying to brush the Berlin proposals under the carpet. It had been difficult enough to get the original proposals for voluntary nursing units accepted, he reasoned. It would surely be wiser not to ask for more. Actually, for once, he was quite mistaken. Everyone was far more amenable to the idea of neutrality than they had been to voluntary nurses. The delegates were well aware that doctors and nurses were sometimes wounded or even killed during the fighting, a practice that was to no one's advantage since they were non-combatants whose role was to tend the wounded. Paradoxically, the biggest, indeed the only stumbling block to the discussion of neutrality was Moynier himself.

Even Dr Boudier dismounted from his mule and joined in the enthusiastic debate, suggesting that neutrality be extended to civilians who went to the assistance of the wounded. This would overcome their fears of being punished for helping the wounded of the other side in the event of the enemy returning, he claimed.

Moynier eventually gave way to these arguments, mainly because he himself suddenly realised that neutrality was an essential prerequisite for the successful functioning of the voluntary aid societies they were proposing, indeed the most fundamental issue of all. The concept of neutrality for medical personnel and their helpers was unanimously adopted by the conference and included in the recommendations annexed to the resolutions which were then approved.

At the close of the proceedings, Dr Basting proposed that the members of the International Conference declare 'that Mr Henry Dunant, in stimulating by his untiring efforts an international enquiry into the means to be adopted for giving effective help to the wounded on the field of battle, and that the Geneva Society for Public Welfare, in supporting by its cooperation the noble ideas put forth by Mr Dunant, have put mankind in their debt and are deserving indeed of worldwide gratitude'.

The entire assembly rose to its feet and applauded Dunant loud and long. Their tribute was well merited for it had been Dunant who had had the vision and inspiration to stir Europe's conscience with his book, the audacity to issue the Berlin proposals on his own initiative, and the extraordinary energy and zeal to travel from capital to capital enlisting royal patronage and support, thereby ensuring an impressive and influential attendance of official delegates at the conference. Moreover, without Dunant and his enthusiastic champion, Dr Basting, under Moynier's discreet and cautious guidance the conference would have confined itself to merely national arrangements for reducing the suffering of the wounded rather than opening the way to the establishment of international law for the protection of victims of war.

But Moynier's contribution had also, in its own quiet way, been considerable. It had been no easy task shepherding such a mixed assembly with their conflicting interests and views, and General Dufour rose and praised the young lawyer for his able chairmanship. This was a proud moment for Moynier who, while already an accomplished speaker, had seemed to grow in stature and confidence as the conference progressed. In later, mellower years, he recorded: 'I remember and I shall never forget . . . how the participants rose to gather round the president's chair, which I was occupying, and stretched out to seize my hands. Their eyes were set on the future and each believed in the efficiency of the decisions which had been reached and which held out the promise of great achievements.' All memory of Henry Dunant had slipped conveniently from his mind.

The conference, which had lasted four days, was over and the delegates, fired with enthusiasm, dispersed to their respective capitals, having tacitly authorised the Geneva Committee to continue masterminding the operation and to act as the coordinating body between the future national committees. On 15 November, the text of the draft resolutions was sent to all European governments and those who had taken part in the conference. Delegates also received a lengthy letter from Moynier confirming the committee's aims and setting out a list of questions they should ask their governments with a view to ascertaining their willingness to adhere to an international convention.

Highly satisfied as they were with the happy outcome of the conference, the committee members nevertheless realised that an uphill task lay ahead. They had to ensure that the demands laid down in the resolutions were put into effect. This would be hard enough, for the delegates and other supporters would need to be encouraged to promote the creation of national committees, and the International Committee had to provide them with means of communication. The recommendations, however, were a different matter. The questions of neutrality and a distinctive universal emblem required an international treaty drawn up by a diplomatic conference which could only be convened by a national government. But which country could be prevailed upon to take this step, and how? The five gentlemen of Geneva left for their respective homes in a sober frame of mind.

FIVE

Europe Initials a Contract

Moynier was aware that in order to persuade the different powers to enter into the mutually binding agreement of a diplomatic convention, the committee would need to engage in active propaganda until such time as it found a government that was prepared to champion the cause and convene a diplomatic conference. He later admitted that such an ambitious scheme seemed almost predestined to failure. 'But contrary to all expectations,' he marvelled, 'the obstacles seemed to vanish from our path as if by magic.' Magic it most certainly was not, for in this astonishingly complacent reminiscence Moynier denigrates and totally ignores the extraordinary perseverance and exceptional negotiating skill of one of his colleagues. If there were any supernatural element involved, it must surely have been the miracle which was to be performed by Henry Dunant in Paris.

After taking a day or two to recover from the strains of the conference, the five committee members came together in Moynier's house beside the lake in Geneva. Their first objective, they all agreed, was to promote the creation of relief societies in as many countries and as quickly as possible. Then, when they approached governments on the issue of the proposed convention, they would have active friends and influence within the nations themselves.

Reactions to the conference were by no means all encouraging. Holland expressed reservations, claiming to be self-sufficient in medical services which it regarded, in any case, as a state responsibility. The Dutch still remembered the assistance that had been given during the 1831 siege of Antwerp when enough lint was contributed to keep all their hospitals going for the next twenty years.

As for Britain, its medical services were now fully capable of coping with the consequences of even large-scale military engagements and Dr Rutherford, the British delegate at the recent conference, wrote to Moynier saying that the Minister of War considered that any outside help appearing to reduce the responsibility of the War Office in this field could have undesirable consequences.

Austria informed the International Committee that there was no need to create a national society since one already existed: the Austrian Patriotic Society for Aid to Wounded Soldiers, War Widows and Orphans. Set up in April 1859, this society raised a large amount of money enabling it to render valuable service during the Italian campaign, evacuating and repatriating the wounded and setting up a number of small hospitals that provided excellent care.

In Russia, the Grand Duke Constantine was willing to support the project and a special commission of army officers and doctors had approved the setting up in peacetime of committees to provide aid to wounded soldiers. However, they were against allowing voluntary medical units on the battlefields. Milyutin, the Russian Minister of War, therefore expressed reservations and reluctantly informed the committee that in the circumstances he could not lend his full backing to the setting up of a national committee in Russia.

These slightly disappointing reactions were nevertheless understandable. As far as Britain was concerned, Moynier assured Dr Rutherford that the committee could only congratulate his government on having official medical services that fully met the requirements of war. The national committees discussed at the conference were intended to make good the shortcomings of official services. But if there were no shortcomings, so much the better!

No such valid reasons could be claimed by France; just the opposite, in fact, as became painfully evident a few years later during the Franco-Prussian War. Yet France was the only country where the International Committee could not rely on the support of the delegates who had attended the October conference. Within a week or two of the conference, rumblings filtered through to Geneva that the French considered the provisions dangerous and impracticable. Marshal Randon, whose hostility was well known, exclaimed:

'Why must these civilians meddle in matters which do not concern
them?'

In November, Dunant – who always felt that little would be
achieved in Geneva and believed that the hub of European activity
was Paris – left for his favourite city with the dual purpose of promoting the setting up of a French central committee, and of con-
tending with the formidable opposition of the French army and
government.

While he was away, some of the other countries started to react.
In December, Moynier was able to announce to his colleagues, with
the fleeting smile that for him passed as excitement, that the first
society had been formed in Württemberg. This was followed, a few
days later, by a second society in the Grand Duchy of Oldenburg, in
Germany, under the patronage of the Grand Duke himself. The fact
that Dunant had obligingly made several small revisions and
compromises in the German edition of *Un Souvenir* may have had
something to do with the speed and ease with which these two
societies were formed.

In February, a third society was created, in Belgium, presided over
by the King's aide-de-camp. And finally, a few days later, the
Prussian society was set up in Berlin, chaired by Prince Henry XIII
of Reuss who had attended the conference. This committee was
extraordinarily active and fertile, producing no fewer than eighty-
five branches throughout the country in the first year alone. The
Prussian authorities and particularly the Minister of War, von Roon,
sensibly welcomed a society that was prepared to train medical
personnel at its own expense in peacetime and place them at the
service of the army in time of war.

Meanwhile, back in Paris, Dunant espied a ray of hope to break
the deadlock of French opposition. Dr Boudier and Préval, who had
shied away from the conference proposals for voluntary nursing
units, had nevertheless raised no objections to the question of
neutrality. Perhaps this issue could serve as a sort of Trojan mule to
carry the French government into subscribing to the proposed convention. His faithful ally, Baron Darricau, advised him to approach

the Minister of Foreign Affairs, who had expressed keen interest. Appreciating that this was the minister primarily concerned with diplomacy, Dunant seized the opportunity and suggested that France should sponsor the plan for an international flag and armband. Enthusiastically, he wrote off to Moynier reporting this development and requesting approval before going ahead.

Moynier, alarm bells ringing in his head at the recollection of the 'unauthorised' Berlin circular, promptly stamped on the idea. He informed Dunant that he considered such a proposal premature and that the committee had at no time expressed the wish that one of the great powers take individual responsibility for sponsoring an international flag and armband. If he had ever had any doubts, Moynier's reaction now confirmed for Dunant that he had been right not to consult his colleagues on the committee before sending his circular from Berlin concerning neutrality.

The more adventurous Dr Maunoir, however, to whom Moynier sent Dunant's letter, regretted that such an offer should not be taken up. 'Here is a unique opportunity,' he wrote, 'to get things moving as a result of a conversation that is in no way compromising, with a man powerful enough to influence the action undertaken by an important country. In what way is it contrary to the general wishes of our conference? We should keep only one thing in mind, the success of our project and, if I might say so, by any means at our disposal.' Did Moynier consult *his* colleagues before taking this decision, or did he use the 'chairman's prerogative' of enclosing the letter with his reply, saying 'I'm sure you will agree . . . ?' We shall never know.

Undaunted by this setback, Dunant turned his attention to the formation of a French national committee. This entailed another sortie into high society and who better to help him than his old friend and compatriot, Huber-Saladin? Together, they again embarked on their social crusade among the beau monde where Dunant and his cause received a sympathetic hearing, particularly from the ladies. 'The Baroness de Staël,' he reported to his colleagues in Geneva, 'keeps a white armband with the red cross on it permanently on the table in her reception room to intrigue her friends and make them ask the use of this strange new decoration. This charming way of publicising a noble idea is most successful!' Whether those Calvinistic gentlemen were impressed is doubtful.

But underlying all these assorted efforts and activities in ministerial antechambers and fashionable salons, Dunant sensed that his trump card to turn the tables in France lay in the Emperor's hand. Early in December, shortly after being turned down by Moynier on the matter of the flag and armband, he sent an appeal to Napoleon III which met with greater success than even he would have dreamt possible. Out of the blue, the Emperor's aide-de-camp replied, informing him that His Majesty warmly approved of the aims of the conference and the resolutions it had adopted to those ends. The Emperor would support his efforts to form a relief committee in Paris and the Minister of War would be asked to authorise a number of high-ranking army officers to become members.

Delighted but beginning to feel the strain of all his energetic campaigning in Paris, as well as the constant stream of correspondence he maintained with the many new friends he had made throughout Europe who might help to further their cause, Dunant returned to Geneva just before Christmas to present the Emperor's letter to the committee and to take a few weeks much needed rest. Shortly after returning, he received a letter from Marshal Randon asking various questions concerning both the proposed convention as well as the composition, aims and duties of the national committees, stating that he could not reach a decision without clarification on these various points. This was clearly a face-saving operation on the Marshal's part.

Uncharacteristically, Dunant delayed almost a month before replying and when he did, it was not to answer the Minister's questions which he claimed could be more satisfactorily dealt with in discussion when he next came to Paris. He was not prepared to give the Marshal the chance to work up new objections. Instead, and this time with the support of the committee, he used this opportunity to apply subtle pressure on France to take an active part in promoting the cause of neutrality. Pointing to the various governments that had confirmed their acceptance of the conference resolutions and stressing that the King of Prussia had undertaken to promote the issue of neutrality, he appealed to France to follow his example, since France had always been in the vanguard with respect to noble and generous ideas and should not be led by others. France had always adopted an enlightened position, he concluded, illustrating his point by enumerating the occasions in recent history when French commanders-in-chief had concluded agreements for the care and protection of the wounded and the exchange of prisoners of war.

As intended, Marshal Randon's pride was piqued by the idea of Prussia taking the lead over neutrality. The matter was referred to the Emperor who was already favourably disposed. In February, Dunant received another letter from the Emperor offering to put him in touch with his Minister for Foreign Affairs the next time he came to Paris, with a view to discussing his suggestions that neutral status be accorded to ambulances, hospitals, the wounded and medical personnel. A heady success indeed: Dunant was well on the way to victory.

At this stage in the proceedings, Prussia and Austria went to war with the Danes over a disputed succession in the partly German duchies of Schleswig and Holstein which had for many years been ruled by the King of Denmark. Napoleon III, a great believer in referendums, had proposed settling the matter with a plebiscite, but such a course of action was far too tame for Bismarck who had set his sights on acquiring a naval base at Kiel. Austria and Prussia marched in. Public opinion in Europe was outraged at this violation of international law. Lint collection evenings were organised in Geneva on behalf of the Danes and once more the cry went up, 'Lint for the wounded, send in your lint.' And once more the stalwart but generous-hearted Genevans tore up their sheets, for better a bare bed than a bleeding Dane. In England, that splendid octogenarian Lord Palmerston thundered that 'if Denmark had to fight, she would not fight alone'. The Cabinet, however, disagreed, so nothing came of that.

Dunant, just back from Paris, suggested that the committee should send delegates to the theatre of operations on an experimental basis. General Dufour approved of the idea but, scrupulously correct as always, insisted that they be sent to both sides, thus underlining the committee's impartiality. Captain van de Velde, the Dutch delegate at the conference, who happened to be in Geneva at that time, volunteered to go to the Danes and Dr Appia, leaping at the chance of practising some field surgery again, immediately offered his services on the German side. These two delegates were thus the first official 'Red Cross' representatives in a theatre of war.

The unfortunate van de Velde had a wretched time. Not only did he suffer from the appalling conditions of a Nordic winter, being almost rendered immobile by the cold on the freezing boat taking him to Malmo and suffocated by dank, icy fog but, after staggering breathlessly ashore, he was met by distrust and violent hostility on the part of the Danes. Their military authorities refused to allow any voluntary medical help and would not even let him visit a Prussian camp to compile lists of the Danish sick and wounded prisoners. Worse still, he and the committee were scathingly attacked by the Danish press who accused them of hypocritical indifference to their cause by simultaneously sending a representative to the Germans in Schleswig. After all this, the long-suffering Captain was probably in more need of relief than the Danes.

The situation was very different for Dr Appia who on arrival at the front was welcomed and given carte blanche by the commander-in-chief of the Prussian forces. Wearing his red cross armband, he busily visited hospitals, first-aid posts and ambulances, going wherever he pleased. If he sometimes had to wallow through deep mud, he scarcely noticed it. Appia was in his element and, whenever the opportunity presented itself, out would come his instruments to perform an operation. He noted with satisfaction that the Prussian and enemy wounded received identical treatment, and that the Prussian army willingly accepted the assistance of voluntary medical staff. He was particularly impressed by the efficiency of three hospitals set up by the Order of St John of Jerusalem which, being a permanent organisation, could call on qualified doctors and well-trained volunteers as soon as the need arose. It was also excellently equipped, with a new type of horse-drawn ambulance and stretchers on wheels which could be brought right on to the battlefield to collect the wounded. In fact, it was doing precisely what the Geneva Committee was aiming to do through its national societies.

Moynier realised that these reports from the front were of more value to their cause than any amount of theoretical discussion. They clearly showed up the inadequacies that had to be remedied, the improvements that were needed and the misunderstandings that had to be resolved. They also demonstrated the importance and need for the kind of services the committee was trying to provide, and how right it was in its way of going about it. The criticism by the Danish press that the committee had failed to condemn the Prussian aggression emphasised yet again the vital need for universal acceptance of the principle of neutrality. During heated discussion, the committee hammered out its position on this issue, which has remained unchanged to this day. Its task was solely to attend to the wounded and suffering, to help the victims of war. To do so, it must refrain from making moral pronouncements or passing judgement on the parties to the conflict.

By early summer, the war was over. The Danes had been forced to submit and the duchies of Schleswig and Holstein were jointly occupied by Austria and Prussia. Meanwhile Dunant had been busy in Paris cultivating his committee. The Emperor had kept his promise and Dunant was granted an audience with the French Minister for Foreign Affairs. The Minister informed him that if the Swiss Confederation would issue an invitation to 'the civilised states' to attend a conference with a view to transforming the idea of neutrality into international law, then France as a major military power was willing to back this enterprise and to recommend to the various states that they accept the invitation. What a triumph for Dunant – to have converted their strongest opponent into the sponsor for their cause. He had pulled off a stroke of genius and no one but Dunant with his extraordinary perseverance and boundless optimism would even have attempted it.

The Minister went on to say that, naturally, the conference should take place in Berne, the seat of the Federal Council. Dunant energetically protested. Geneva was where the movement had come into being, Geneva was where the first conference had been held, Geneva was where the International Committee had its headquarters. Furthermore, as promoter of the project, his heart was set on this conference being held in his birthplace. The Minister gracefully gave way, although Dunant later discovered that he would have preferred the conference to take place almost anywhere other than the city of Calvin.

The next point to be discussed was which states should attend. The Minister was staggered to hear that Dunant wished to invite separately all the small German states that had attended the first conference, as well as the United States, Mexico, Brazil and Japan. After considerable hesitation, he was finally persuaded to agree, but he drew the line at the idea of inviting the republics of South America.

Dunant immediately wrote off to Geneva with the good news. Moynier, incredulous that Dunant almost single-handed had succeeded in getting the French government to take the initiative for a diplomatic conference, asked the French consul in Berne for confirmation. Yes, he was told, they had themselves just received instructions to that effect. He and General Dufour then approached the Federal Council and were informed that the Swiss government would be pleased and considered it a great honour to convene a diplomatic conference. On 6 June 1864, a formal invitation to the Diplomatic Congress to be held in Geneva on 8 August was sent out to twenty-five states, a letter from the French government backing this invitation following a few days later.

Before returning to Geneva to take part in the preparations for the conference, Dunant wanted to make further progress with the setting up of a French central committee. Convinced that the international focus of the movement would one day shift from Geneva to Paris, he was determined that this committee should be composed of the most eminent and influential people. Beautifully printed cards went out to all the illustrious and aristocratic names that had promised their support, inviting them to a meeting on 25 May in a board room that a banker friend had kindly placed at his disposal.

63

In this company, his inhibitions about public speaking seemed to evaporate and he waxed eloquent on the sublime role civilians could play in alleviating the ills of war. He told his audience about the Emperor's support for a diplomatic conference and persuaded them that the time was ripe for the statutes of the French committee to be established.

A few days later, Gustave Moynier received a letter from Dunant in Paris announcing the formation of the sixth aid society and proudly enumerating the names of its distinguished committee members. Then came a bombshell: 'And now dear Monsieur Moynier, I feel that I have done everything that is within my power to ensure the success and continuity of our venture. I now wish to withdraw. Please therefore do not count on me for active support in the future. I shall be retiring from the scene. The organisation is launched and in this I have been no more than an instrument of God's will. It is now for others better qualified than myself to promote its aims and ensure they are effective.'

Why did Dunant choose this moment to resign from the movement he had done so much to create? Was it that he felt that his visionary role was drawing to a close? Did he foresee endless administrative chores ahead for which he had little taste? The cries from the battlefield would no longer go unheeded but would be heard by those whom he had taught to listen and who were now more suited than himself to carry on the task. Was it Moynier's unremitting disapproval that was souring his life and eroding his fragile veneer of confidence? In such a complex character as Dunant there is seldom a simple answer.

Or was it money? The spectre of his disastrous Algerian venture was once again rearing its ugly head, and this must also have been a drain on his mental reserves. For the past two years, he had been paying for two secretaries as well as his manservant, had covered his own considerable travelling expenses and contributed to those of the committee. His financial situation was becoming precarious, as was the state of his health. He simply could not afford to neglect himself or his business concerns any longer. He had to withdraw and put his own house in order.

As for Moynier, any transitory twinge of triumph he may have experienced at the prospect of a permanent eclipse of the man he covertly despised for his undisciplined mind and commercial ineptitude was rapidly replaced by alarm and dismay. Moynier was quite shrewd enough to recognise that Dunant really was unique. Moreover, Moynier sensed that it was the very weaknesses in Dunant's make-up that strengthened his own position, by providing an essential counterbalance. His dry legal mind was the perfect foil to Dunant's visionary fire and enthusiasm. Together they worked well. But one without the other might be a different matter.

He immediately wrote back to Dunant, asking him to change his mind. 'We find it hard to believe,' he wrote, 'that you are seriously considering depriving us of your invaluable assistance. We are merely your helpers and not here to take your place. To abandon us would be the surest way to jeopardise the success of our work at the very moment when it seems to be coming to fruition . . .'

This appeal won Dunant over and he returned to Geneva where preparations for the conference were now in full swing. Apart from sending out the official invitation, the Federal Council left all the organisation of the conference to the International Committee, including drawing up the draft convention which would serve as the basis for the work of the assembly. Moynier and General Dufour laboured long into the summer evenings, laying the groundwork for what was virtually a revolution in the practice and the law of war, which up to that time had been based only on customary usage and legal opinion. The aim now was to grant neutral status to medical personnel, ensuring that they were not taken prisoner, and to incorporate this into an international treaty. No such treaty had ever before been concluded in time of peace or been anything other than transitory and limited to the two conflicting parties concerned.

At 1 o'clock on 8 August, the International Conference for the Neutralisation of Army Medical Personnel in the Field was opened by General Dufour. It was attended by twenty-four duly accredited government delegates, many resplendent in full dress uniform, representing sixteen states (Baden, Belgium, Denmark, France, Great

Britain, Hesse, Italy, the Netherlands, Portugal, Prussia, Saxony, Spain, Sweden, Switzerland, the United States of America and Württemberg).

There were quite a few familiar faces from the previous conference: Dr Rutherford from Britain, Dr Loeffler from Prussia, and 'our Boudier' as Moynier called him, together with M. Préval from France. This time, the Republic and Canton of Geneva formally provided two large rooms for the occasion in the Hôtel de Ville, or city hall, in the heart of the old city: a suitably noble setting for an historic occasion, where the ingenious circular seating arrangement pre-empted any possible grounds for jealousy or resentment and ensured nobody could take offence.

In his opening address, General Dufour recalled the purpose of the conference: 'We seek only one thing, the neutralization in war of field dressing stations, medical personnel and their helpers . . .' Unlike the previous year's assembly when the committee had had to fight every inch of the way to get its ideas accepted, everyone now was surprisingly in agreement.

One of the few points of dissension arose over the definition of the term 'medical personnel'. Dr Loeffler, the Prussian delegate, wanted voluntary assistants specifically included in this group so that they would also benefit from neutral status. But the French delegates had been forbidden by Marshal Randon – still fighting a rearguard action – to accept the neutralisation of voluntary medical assistants.

Faced with this apparent stalemate, the conference found an ingenious way round this hurdle. Since voluntary medical helpers would be subject to army discipline and, to all intents and purposes, incorporated into its ranks, it argued, they would be almost indistinguishable from their military counterparts and almost certainly would be treated in the same manner. Why, then, was there any need to single them out? They were in effect included within the terms of the Convention.

Strangely enough, there was no opposition to the granting of neutrality to householders aiding and lodging the wounded, whether friend or foe. The presence of a wounded person in a house would ensure neutrality and liberty for its inhabitants and exonerate them from the necessity of lodging troops, as well as from paying part of any war contributions that might be levied. These generous inducements were intended to help the wounded – who were also accorded neutral status – by providing them with readily available food and lodging. Unfortunately, this led some years later to one of the most flagrant examples of abuse of the Red Cross emblem. An emblem, incidentally, which was now tacitly adopted by the conference as designating not only the voluntary aid societies but also the army medical services and all persons and installations accorded the status of neutrality.

The conference lasted fifteen days, much of which was taken up by lavish and splendid entertainment for the delegates – garden parties, trips on lake steamers, glittering receptions in country residences, illuminated regattas, concerts, official banquets and firework displays. The *Carillon de Saint-Gervais*, a satirical Geneva newspaper, chose to make fun of the meetings, presenting them as a series of sumptuous social gatherings:

> First meeting Tuesday. Two thousand dead bottles lying on the floor, five hundred partridges, trout, pâtés, etc. buried or tended . . . a veritable Solferino. . . .

Other reporters were more favourably impressed by this elegant hospitality, all beautifully orchestrated by Dunant whose role in the conference seems to have been confined to that of a master of ceremonies. In hindsight, it would seem that his instinct in trying to resign when he did was once again uncannily correct, and it might well have been far better for all concerned had he made a dignified departure from the scene at this stage. His work, perhaps, was done. The Convention for the Amelioration of the Condition of the Wounded in Armies in the Field was completed. All that remained was for the delegates to add their signatures.

On 22 August, the delegates in full regalia assembled in the Hôtel de Ville for the signing ceremony. Some of the government representatives displayed reluctance and last minute hesitations. And not all of them even had full powers to sign. The British delegate, for one, declared that he could not possibly sign without a seal. But General Dufour had a simple answer to that. Drawing out his penknife, he neatly cut a button from the delegate's tunic and presented it to him with the words: 'There, Your Excellency, you have the arms of Her Majesty.' This was not only one of the most significant uses to which a Swiss army knife has ever been put, but also explains why the seal to the British signature on the first Geneva Convention bears the imprint of a British army uniform button.

While this solemn ceremony was in progress, and almost at the very moment that the last of the signatures was finally being appended to the Convention, delegates were startled by the roar of a mob in the courtyard below. Recent elections in the city had given rise to angry demonstrations and even gunfire, during which several people had been wounded. The furious crowd then marched on the Hôtel de Ville with the intention of airing their grievances and perhaps even taking hostage some of the town councillors whom they assumed to be in session in their usual premises. Seeing them surge into the courtyard, Dunant rushed to lock the doors of the vast antechamber and to close the windows, but some of the more active and agile among the invaders had already scaled the walls and nearly beat him to it. Frantic attempts by Dunant to repel the enraged demonstrators were interrupted by General Dufour who quietly but authoritatively took command of the situation and ordered the crowd to withdraw, explaining that there were no town councillors present and that a meeting of foreign diplomats was taking place.

After the demonstrators had dispersed, the signing ceremony was completed and the Geneva Convention was ready for ratification. To the delegates, as they slowly descended the broad marble staircase, this dramatic finale to the proceedings came as a stark reminder of the violence ever simmering beneath the surface, even in sedately civilised Geneva, impressing on them the gravity of their mission and the formidable nature of the task that lay ahead.

SIX

What a Waste of Lives

Gustave Moynier sat looking out through his study window across the calm, sun-flecked waters of Lake Geneva to the craggy mountains beyond. Before him on his desk lay the Geneva Convention, but it was not this handsome document with all its seals and signatures that was engaging his attention. As his gaze took in the distant snow-capped peaks of Mont Blanc, his mind was travelling into the future. He was stirred to a degree of enthusiasm rare for him. Not only was he convinced that the Convention would significantly reduce the suffering caused by war, he even saw it as the first step in bringing about the condemnation of war and, ultimately, its gradual disappearance altogether.

The sound of the doorbell jolted him back to the present. His colleagues on the International Committee had arrived for their first meeting since the conference, all except for Henry Dunant who had hurried off once again to Paris as soon as the delegates had left. As they exchanged greetings and settled themselves into their chairs, the members smiled at each other as if in mutual congratulation and there was an air of self-satisfaction in the room as of a job well done. Moynier brought them down to earth with a thump.

This fine and impressive Convention lying on the table in front of them and to which their eyes kept straying so proudly was quite worthless, he pointed out solemnly, until the states formally confirmed their intention to abide by it. They must therefore be persuaded to ratify it at the earliest opportunity. Moynier was under no illusions that this would be an easy task; indeed his sentiments were very similar to those of Winston Churchill nearly eighty years later when he said, 'This is not the beginning of the end, it is the end of the beginning.'

Article 10 of the Convention specified that ratifications should be exchanged at Berne within the next four months, or sooner if possible. The committee therefore wasted no time. Three weeks after the end of the Diplomatic Conference, a circular was sent to the nine existing aid societies, urging them to do all they could to convince the authorities of their countries of the advantages of adhering to the Convention. With it went a memorandum clearly explaining the reasoning behind each clause and the expected results of its application. This showed remarkable foresight on Moynier's part, for only two years later thousands of wounded soldiers were to suffer untold agony, and many lose their lives, simply because their commanders did not understand the benefits that could be derived from the Convention.

The committee members used all their ingenuity to persuade the national governments to commit themselves, and exactly one month to the day after the Convention had been signed news of the first ratification, that of France, came from Paris. Henry Dunant had not been idle. One after another, the European nations began to follow suit and by the end of the year nine countries had ratified, with five more in the following year.

While the International Committee was engaged in this diplomatic activity, Moynier and his colleagues were also working hard to promote the formation of new national societies and coordinate their activities. Nine societies had already been formed before the Geneva Convention was signed and nine more were set up in the following two years. The International Committee played a vital part in ensuring a basic uniformity in their principles and ideals, while allowing for the necessary slight divergences in details and organisation from one country to another. Without the committee's perseverance, guidance and vigilance, the family likeness and unity of the various Red Cross societies, so taken for granted today, would simply not exist.

One of these nine new aid societies set up in 1866 was in Switzerland itself and Moynier was at pains to emphasise that its role was entirely separate from that of the International Committee, and that the two should not be confused. Although the International Committee had its headquarters in Switzerland, he informed the central committees, its role did not include assistance to the army of this country. It was intended simply as a link between the committees of various countries, providing them with communication facilities. It had been for this purpose that it was set up by the 1863 conference and it would continue to function as long as it could be of use in this way. Its position with respect to the Swiss committee in Berne would be the same as that *vis-à-vis* any of the foreign committees.

With his legally trained and logical mind, Moynier paid meticulous attention to defining the role of the aid societies in peacetime, insisting that they should not allow themselves to be diverted into supporting other causes, however deserving these might appear. For he could see them losing their unique status and becoming indistinguishable from the plethora of philanthropic and charitable societies which existed at that time. Their mission was the improvement and support of military medical services, as well as the building up of reserves of cash, equipment and medical resources in readiness for use in war.

And war was once again on the horizon. Bismarck's long-term plans for Prussian supremacy in Germany, followed by Prussian domination of Europe, were slowly but surely taking shape and he was carefully cultivating the growing tension between his country and Austria over the administration of Schleswig and Holstein which they had jointly held since their victory over Denmark in 1864. In April 1866, an ominous treaty was signed with Italy, ensuring her alliance in the event of war with Austria and promising her the long-awaited prize of Venice which Napoleon had failed to deliver in 1859.

Despite an impassioned letter from Queen Victoria at Windsor Castle to King William I of Prussia, asking him to use his powers to avert the impending war, and Queen Augusta's own pleas to her husband to resist the plans of his ministers, the King had been too thoroughly indoctrinated by his ambitious Chancellor and was too

71

obsessed by the military destiny of his country, as well as the achievements of his illustrious forebear Frederick the Great, to heed any such requests. The Seven Weeks' War was declared on 15 June 1866.

By the outbreak of war, fourteen nations had ratified the Geneva Convention, including Prussia, but Austria, the other belligerent, had actually refused to sign. This was precisely the kind of situation the International Committee had always feared might arise: war breaking out without all the parties involved being bound by the Convention. Ratification became an even more urgent priority. In Paris, Dunant was active. He had already appealed to the *duc* de Fézensac, President of the French Central Committee, to press the French ambassador in Vienna to urge the Austrian government to sign. He also advised General Dufour to intercede with the Swiss Federal Council with a view to approaching the governments of various other states. For once a war was started there was no knowing which other nations might not be drawn in.

Not only were these approaches unsuccessful but they revealed that Austria, for one, had completely failed to understand what the Convention was all about, claiming to have no need of the intervention of an international committee which would be inconvenient to the military without contributing to the efficiency of their own measures to look after the wounded. The fact that the Convention was concerned solely with the neutrality of medical personnel seemed to have totally escaped them. Moynier was furious, declaring that such misconceptions not only illustrated the ignorance of those putting them forward, but above all their lack of responsibility.

In comforting contrast to such pigheadedness, Prussia was a model member of the Geneva Convention. The Prussian generals received orders to apply the Geneva Convention regardless of whether Austria did likewise. The Prussian Society with its 120 local branches had been busily amassing huge stocks of medical supplies and had raised vast amounts of money from charitable contributions. The government, appreciating the enormous help this would be, provided generous facilities: parcels were exempted from postal and carriage charges, duty was waived on imported goods and the society's staff were fed and lodged at the army's expense. A member of the central committee was even appointed liaison officer and was kept permanently informed of troop movements so that he could quickly direct aid wherever it was needed. Such was the efficiency and speed of the Prussian committee that their doctors and voluntary helpers sometimes arrived on the scene before the military medical services.

After the battle of Sadowa, which clinched the Prussian victory, 40,000 soldiers, mostly Austrian, were left dead or wounded on the battlefield. By the same evening, the Berlin Central Committee had taken in hand the mammoth task of collecting the wounded and transporting them to field hospitals where they were treated with the greatest care and expertise. Refreshment centres were set up at railway stations to serve the wounded arriving in hospital trains. Hospitals were built at the committee's expense, artificial limbs supplied, books and games distributed, and preventive measures adopted to combat the threat of cholera. The committee even tended to what was described as the spiritual and psychological welfare of the troops, as if being wounded was not irksome enough!

Although the Patriotic Society in Austria provided assistance to the wounded, its lack of pre-planning, adequate resources and qualified staff severely limited its usefulness and resulted in relief supplies arriving hopelessly late, if at all. Their efforts, pathetic in comparison to those of the central committees, proved the need for careful preparation and planning and the wisdom of Moynier's oft repeated phrase: 'Charity should not be caught unprepared.'

Despite the fact that the Austrian commanders had been informed that the Prussian troops would expect their adversaries to reciprocate in applying the Convention, the Austrians took no notice whatsoever and went on behaving as they had always done. There was not a single Red Cross flag or emblem to be seen in their ranks. They failed to recognise the neutral status of Prussian doctors and took them prisoner. And, assuming the Prussians would do the same, they ordered their own medical staff to abandon the wounded and field hospitals and retreat with the rest of the army. Eight hundred such men died as a result of being abandoned after the battle of Sadowa. What a waste of lives! Yet if Austria had only signed the Convention, all these lives and many more would have been saved. The Austrian doctors and nurses would have remained behind with their wounded until the arrival of the Prussians. They would then have been returned to their own side while the Prussians took over the task of tending the wounded.

Now it was Italy's turn to join the fray. No doubt believing that the campaign in the north would divert Austria's attention, she decided the time had come to honour the treaty signed with Prussia two months earlier. Full of confidence, Italy declared war on Austria and was promptly defeated. For by an uncanny coincidence, on 24 June 1866 – seven years to the day since the battle of Solferino – the Italians again confronted the Austrians in almost exactly the same place and with the same thunder rumbling around the nearby hills. The only differences were that, this time, the fighting was centred a few miles to the east of the Mincio river instead of to the west and, this time, the Italians did not have France fighting alongside them, so the Austrians won. But the defeat of King Victor Emmanuel's troops did not end the conflict. The Italian national hero Garibaldi raised an army of guerrillas and marched against the Austrians, pushing them back and regaining much lost territory.

Although Italy was a signatory to the Geneva Convention and her central committee in Milan had been active in their preparations even before the outbreak of war, the knowledge, or at least the fear, that Austria would not apply the provisions of the Convention again resulted in unnecessary suffering and loss of life. After one particular defeat, Garibaldi's wounded troops were crammed into a church in a small town where the local population, fearing reprisals from the advancing Austrian army, turned their backs on the unfortunate soldiers. Two days after the battle, believing the Austrians were about to attack, an order to evacuate the wounded from the church was given at 2 o'clock in the morning. By the feeble light of a few candles, the wounded were thrown in conditions of panic and chaos into carts jolting their way out of the battle zone, many unfortunate wretches dying in agony on the way. Had the Geneva Convention been applied, most of this suffering and unnecessary waste of life would have been avoided.

The Seven Weeks' War also introduced a new element, naval warfare. On 20 July, the Italian and Austrian fleets fought an important naval engagement in the Adriatic, near the island of Lissa, when ironclads equipped with steam engines were used for the first time in battle. Despite having one of the best fleets of its time, Italy was defeated and one of her battleships, *Re d'Italia*, sunk with appalling loss of life, no attempts being made to rescue the hundreds of drowning men. This tragedy highlighted the need for the Convention to be extended to war at sea. An article to this effect had actually been included by Moynier and General Dufour in the draft convention prepared for the Diplomatic Conference in 1864 but, probably because there had been no naval equivalent of Solferino in recent times, the question was shelved. The issue was to be raised from unexpected quarters and with unusual passion the following year.

The Seven Weeks' War proved the advantages of adherence to the Geneva Convention so convincingly that three more states immediately added their signatures. These were the Grand Duchy of Hesse, Bavaria and, finally, Austria. War had proved a more effective advocate than even Moynier himself.

Austria's signature seemed to set the ball rolling and Portugal, Royal Saxony and Russia quickly followed suit. Three further aid societies were also set up, in Russia, Austria and the Netherlands. A lot of water had flowed down the Rhône and through Geneva since that first meeting of the Committee of Five four years earlier, and a great deal more had been achieved than its members had ever dared hope. In fact, everything seemed to be running so smoothly that the International Committee wondered whether it was not time for it to withdraw from the scene. After lengthy discussions on the subject, they decided they should continue as long as the national societies needed them. A fortunate decision since, in the event, without the impartial guidance and mediation of the International Committee, as well as its skilful negotiation around all the obstacles that lay ahead, the Red Cross movement would not have acquired the stature or universality it enjoys today, and would probably never have survived at all.

One of Moynier's chief concerns was to encourage the different aid societies to work more closely together, guided by a common philosophy. To this end, and together with Appia, he wrote a 400-page manual entitled *La Guerre et la Charité* which dealt with all the problems connected with the organisation and management of aid societies. He was extremely concerned about the question of whether societies of neutral countries should go to the assistance of countries at war. A good opportunity to discuss this arose when the French Central Committee announced that the next Universal Exhibition would be held in Paris in 1867 and suggested that the work of the aid societies should be put on display, as it was one of the great achievements of modern times. The committee also suggested that this would be a good time to convene a conference of delegates from all the national societies.

Moynier welcomed this idea and in a letter to the *duc* de Fézensac, emphasised the importance he attached to jointly studying the relations to be established between the committees of various countries. He added that the honour of organising this conference rightly rested with France, expecting them to agree to undertake this task. But he had reckoned without the inspirational influence which Henry Dunant had exerted on the French committee in Paris.

To Moynier's dismay, the French Committee went overboard and invited to Paris not only the central committees of the various countries, but also assorted medical men, representatives of various charitable and religious institutions, delegates from signatory states, scientists, philanthropists, Old Uncle Tom Cobbleigh and all! In such a vast and motley assembly, there seemed to Moynier little scope for constructive discussion.

Among the items included on the proposed agenda for the conference were suggested revisions to the Geneva Convention. Having fought so hard for the Convention and its ratification, Moynier was reluctant to jeopardise it for the sake of a few dubious improvements. He therefore felt obliged to go to Paris himself to ensure that all the good work he and his colleagues on the International Committee had accomplished was not thrown to the winds. As it turned out, the points put forward for revision were relatively minor, requiring clarification rather than drastic change. Moynier left Paris with a lighter heart, reassured that the Convention would emerge from the coming conference unscathed. He returned to Geneva in good spirits, unaware that a time-bomb was ticking away there, the explosion of which a few days later was to rock the International Committee to its very foundations.

SEVEN

The Felfela Affair

While Moynier toiled away in Geneva supervising the setting up of national aid societies and wrestling to win further ratifications for the Convention, Dunant was basking in the bright lights of his beloved Paris where he had escaped as soon as the conference was over and the Convention safely signed. Having been relegated to the role of 'Entertainments Officer' during the Convention ceremonies, at what should have been the apex of his fame in Geneva, Dunant felt that it was only right he should enjoy somewhere else the applause he so richly deserved.

And Paris did not fail him. Here he was warmly welcomed and encouragement and praise lavished upon him, not only by the great ladies of high society for whom he seemed to have peculiar appeal, but by the press and those in intellectual and literary circles. On one occasion, at the Institut de France, after listening to a tedious and long-winded peroration from the writer Ernest Renan justifying his own claim to fame, he was rewarded for his patience – or, more likely, roused from his slumbers – by the writer finally declaiming: 'You have created the greatest work of the century. Europe perhaps will stand in dire need of it.' Bishops and archbishops flocked round with their blessings and there were invitations to give lectures to various prestigious organisations, and glowing praise from all sides. He wrote proudly to his mother, regaling her with tales of all these tributes, but adding modestly that the merit was not his alone, 'for the hand of God guided my pen in writing *Un Souvenir de Solferino*'.

Further encouragement came with the news of the growing number of ratifications. In January 1865, he received a personal letter from Sir Thomas Longmore, telling him that Great Britain was ratifying the Convention This he took great pleasure in sending on to Moynier in Geneva. Another letter, from the French Minister for Foreign Affairs, announced that the Emperor was awarding him the Légion d'Honneur as a token of his high esteem on the occasion of the international agreement recently concluded in Geneva. Such an honour coming from his longtime hero, from Napoleon III: this was heady stuff indeed!

Then came the announcement that the Emperor would be visiting Algeria in the spring. Dunant, who had never relinquished his dreams or unpinned his hopes where Napoleon and his business ventures were concerned, set off for Algiers with the intention of seeking an audience on the spot. On 10 May, he attended a fête given in the Emperor's honour by Marshal MacMahon, his old friend and recently appointed Governor-General of Algeria. This was a magnificent affair, held at the white marble Moustapha Palace in its setting of gushing fountains and avenues of orange trees. All the ships in the harbour, all the mosques and public buildings were brilliantly illuminated for the occasion; a mock attack was staged on the fort and rockets shot into the sky. At midnight, there was a feast for fifty with a menu including ostrich eggs, roasted gazelle and antelope, and drumsticks of lion, although perhaps some of the Arab potentates present might have preferred a lightly poached sheep's eye!

He was given a great welcome by Madame MacMahon who cornered him and asked eagerly about the progress of his work for the wounded, declaring ardently: 'I am one of your disciples, Monsieur Dunant.' A sentiment he might well have echoed towards the Emperor as he took his place in the procession, waiting to be presented, his Légion d'Honneur proudly displayed on his breast.

After all the attempts he had made, all the miles travelled and all the traumas undergone to arrive at this moment, here he was at last, face to face with Napoleon III. With an enigmatic smile hovering on his lips, the Emperor listened to Dunant's appeal for patronage of the French aid society and suggested he come and make it at the Tuileries, together with members of the committee. Then Dunant broached the matter of his Algerian business and, here too, the

Emperor promised him 'Your company will be protected by my government'.

Taking Napoleon's words as gospel, brimming with renewed confidence and optimism, Dunant went on to Setif to visit his associate, Henri Nick. His Algerian affairs seemed to be looking less bleak since his banker friend, Théodore Vernes, decided to play an active part, and the Société des Moulins de Mons-Djemila had been merged with a group with similar interests to form a company called L'Omnium Algérien. Now, with the added bonus of the Emperor's promise of protection, Dunant felt that things were really looking up. Listening to his eager enthusiasm, the wily Nick sensed an opportunity to make a quick buck. He suggested to Dunant that he persuade his friends in the Crédit Genevois, a recently founded private bank in which Dunant had connections, to take a half share in some marble quarries at Felfela for 200,000 francs. The idea was that the quarries would then be sold to L'Omnium Algérien for 500,000 francs – a sum nearer their real value, according to Nick – and he and Dunant would make 50,000 francs on the deal, the money going to finance the Mons-Djemila mills. Nick, rogue that he was, omitted to mention that he had acquired these quarries for a mere 95,000 francs.

To raise the money to pay for these quarries, the Omnium needed to obtain some concessions in Algeria from the French government and Dunant was confident that these would be forthcoming. Alas, there is a world of difference between an Emperor's benevolent intention and a ministerial permit, and big business interests made sure L'Omnium was cut out. Only a matter of days after the Emperor's promise of protection for L'Omnium, the French government signed an agreement with two powerful contractors for the formation of the Société générale Algérienne which would be engaged in public works to develop the colony. With a capital of 100 million francs and government backing, this company reduced the prospects of L'Omnium to virtually nil. Amazingly, however, Dunant still retained his own faith and, even more surprisingly, that of his shareholders. Apart from his own eloquence and persuasive-ness, their confidence was undoubtedly bolstered by the knowledge that the highly able banker Théodore Vernes was involved in the project.

In high spirits, Dunant returned to Paris to take up the Emperor's invitation for the committee of the French Society to visit the Tuileries. Headed by the ancient *duc* de Fézensac, the party was received by the Emperor, who paid particular attention to Dunant and made a generous contribution to the society's funds. The committee then proceeded to the Ministry of War to call on Marshal Randon and express its gratitude to him for accepting the honorary presidency of the committee. The Marshal immediately launched into a tirade against those 'meddling men from Geneva'. Then, seemingly unaware of Dunant's presence, he went on to complain angrily about a certain Monsieur Dunant who had had the cheek to criticise the French administration in a recently published and grossly overrated book. Without revealing that he was present, his colleagues eventually succeeded in pacifying the irate Minister and the audience ended on a subdued note. An unfortunate anti-climax after such a splendid start to the day.

His confidence was again shaken several weeks later when George Sand challenged his right to the credit for the Geneva Convention. Writing in *L'Opinion Nationale*, he claimed that this rightly belonged to Henri Arrault. Although Dunant was unaware of it at the time of writing *Un Souvenir*, Arrault had indeed published a paper in 1861 on the neutralisation of the wounded and medical personnel. And, in the same year, in Italy a Dr Palasciano had also advocated the same thing. But, in both cases, their proposals had got no further than the printed page whereas Dunant's, at the price of extraordinary perseverance and despite enormous difficulties, had been propelled into action.

Unfair and unwarranted as it was, this attack coincided with various other signs that seemed to indicate a turning point in the tide of Dunant's fortunes. Nothing appeared to be happening to justify the Emperor's promises in regard to his Algerian affairs. As if to emphasise the point, a series of natural catastrophes occurred and Algeria, in 1865, suffered one disaster after another. War was followed by cholera, locusts, earthquakes, drought and an exceptionally dreadful winter. The mills and assets in Mons-Djemila were not only lying idle but deteriorating by the day.

Still Dunant did not despair. Hearing that the two contractors who had formed the Société générale Algérienne were going to see the Emperor, he asked General Dufour to write a note to his former pupil, suggesting that Dunant be made a director of their company. But the scrupulously correct General demurred, unwilling to presume upon his friendship with the Emperor. Gradually the already minimal activities of the ill-starred Omnium ground to a halt.

With the outbreak of the Austro-Prussian War, his business anxieties were compounded with anguish as he read reports from the front, imagining only too vividly the dreadful scenes being enacted on the battlefield. All that he could do was fight for Austria's signature to the Convention and this was finally secured in July. He comforted himself with the thought that at least Prussia had the benefit of an active central committee in Berlin under the personal guidance of Queen Augusta who, finding that she had been unable to prevent war, resolved to do all in her power to relieve the suffering it caused. Under her supervision, committees were set to work in many German towns, groups of voluntary nurses formed and vast amounts of money raised with which medical and other supplies were purchased and forwarded to the front. Despite the risk of cholera, she visited the wounded in hospital every day and it was due to her untiring efforts and dedication that the Prussian aid society operated so efficiently and harmoniously with the army medical services. At the end of the war, Queen Angusta insisted that Henry Dunant, the man whose work had so inspired her, be invited to the victory thanksgiving celebrations.

Dunant hurried to Berlin where he was quickly caught up in the general mood of exhilaration and excitement. It was a day for rejoicing and the streets were gaily decked with flags and garlands. Taking his place among the royal guests to watch the parade of the victorious army, he saw with pride and emotion that, side by side with the national Prussian flag, fluttered the white flag with the red cross for which he had fought so hard. It was everywhere – adorning the rostrum, the palace, the houses, the triumphal arches, even the royal pavilion.

That evening there was a huge gala banquet at the palace to which all the generals and senior officers were invited, and Henry Dunant too. A slightly incongruous figure in his sober black attire among all the resplendent uniforms and the glittering crowd, he tried to make himself as inconspicuous as possible and found a seat at a distant table in the furthest hall, unaware that he had been assigned a place quite near to where the King was sitting.

After the banquet, the Royal Family gave a reception. Count Stolberg, the President of the Prussian aid society, located Dunant and led him to the main reception room where among all the princes, princesses and noble lords, he caught a glimpse of the pale and disdainful face of Count von Bismarck. Wearing the uniform and helmet of the White Cuirassiers, he stood rigidly aloof and silent, with the air of contemplating those around him as so many puppets to be manipulated at his will. From his lofty eminence, his eyes rested momentarily on Dunant, puzzled perhaps at the identity of this modest stranger, the only person present in civilian clothes, being welcomed so warmly by Their Majesties.

The King spoke graciously to Dunant, reminding him that he had been the first European sovereign to encourage his work, and telling him that the Austrian wounded who had been left to them were being cared for even better than their own. Then the Queen greeted him enthusiastically. At that moment, the Crown Prince approached, with the intention of presenting three bishops to the Queen. Paying no attention to them, Her Majesty advanced towards her son, exclaiming eagerly: 'Here is Mr Dunant who has finally arrived.'

'Ah, we are old friends, Mr Dunant and I,' said the Crown Prince, his face lighting up as he recalled their long conversation at the lunch in Potsdam three years earlier, and he smiled and shook Dunant warmly by the hand. Next to pay tribute were the Queen's brother, the Grand Duke of Saxe-Weimar, who confided that he had always wanted to meet him, and the King's sister who spoke glowingly of his work. Dunant was intoxicated by so much honour and royal praise, in such striking contrast to the disappointments and disapproval that had become his daily fare in Geneva. This was the tonic he needed. And there was more to come.

Two days later he was invited to dinner at the royal palace with about thirty other people. He was standing by one of the large windows overlooking the palace gardens when the arrival of the King and Queen was solemnly announced. The Queen immediately went over to Dunant and drew his attention to her Red Cross armband, proudly telling him that she had worn it throughout the war and that she had put it on that day in his honour. This time, unlike the armband displayed by Madame de Staël in her salon in Paris some years earlier, everyone knew what the Red Cross denoted.

At dinner, he was seated between two chamberlains and almost opposite the King and Queen, who continued to wear the armband on her bare arm throughout the evening. Ironically, the topic of conversation was war and the King held forth with great enthusiasm on the best ways of annihilating columns of infantry. Dunant found little to contribute to such a discussion. After dinner, the Queen received Dunant in her boudoir where, after a long discourse on her work for the wounded during the war, she presented him with an alabaster statue of St Michael with a red cross emblazoned on its breast – a fitting adornment for his mantelpiece, no doubt.

Pleasant as it was for Dunant to receive such acclaim and royal approval, it was nevertheless time to face once more the everlasting problem of his Algerian affairs, and he reluctantly returned to Geneva. With the Société Algérienne flourishing under able management and his own Omnium beyond all hope of resuscitation, he decided to set up a wholly Swiss company, the Compagnie Algérienne, with the purpose of acquiring and exploiting industrial and agricultural enterprises in Algeria. It was also hoped that this new company could collaborate with others, notably the Société Algérienne. Again he found little difficulty in rallying support for his cause. The board of the new company boasted a list of distinguished Geneva names and even the Crédit Lyonnais took up a substantial holding.

It seemed a good omen when Prince Jerome Napoleon – that magic name – came to stay at his residence in Prangins, on the lakeside near Nyon, in the summer of 1866. He had commanded the 5th Corps during the Italian campaign and had also for a time been Minister for Algeria. Dunant visited him before attending the victory celebrations in Berlin and they had had the friendliest discussions. Back in Geneva at the end of September and trying desperately to find ways to promote his new company he told his mother that he intended to appeal to the Prince and thought the best way of going about it would be to entertain him at their elegant home on the outskirts of Geneva. The Prince accepted their invitation to a dinner party at La Monnaie and all went well until Dunant began telling their illustrious guest about his difficulties in Algeria. Abruptly stabbing his Havana into a delicate Sèvres ashtray, the Prince coldly informed him that he could take no hand in Algerian business affairs since – as Dunant himself should remember – he had been responsible for administering the colony some years ago. Another door was thus closed firmly in Dunant's face.

Apart from all the calamities in Algeria, the war in Austria had sent shudders through the Paris Bourse and made 1866 a disastrous year for business. In February 1867, the Crédit Genevois, suffering from the general crisis and an alarming shortage of cash, reneged on the deal over the Felfela quarries and asked for their money back. Naturally, it was not available. Dunant and Nick had been relying on concessions, which they had failed to get, to provide them with working capital. In a last-ditch attempt to save the situation, Dunant speculated on the Bourse, engulfing himself still further in trouble.

Meanwhile, the Crédit Genevois, faced with the spectre of bankruptcy, went into liquidation. Accused of mismanagement by an irate group of shareholders, the directors were summoned before the commercial court, and Dunant with them, for it transpired that he had been appointed to the board some time earlier. The verdict was that all the directors were guilty of incompetence but not criminally so, and therefore the plaintiffs had no claim on them in law.

The news of the collapse of the Crédit Genevois exploded like a bomb in Geneva, a city where financial failure is considered a cardinal sin. And Dunant's involvement in the affair seemed a catastrophe for the International Committee which, according to Moynier, 'believed its last hour had come'.

Even before the verdict was known, as soon as the bank went into liquidation, Dunant sold all his considerable assets in Algeria and paid in the proceeds to reduce the loss. By doing so, he honourably acknowledged his responsibility as a director of the bank, regardless of whether the court would establish any legal liability. There is no evidence that the other directors, who were responsible for vastly greater losses, contributed a single penny.

The shareholders, however, were not prepared to let the matter rest. They were out for blood and appealed against the verdict. In doing so they launched a train of events which resulted in a scandal that rocked the International Committee and disgraced its founder. As for Dunant himself, he was utterly ruined. Virtually banished from Geneva, he was exiled in Paris where he lived in abject poverty, knowing that he would never be able to set foot in his native city again.

EIGHT

Dunant Dusts Himself Off

In April 1867, all Europe was talking about the fabulous Universal
Exhibition that had just opened its gates in Paris on the Champ de
Mars. Here, the splendour and the proud achievements of the
Second Empire were on display for all the world to see. Napoleonic
magnificence was mirrored in the lavish decorations and glittering
military parades, Napoleonic munificence in the welcome extended
to all other countries to exhibit their latest weapons and wares.

Crowned heads from all over Europe converged on Paris,
attracted by the city's glamour and brilliant social life as well as by
the exhibition itself. The King of Prussia arrived, accompanied by
the sinister but resplendent Bismarck in his uniform of the White
Cuirassiers and in unusually affable mood, surprising Paris with his
gallantry and charm at all the balls and gala receptions he so eagerly
and unexpectedly attended. Tsar Alexander II turned up with his
sons and even the Sultan of Turkey succumbed to the temptation of
leaving his realms for the first time. There were certainly some
amazing sights to see, and inventions to marvel at, such as the
machine that swallowed a rabbit skin and returned it, a few
moments later, transformed into a stylish felt hat. In striking
contrast, there was a colossal cannon weighing 100,000lb and cost-
ing 3 million francs, attracting suitable awe and admiration from the
passing crowds, as did the bust of its creator, Alfred Krupp.

Nearby, on a pedestal of honour, stood another bust, handsomely
garlanded with laurels but unrecognised by most passers-by, except
for those who stopped to peer at the engraved inscription: 'Henry
Dunant; founder of the Movement for the Relief of the War
Wounded'. This formed the centre-piece of an exhibition within the

exhibition, arranged by the Geneva Committee in collaboration with the French Committee, to display the organisation and equipment of the aid societies.

Visitors to this stand were fascinated by the array of surgical instruments, stretchers and scale models of horse-drawn ambulances and field dressing stations, many responding spontaneously to the collection of contributions – contributions that the real-life Dunant, shivering with cold and hunger only a few miles away, would have been only too happy to garner for himself.

Henry Dunant had indeed been plunged to the rock bottom of the abyss. In bold but somewhat shaky handwriting, he heads this page in his memoirs: '1867. Catastrophe! Ruined!' He went on: 'I had not even entered my thirty-ninth year when everything collapsed around me. . . . Sick with grief, and not having even enough money to pay a hotel, I was obliged to take refuge in a cheap district at the far end of the suburb of Saint-Antoine. . . . I had been left to drown without help and in the most atrocious agony. I would not wish for even my worst enemies to suffer the hundredth part of what I suffered then. . . .'

By a cruel irony of fate, it was in his beloved Paris where he had so recently enjoyed acclaim and praise that he now eked out a miserable and humiliating existence. Sometimes unable to pay even the peppercorn rent for his outhouse in a garden in the rue de Neuilly, he frequently spent the night in station waiting rooms. As for food, his stomach 'ached with hunger and seemed to swoon when passing those delicious Parisian bakers' shops'.

Hearing about the tributes paid to his laurel-wreathed statue at the Universal Exhibition only served to exasperate the half-starved Dunant. He got a friend to steal in one night and carry the offending object away. Finding it too heavy to bear unaided out of the hall, this gentleman borrowed a nearby trolley to which he strapped his friend's statue, thereby unwittingly giving Dr Appia's beloved mobile stretcher its one and only active tour of duty.

One might have thought that his colleagues would have come to Dunant's aid in some way, even if they had chosen to keep quiet about it. Far from it. Moynier did everything he could publicly to dissociate himself and the committee from their disreputable

Secretary. In June, he wrote to the organiser of the Universal Exhibition to warn him against the possible intervention of Henry Dunant, concluding with the words: "We have very good reasons for not wishing to be represented by him henceforth. If, therefore, he offers to act on our behalf, I would be obliged to you to get rid of him . . .' Finally, on 15 August, Moynier wrote to Dunant, inviting him to tender his resignation. Ten days later, he complied, whereupon Moynier wrote back that his resignation as Secretary had been accepted and that it was assumed it also covered his membership of the committee.

Shunned by his colleagues, even by most of those on the French central committee to whom Moynier had also been careful to write, Dunant found himself in the paradoxical situation of still being held in the highest esteem by delegates to the forthcoming International Conference of Aid Societies in Paris, who knew nothing about the goings-on in Geneva and who would probably have been highly amused if they had. Several of the monarchs visiting the exhibition wanted to meet and congratulate the man about whom they had heard so much, but their enquiries as to his whereabouts were met with blank looks and vague or non-committal replies. It was sometimes even inferred that he might be dead. Only Queen Augusta, who had heard of Dunant's plight from Loeffler, sent him assurances of her continuing interest, together with a gift of 3,000 francs, a sum that Dunant privately regarded as not exactly royal.

Moynier's conduct was not, in fact, motivated solely by concern that the disgrace connected with Dunant would rub off on the committee. He also had a shrewd suspicion that, behind the scenes, Dunant was at work to move the headquarters of the International Committee to Paris. In June, Théodore Vernes, the banker and now treasurer of the French aid society, had written to Moynier, confiding in him that his colleagues would like to withdraw its title from the Geneva Committee and transfer it to the Paris Committee. The Frenchmen were also feeling rather sour over the jury of the Universal Exhibition awarding a Grand Prix with gold medal to the Geneva Committee for the exhibition of medical equipment rather than to Count Sérurier of the French committee who had organised it.

The first International Conference of Aid Societies thus opened on 26 August with rather strained relations. It was attended by delegates from sixteen central committees and representatives from nine governments. Dunant was present, Moynier having informed Théodore Vernes that he had no objection to his being invited as a private individual, but that he could not under any circumstances consent to sit beside him in his capacity as Vice-Chairman.

One of the main subjects on the agenda was the revision of the Geneva Convention. A lengthy draft had been drawn up by a sub-committee which Moynier urged the assembly to adopt, reminding his listeners that they were not in any case empowered actually to revise the Convention, merely to prepare a text for submission to the states. But the delegates protested that this would be premature. Following a conference in Berlin, the Prussian central committee had also prepared proposals for modifications to the convention. And the central committee of Hesse came up with a third text which it submitted to the conference. After three days spent reading these various proposals and counter-proposals, Moynier became so hoarse that he had to ask Dr Appia to take over as Chairman. A fourth text was finally agreed upon, adopting the main arguments of the committee and adding some new ones, notably relating to law and order on the battlefield, to put a stop to the horrific plundering that regularly took place, and identification of the dead and their notification to the respective authorities as well as to their relatives.

Then came discussion over the structure and responsibilities of the International Committee. Convinced that most national committees wanted a revision of the 1863 Resolutions concerning the role of the Geneva Committee, Moynier himself proposed replacing it by a supreme council which would include members elected by the national committees of various countries and would be situated in a place where no committee could exert a dominating influence. This gave the French committee just the opening it was looking for. Geneva has none of the necessary attributes to be the headquarters of the International Committee, they claimed. Even its much vaunted neutrality was not all that secure, to judge by the unrest in the Italian canton during the Italian war and the uncertain future of the French-speaking cantons in view of their possible reversion to France. Paris in their view was a far safer bet and possessed all the necessary resources to make an ideal base for the International Committee.

The committee appointed to study Moynier's proposal finally recommended that the conference maintain the headquarters of the International Committee in Geneva. But it tactfully suggested the creation of an International Subcommittee in Paris where all the equipment and material could be collected together, forming a sort of university or museum, thus taking advantage of all the facilities offered by this great and beautiful metropolis. The assembly immediately applauded, thanking the French committee for its generous offer and the French spokesman bowed to the conference with a sardonic smile, inwardly acknowledging defeat.

At this stage in his life at least, Henry Dunant seemed to belong to that happy breed of people whose energy, resilience and ability to blank out unpleasant facets of reality ensure that they never stay under for very long. In Paris, after the initial shock of the débâcle in Geneva had begun to subside, he bounced back into commercial activity as if all his career until then had been one long and unbroken success story. Within a matter of weeks, he had acquired a new clutch of projects with which to sail confidently into the future and, hopefully, salvage the disasters of the past. His resurrection was due in large part to several friends, all colourful characters like himself and ready to give him generous and unstinting help at the time he needed it most, and to his mother's short but timely visit from Geneva.

First to appear on the Paris scene was Charles Bowles, an American banker and the European representative of the United States Sanitary Commission, an organisation with similar aims to those of the International Committee. He had also been a delegate to the 1864 Diplomatic Conference at which the Geneva Convention had come into being. Bowles was a great admirer of Dunant 'With all his resources, mental, influential and pecuniary, and with his courage and great energy, he has been at once the pioneer, prop and successful promoter of this work.' Bowles and Dunant had a great deal in common, notably an incurable tendency to mix philanthropy and business – a dangerous blend that would lead Bowles in his turn down the road to bankruptcy later in life. At this point in time (as he might have put it himself), everything was prospering around him and the banking house of Bowles Bros. & Co. had flourishing branches in London, Paris, New York and Boston. He generously offered Dunant a comfortable office in the rue de la Paix, invited him to become his associate and gave him a token salary that set him afloat and at least enabled him to keep the wolf from the door.

Now that he had found his feet again, Dunant felt able to invite his mother to visit him in Paris. He had kept in touch with her throughout his period of despair, humiliation and degradation and the tone of his letters clearly reveals how much he missed her. Meeting her at the Gare de Lyon, he was delighted to find that she had brought with her several trunks containing much needed clothes, left behind in his precipitate departure from Geneva.

Staying in the comfortable and elegant Hôtel Meurice facing the Tuileries Gardens, she provided a focal point for his new hopes. Discussing his plans, he drew strength from her understanding and encouragement while her quiet charm and aristocratic dignity provided the respectable background he badly needed to project to his new friends.

Together they explored Paris, a Paris far divorced from the high society which Dunant had hitherto frequented. Visiting Notre Dame and the Louvre, drinking coffee in one of the colourful cafés of the Latin Quarter, strolling through the Bois de Boulogne on sunny afternoons . . . with his mother in Paris, Dunant experienced one of the last periods of peace he was to enjoy in his long life. For little did he know, as he cheerfully saw her off at the station, he was never to see her again.

Another friend who was destined to play an important part in Dunant's life was Jean-Jacques Bourcart, an enlightened and generous-minded businessman from Alsace, dedicated to the cause of social reform and a friend of Cobden and Bright. He had written numerous books, including one on workers' participation in business enterprises. Unfortunately, he attempted to apply the system in his own company and ruined himself in the process. He had first set eyes on Dunant during a lecture he gave on behalf of the French aid society, and had been struck by his shabby appearance. On closer acquaintance, he found Dunant an engaging companion with whose ideas and ideals he was completely in tune.

Bourcart had been scandalised by a scene he witnessed at the Exhibition of Aid Societies when he had overheard a conversation between two men unknown to him personally but whom he later discovered could have been none other than Moynier and Count Sérurier, making derisory comments in front of Dunant's bust. This incident resolved him to do all he could to reinstate him. Helping him generously from his own resources, he even went to the Tuileries to solicit those of the Emperor, who offered to pay half Dunant's debts if other charitable persons did the rest. But the letter Bourcart wrote with this good news mysteriously failed to reach its destination. Some years later, he recalled how it was as if all his efforts to help were foiled by unseen hands.

But the man who turned out to be Dunant's most loyal and devoted ally in the bleak spring days of 1867 was Max Grazia, a scholarly and highly cultured Italian from Rimini, who gave him moral and material support, encouraged him in his moments of black despair and helped him to write the painful and difficult letters to his creditors. Not only was Grazia a Good Samaritan but he also offered Dunant the means to make a living as secretary of an ambitious new undertaking he was promoting, the International World Library which aimed to publish a collection of all the masterpieces from every period and every country in the best French translations. This was a project very much after Dunant's heart and tailor-made to his tastes for internationalism and commercial philanthropy. (Grazia also, for a welcome change, failed to go bankrupt!)

The job of secretary to the International World Library, which brought in a small income, together with partnership in Bowles's banking house, would probably have been enough to keep anyone else in similarly straitened circumstances busy and content. But Dunant's sights, as always, were set on wider horizons and loftier schemes. The presence in Paris of the Sultan of Turkey, Napoleon's guest of honour at the Universal Exhibition, reawoke in him all his long-cherished dreams for the development of the Orient – the very sound of the word Orient held irresistible appeal to someone of Dunant's austere Calvinist background. This scheme, hatched the year before in a pamphlet published in Paris, actually embraced the whole of the Near East but the emphasis was on Zionism.

The return of the Jews to Palestine, the development of agriculture, industry and trade, the granting of concessions of land by the Turkish government and their colonisation by Jewish families from Morocco, Poland and Romania, the construction of a port at Jaffa and a road and railway linking it to Jerusalem, international cooperation in the restoration of the holy shrines . . . his plans branched off in all directions, each more ambitious than the last, culminating in the proposal that the new colonies should be diplomatically neutralized in the same way as Switzerland, by convention. France would have the lion's share in these colonial undertakings with Napoleon III magnanimously repatriating modern-day Jews to the Promised Land.

Once again began the all too familiar quest for concessions. No *arrière-pensée* of apprehension, no twinge of doubt, ever seems to have crossed his mind. The Sultan being in Paris should make things easier and Dunant started by trying to reach him through his friends on the French central committee, Count Sérurier and the *duc* de Fézensac. An engineer by the name of Conrandy had meanwhile approached him with his plans for the reconstruction of Solomon's aqueduct to provide a water supply for the Holy City, and even his business-like friend Bourcart considered that if Dunant could get the concession for this project, he should be able to sell it to Conrandy for a sum that would comfortably cover all his debts. A rich Russian also expressed interest in buying land in Palestine to set up Jewish colonies. The overjoyed Dunant wrote ecstatically to his mother with the good news.

The lucky streak continued with a summons from Empress Eugénie to the Tuileries on 7 July. The Empress had been horrified by a story she had heard from an Admiral in the Austrian navy who had been in the battle of Lissa the year before when the *Re d'Italia* went down with a thousand men aboard. Emotionally she recalled how hundreds of panic-stricken sailors had perished without any attempt having being made to help them. Yet if only there had been a lifeboat on hand, she added, under the protection of the international flag, they could have been saved.

The Empress insisted that provisions be made to extend the Geneva Convention to cover wounded and shipwrecked sailors. Dunant told her that he was no longer the secretary of the Geneva Committee but that the French government could take the appropriate action. 'No,' retorted the Empress, 'it must be you.' And the sovereign pointed an imperial forefinger straight at Dunant's chest. Left with little option but to obey, Dunant visited Count Sérurier the same day and ensured that the Empress's request would be submitted to the International Conference of Aid Societies the following month.

By a strange coincidence, the French Ambassador to Constantinople, M. Bourée, was also present at this audience and, after the matter of naval warfare had been dealt with, the conversation happened to turn to the subject of Palestine. Dunant grasped this opportunity to interest the Emperor, via the Empress, in his oriental project which diplomatically included the building of a hospital in Jerusalem which would be placed under Her Majesty's own protection. The Ambassador promised to make the necessary enquiries on his return to Turkey and the Empress graciously bestowed official patronage on his project.

Only a week afterwards, Dunant received a letter that would have dampened anyone else's ardour and extinguished their hopes for good. A Dr Zimpel who had bitter experience of Turkish bureaucracy, having attempted a similar scheme some time ago, wrote in withering tones to pour scorn on the plans outlined in his pamphlet. He implied that Dunant must be out of his mind to contemplate colonisation in Palestine which was under the most corrupt administration imaginable.

Amazingly, Dunant brushed aside these warnings and calmly continued with his plans to form a Universal Oriental Company under the patronage of the Emperor with a capital of 500 million francs. The money would be raised from wealthy Jews all over the world, as well as from investors in Europe and America. In an 'open letter' on the subject, evidently intended for a fairly select audience, if not for the Emperor himself, there was a reassuring sprinkling of names like Rothschild and Montefiore. He was momentarily diverted from this programme by the invitation he received from Count Sérurier to attend the first International Conference of Aid Societies where he rapturously heard himself described as the founder and promoter. In the past few months, he had also been named vice-president of several newly formed national societies and honorary member of others.

By this time, Ambassador Bourée was back in Turkey sounding out local interest in Dunant's project. The information he received from the French consul in Jerusalem were scarcely encouraging. There was little scope for agricultural development in the area. The building earmarked for the new hospital under the patronage of Empress Eugénie had been taken over for government offices. The proposed reconstruction of the aqueduct was a hopelessly impracticable pipe-dream. A snort of contempt for such idiotic schemes was almost audible in the consul's tone.

To judge from a letter to his mother at the New Year, this was all water off a duck's back. The prospects for his Oriental Company were brilliant and the rich and royal all over Europe were scrambling to buy land in Palestine. He was convinced that 'with the help of God' he could settle all his debts and start on the road to fortune again. The first few days of 1868 were so cold that the Seine was frozen over and he thanked his mother for sending him a fur coat, telling her how in the omnibus one day a little boy was shivering so much that he had wrapped him up in it. He had received 126 cards for the New Year, from a host of distinguished people. His new year had got off to a fine start.

Even before the end of the old year, he had been approached by representatives of the 'Temple', a Protestant sect from Württemberg that was seeking permission for its members to settle in Palestine. Dunant, they thought, could obtain the necessary concessions from the Sultan. Since their plans to colonise Palestine did not conflict with his oriental schemes and appealed to Dunant's Protestant loyalties, his new company signed an agreement with the Council of the Temple and received an initial payment of 2,500 francs. As if resettling Jews in Palestine were not enough, he seems to have been quite oblivious to the reception a Muslim potentate would be likely to give to a proposal to settle a further influx of Protestant Christian Germans!

Meanwhile, work to get the International World Library on to a sound financial footing continued, an undertaking that was proving far more difficult than he and Grazia had anticipated. But promoting it was right up his street and he busied himself writing a programme. In fact this project never really got off the ground, at least not in Dunant's lifetime. But it would be a mistake to consider all the ventures into which Dunant launched with such enthusiasm as far-fetched and impracticable. His proposals for setting up aid societies for the wounded might also have sounded pretty absurd at the time. It is quite conceivable that if Dunant had found others like Moynier as partners in his later projects, the State of Israel and UNESCO (United Nations Educational, Scientific and Cultural Organisation) might have become realities a century earlier.

Early in 1868, his doctor brother Pierre, who had already written warning of their mother's illness, now informed him of her death. Dunant was devastated. She had been everything to him: his adviser, admirer, guardian angel, the one person who had always believed in him and stood by him, the only person he had ever loved. He could not even go to Geneva to attend her funeral. In any case, he did not have the fare.

NINE

Moynier is All at Sea

In September 1867, the International Committee met for the first time without Dunant, Louis Appia being appointed Secretary in his place. The meeting was held early in the morning in Moynier's house, to which he summoned his colleagues several times a month. The office equipment consisted of one file containing correspondence and two green, leather-bound tomes, one to draft the committee's letters, the other to write reports on the meetings held. By common consent, no mention was made of their erstwhile colleague, for they were all aware of his enormous contribution in bringing about the Geneva Convention, and as gentlemen they were acutely embarrassed by the circumstances of his disgrace.

If you ask around Geneva today, you will find most people believe that Dunant was involved in some rather suspicious dealings with a bank which subsequently went bust, as a result of which many citizens of Geneva lost their money. They will usually add that he was probably not entirely to blame as he himself was taken for a ride by an unscrupulous operator in Algeria. But was Henry Dunant really this rather shady character who used dubious methods in business, or was he in fact the innocent victim of an elaborate and sinister plot perpetrated by a group of ruthless bankers to save their own miserable reputations?

Dunant pursued his business enterprises with the same boundless enthusiasm, extraordinary ingenuity and negotiating skills he had applied to the founding of the Red Cross. If somewhat naive and over-confident, he was not unlike many others of his generation in this respect. When he encountered difficulties and obstacles, as anyone building a business inevitably will, especially in a new colony, he did not try and evade them but paid the shareholders a dividend from his own pocket to maintain their confidence while he fought on as he knew best to bring his projects to a successful conclusion. Up to the time of the collapse of the Crédit Genevois, nobody doubted that his integrity and honour were of the highest order. So what went wrong?

The whole scandal had blown up when a group of shareholders sued the directors for their losses in the commercial court. The directors had come out of this rather well. Cleared of all charges of criminal negligence, they could doubtless have passed their incompetence off as poor commercial judgement and bad luck.

The affair might have ended there had not the shareholders decided on their appeal, which was heard the following year in the Court of Civil Justice. The directors, fearing that this time the full extent of their mismanagement would be exposed and that they might be held liable for the losses incurred, saw a way out. Taking care not to arouse Dunant's suspicions which might bring him back from Paris to speak for himself, they ruthlessly accused him in court of having deliberately deceived them over the value of the Felfela quarries. At the same time, they grossly exaggerated the importance of this transaction.

The court was completely taken in by this deception. While declaring the directors guilty of rash conduct and grave errors of judgement in concluding such a transaction without having made any enquiries whatsoever on their own behalf, it ruled that 'Mr Dunant who knowingly deceived his colleagues should be held responsible for all the losses occasioned by this affair, and that the other directors should each be responsible for only one seventh of the loss . . . but that each of the other six directors should claim from Mr Dunant all that he will have to pay as a result of this judgement.'

So cleverly was the plot conceived that it escaped everyone's notice, and has done to this day, that a default on a few quarries involving some 200,000 francs could hardly be the sole or even the main cause of the collapse of a bank with a capital of 25 million francs! The other directors had skilfully managed to divert attention from the true cause of the crash, their own disastrous mismanagement, and lay all the blame at the door of Henry Dunant.

Had Dunant been able to tell the court about Napoleon's promise which should have made success a certainty, it would have become apparent that he had genuinely and with justification believed in the potential of the quarries. His colleagues must have been well aware of the Emperor's undertaking when they agreed to purchase, but they studiously kept quiet about it in court. Furthermore, the Société Algérienne shortly afterwards bought the quarries from Dunant for 100,000 francs, at a time when he was in no position to argue the price. If they were prepared to offer this when they had him over a barrel, his original valuation to the Crédit Genevois was probably pretty accurate.

Having successfully misled the judge and laid a smokescreen over the real reason for the crash, these worthy gentlemen then used their influence to ensure that the verdict was interpreted in their favour. The press gloatingly emphasised those passages from the judgment incriminating Dunant, painting him in the villainous light of the man mainly responsible for the financial losses of so many respectable Geneva citizens. Every effort was made to discredit him and to make sure he was never again accepted in Geneva, lest the truth come out. Bourcart's letter concerning Napoleon's offer to pay half Dunant's debts went mysteriously astray and there can be little doubt that Moynier and his colleagues on the International Committee were discreetly advised to protect its reputation against the damaging effect of Dunant's villainy.

An extra turn of the screw was applied from unexpected quarters, for the attractive raven-haired niece often seen with the Crédit Genevois chairman turned out to be none other than Louise Dubois! Delighted at this opportunity to support her uncle and simultaneously get her revenge on the man who had spurned her in her youth, she busily began spreading the word among her society friends that, of course, the bank scandal wasn't the *only* reason why Henry Dunant had to leave Geneva. She knew for a fact that he wasn't interested in women. . . .

Thus Henry Dunant, one of mankind's greatest benefactors, was made to suffer years of untold misery and persecution for a crime he never committed, while those sanctimonious scoundrels whose crass incompetence had caused this financial disaster got away scot-free.

In his memoirs, Dunant tells of his poverty-stricken life in Paris, reminiscent of the picturesque accounts he had read in novels as a child but which he had considered at the time as far-fetched and incredible. But now he himself, after the setbacks of fortune, lived the humblest of existences and endured all sorts of hardships and privations. He joined the ranks of those

who almost surreptitiously devour tiny mouthfuls of a penny bun hidden in their pockets, who are obliged to blacken their clothes with ink and whiten their shirt collars with chalk; who stuff their hats that have become too big and too shabby with paper, whose shoes let in water; who see their credit cut off at the cheap restaurant where they dine, and the key of their lodging refused when they return in the evening because they cannot pay the rent; who lie down at night without light or warmth; who ruin their health with insufficient and poor quality food. I have often spent the night out in the open, and sometimes, overcome with tiredness, in the waiting rooms of railway stations that stay open all night because of the trains arriving and leaving Paris all through the night.

Almost the worst, as far as material things are concerned, even if one's tastes are simple yet refined, is to see one's clothes fall into tatters without any hope of replacing them. It is really impossible to imagine how agonising it can be for someone who has lived a life of relative ease to be suddenly plunged into the most abject poverty but who must somehow or other keep up appearances if he wishes to recover his position and be able to move in the sort of circles of society to which he is accustomed. It is terrible to feel oneself scorned simply because one is not smartly enough dressed, to have the door closed in one's face because the domestic judges your dress inadequate or smelling of poverty. One cannot approach 'respectable' people, make visits which are indispensable to obtain a job or plead one's cause. There is absolutely nowhere to turn, nobody from whom one can borrow even a franc in a big city like Paris. Naively, too naively, I thought someone would extend a helping hand, remembering that I was the founder of the Red Cross.

Dunant was not the only absentee from the original committee meeting in Moynier's house that September morning. General Dufour, by now in his eighties, only rarely appeared on the scene these days and it was decided to start looking for another experienced military man who could gradually relieve the General of his functions. Their choice finally settled on a colonel in the Federal army, Edmond Favre. The committee then discussed the various matters raised at the recent conference.

In Paris, Moynier had suggested enlarging the International Committee to include a member from each central committee. What might have happened within such a committee in the case of war, with subjects from belligerent countries sitting cheek by jowl – or, more likely, engaged in a stand-up fight if not actually at each other's throats – is something that never seems to have occurred to him. Although favourably received by thirteen national societies at the time, perhaps it is just as well that this idea never took root.

Another proposal that met with an enthusiastic response was the publishing of a journal to keep national societies informed of each other's news and activities. But after careful study of everything involved, the committee found that this would cost 4,000 francs for the first year alone. Since the International Committee had no financial resources to draw upon, receiving no contributions from its supporters as the national societies did, and having to pay all its expenses out of its own five pockets, it asked the national societies how much they were prepared to contribute. At this point, their interest in the matter abruptly evaporated. It took six months to persuade them to share in the cost of publishing a 'bulletin', destined to retain that title to this day. It took slightly longer to reach a decision concerning the creation of a museum, another of the ideas discussed at the Paris conference: 121 years to be precise!

So much for internal reorganisation. But Moynier also aspired to expand the movement and, while in Paris, tried his hand at Dunant's tactics of personal persuasion. The hapless Dr Abdullah-Bey was approached with a view to starting a society in Turkey, perhaps the last country on earth to be amenable to such an idea and whose adherence to the Convention had only been obtained after incredible difficulties. After ten months' nerve-fraying negotiations, attended by endless delays and frustrations, during which Abdullah-Bey was frequently tempted to give it up as a bad job, he eventually and much to his own surprise succeeded in founding an interim committee for relief of the wounded – the first ever set up in a non-Christian country. Moynier lost no time in circulating this momentous news to all central committees, proudly introducing the exotic newcomer.

The next and most important matter to be dealt with was the revision of the Geneva Convention which had given rise to so many proposals and counter-proposals in Paris and been adopted so enthusiastically by the conference. The committee therefore rather wearily requested the Swiss Federal Council to convene another diplomatic conference in Geneva. But Moynier could not help feeling distinctly uneasy. Was it really wise to throw everything back into the melting pot and start again? The more he thought about it, the more dangers he foresaw in replacing the hard-won Convention with a new one that might not be to the liking of some countries, which would then jump at the opportunity to release themselves from their former commitments and withdraw.

The committee's misgivings seemed well founded in view of the reservations already expressed by France, which reiterated its opposition to official recognition of voluntary medical personnel. Then, three weeks before the opening of the conference, the French government wrote to the President of the Swiss Confederation, declaring it would only send representatives to the conference if the discussion was limited to a number of points determined by itself.

That did it. After hasty consultation, the committee decided to backtrack while there was still time. There would be no revision of the Convention as such, merely the inclusion of some additional clauses. Unfortunately, on its own request, the Federal Council had already sent all governments concerned the text adopted in Paris concerning complete revision of the Convention. With any luck, it would still be lying on their desks unread. If not, they must be made to forget it. As they arrived in Geneva, the delegates were each handed an important-looking letter signed by the five committee members, warning them of the hazards involved in revising the Convention and proposing a series of additional clauses instead.

As so often happens when enormous problems and difficulties are anticipated, none arose. After General Dufour in the chair had read out the committee's message to the conference, the assembly endorsed it without more ado and calmly started drafting the first additional clauses, which were concerned with redefining the role of military medical personnel and extending the scope of the principle of neutrality to the wounded.

As is also so often the case when everything is expected to be plain sailing, all kinds of completely unexpected complications crop up, together with a shoal of red herrings. This is what happened when the conference turned to the proposal of extending the principles of the Geneva Convention to naval warfare. Like everyone else, Moynier had supposed this would involve nothing more than simply adding the words 'and hospital ships' every time the Convention mentioned field hospitals. He actually considered it somewhat of an oversight that this had not been included in the original treaty. In fact, the issue turned out to be so complicated that, had it been raised at the 1864 conference, the Geneva Convention might never have been agreed at all.

The seafaring men attending the conference declared that a simple extension of the Convention would not solve the problems encountered in naval combat, which were quite different to those of land warfare. They proceeded to draw up nine clauses to form a separate section in the additional clauses. First of all, the experts thought that it would be impossible to grant the wishes expressed by Empress Eugénie and Queen Augusta that small craft going to the help of the shipwrecked should benefit from neutrality, since this would inhibit the freedom of combat. Nevertheless, they did their best and laid down that small craft which at their own risk picked up the shipwrecked and wounded should benefit from such neutrality as was possible in the circumstances. How this was applied would be left to the humanity of the combatants.

Three different categories of ships carrying the wounded and shipwrecked were defined: military hospital ships belonging to either of the belligerents, merchant ships of different nationalities, and hospital ships fitted out by the aid societies. All should fly their national flag as well as the white flag with the red cross and all should be considered as neutral. But the French delegation objected, refusing to sign if military hospital ships were immune from capture. To satisfy their demands, it was agreed that such ships remained subject to the laws of war and became the property of the captor.

By granting their ships, together with all their personnel, neutrality, the conference had given the relief societies official recognition which they did not enjoy on land. Absurd though it seems, their presence was accepted at sea, where they had yet to prove themselves, but unacknowledged on land where they had already rendered invaluable service. For, contrary to a widely held belief, there was not a word about relief societies in the Geneva Convention. This was because the French military authorities, as always, objected to the intervention of voluntary relief workers and refused to sign a convention implying their existence.

After adopting these naval clauses, and the main body of additional clauses, the delegates dispersed to their respective countries. But, although they had been agreed by the fourteen powers represented at the conference, the naval clauses were never ratified and it was not until 1899 that the Hague Convention extended the provisions of the Geneva Convention to maritime warfare.

At about this time, Tsar Alexander II entered the arena, convening an international conference in St Petersburg, the aim of which at first sight was very akin to that of the 1864 Geneva Conference. The person responsible for this was the Russian Minister for War, a very enlightened man called Milyutin who had corresponded with Dunant and was very much in sympathy with the Geneva Convention. He had been propelled into action by the hollow bullet which burst into flames on impact, and the newer, even deadlier explosive bullet, both of which had recently been introduced into the Russian army. He was horrified by the wounds inflicted by these bullets and wanted them banned. The Tsar, however, would only agree to this if other sovereigns followed suit, so he invited the other European countries to St Petersburg to discuss the issue.

The outcome of this conference was the Declaration of St Petersburg, the next most important treaty mitigating the ills of war after the Geneva Convention. It is rather apt that it came into being as a result of the invention of a bullet, because it is precisely the moment of a bullet's leaving the barrel that marks the dividing line between the targets of the two treaties. While the Geneva Convention was concerned primarily with the results of wounds and the alleviation of the pain and suffering they cause, the Declaration of St Petersburg aimed to prevent at least the worst of such wounds being inflicted. Rather than remedying an evil that had already been committed, it sought to prevent the evil being committed, to change the way war is waged and restrict the means employed. It laid the basis for the future Hague Convention and was the precursor of modern disarmament treaties. There were other significant differences too. The Geneva Convention was a collective protest by the people, springing from the great mass of the population and channelled through their governments. The Declaration of St Petersburg was a civilised and generous humanitarian gesture, prompted by a prince.

As for the growing number of national aid societies, their first international conference in Paris had been such a success that, even before parting, its delegates had fixed a time and place for their next assembly, April 1869 in Berlin. They realised how valuable it was to establish friendly relations in peacetime between people who could be called upon from one day to the next to busy themselves among the enemy ranks. The wounded themselves would be the first to benefit from the resulting harmonious relations that would blunt and overlay the usual bitterness born of war.

The delegates received an extraordinarily warm welcome in Berlin. Several members of the Prussian government, including

Bismarck and von Roon, the Minister for War, personally attended the conference which was held in the Chamber of Deputies. Had these ambitious men curtailed the plans they were secretly hatching for the expansion of Prussia, the future work of the aid societies would have been dramatically reduced. Queen Augusta, of course, followed all the proceedings with great enthusiasm. Entertainments and lavish festivities were laid on, demonstrations and military inspections organised and prayers said in all the churches of the capital calling for guidance and blessing from the Almighty, since everyone else was already in attendance!

The conference first set out to define the scope and limits of the relief societies' action in war. The committee's old ally, Dr Loeffler, pointed out that, while it would be a mistake to try to control the activities of the different societies too rigidly, if they were to work efficiently and be accepted by the military authorities, some sort of broad framework should nevertheless be drawn up within which they should all operate. He proposed that they should support the official medical services in the theatre of war but keep clear during the actual fighting. Only when the fighting was over should they collect the wounded from the battlefield and treat them in their field dressing stations behind the lines, while their base hospitals should always be set up within their own borders. After some discussion, these proposals were adopted.

Before proceeding to the next item on the agenda, Gustave Moynier rose to address the assembly. In his quiet, precise manner, he stated quite simply that he was concerned for the proper application of the Geneva Convention. This caused a stir among the delegates who were expecting to discuss something more positive. With his uncanny instinct for future pitfalls, Moynier went on to say that it was his belief that only if the soldiers themselves and the administrators in the battle zone understood the benefits would it be properly observed. And he urged the societies to step up their efforts to disseminate information. He stressed, however, that as the Convention became better known, firm control must be exercised over the use of privileges and insignia lest they be abused and the Convention fall into disrepute.

His remarks duly noted, Moynier resumed his seat and the conference went on to the main subject on its agenda: war at sea. The relief societies had approved in general the provisions passed by the Diplomatic Conference the previous year. But now that they had had time to think about it, they realised just how difficult this issue was. Were they to wait until the fighting stopped before entering the battle zone, as was the case on land, their efforts would be virtually useless. If the ship remained afloat, the wounded on board would be treated by the ship's own medical facilities. If the ship sunk, all hands would be thrown into the sea, fit and wounded alike, and would almost certainly drown before the battle was over. Even if they went in before the end of the battle, how could the relief societies' ships avoid getting in the way of the combatants?

Considerably more study and research were needed to solve this knotty problem which, it was hoped, would be settled at the next conference, scheduled to take place in 1871. Little did the delegates know that intervening events would result in them not meeting again for another fifteen years.

While his colleagues struggled somewhat out of their depth in Berlin, Dr Maunoir quietly passed on to a higher place. His loss was keenly felt and with heavy hearts Moynier and Appia set about the difficult task of finding a worthy successor. The French central committee, always slightly irritated at the exclusively Protestant composition of the committee, tried as they had tried before to introduce a Catholic. Moynier realised it was high time to make the position clear. He wrote to Théodore Vernes claiming that, although it happened to be entirely Protestant, the committee had never been influenced by religious considerations and never would be. Its attitude in the matter was strictly neutral. After careful consideration of the French proposal, it had decided that given the choice of two candidates of equal merit but different religions, they would choose the Catholic, but they would not elect someone simply because he represented Catholicism. Otherwise, they would also need to include a Muslim, a Greek, a Jew and various other nationalities and would soon find themselves bogged down with conflicting viewpoints and unable to agree on anything. They were convinced, he concluded, that it was better to remain few in number but united in heart and spirit. Moynier conveniently overlooked his own proposals to the Paris conference to enlarge the International Committee somewhat along the same lines, and the committee proceeded to nominate a Geneva city councillor, Louis Micheli de la Rive.

But Moynier was not the only one to overlook an earlier stance. France now surprised everyone by suddenly reversing her position regarding hospital ships. At the Diplomatic Congress in 1868, France had refused to sign the additional articles unless military hospital ships remained subject to the laws of war and became the property of the captor. Now she demanded the exact opposite, refusing to ratify the additional articles unless the capture of hospital ships was forbidden!

This turn-about occasioned an endless exchange of correspondence between the Federal Council and the other countries involved. Moynier urged the central committees to lobby their governments in an attempt to speed matters up. But he himself was rapidly in danger of becoming submerged under the enormous volume of paperwork which this added to their other commitments. In May 1869, the committee engaged its first employee to work for ten hours a week at Moynier's house; it would be some considerable time before they could afford the luxury of office premises. Equipped only with these meagre resources, the International Committee sailed inexorably towards one of the greatest challenges to its survival.

TEN

Vive la Neutralité!

Bismarck's plans for Prussian domination of Europe were coming along nicely. Since his spells as ambassador to St Petersburg and subsequently in Paris, he had become adept at assessing the European situation and now he surveyed recent events and possible future developments with distinct satisfaction. After using the dispute over Schleswig-Holstein to provoke war with Austria and bring about her defeat in 1866, Prussia had annexed Hanover and several other small states misguided enough to fight on the Austrian side. Then, in 1867, he formed the North German Confederation, an ominous configuration on the European skyline.

The opportunity Bismarck was waiting for came in 1870 during a dispute with France over a German candidate for the Spanish throne. He cleverly contrived to make a perfectly reasonable refusal from the Prussian King to an utterly unreasonable request from France appear in a form which the French considered an insult to their ambassador. France rashly declared war on 2 August 1870, forty-four years before the powerful new Germany that emerged from this struggle would propel the entire Continent and beyond into the First World War.

Napoleon, whom everyone had thought to be on his deathbed the previous summer, clambered painfully on to his horse at the head of his army in a last desperate attempt to deserve the name he bore. Marshal Niel, succumbing to the same illness that ailed his Emperor, was succeeded as Minister of War by Marshal Leboeuf, who proudly proclaimed that the army, now equipped with its chassepot rifles and *mitrailleuse* (machine guns) was ready and 'not a gaiter button is missing'. Regrettably, those were just about the only items that were not missing! Their hopes and confidence would lie in shreds only a month later, by which time the world's most efficient engine of warfare had battered its way 100 miles inside French territory and beaten France to her knees at the battle of Sedan.

The Prussian military medical services and their aid society are worthy of note because they were the first to carry out almost to the letter what the International Committee had been advocating. Great importance was attached to health and hygiene and each soldier was issued with a first-aid kit to carry into battle. Because the increasing range of artillery meant that field dressing stations had to be moved a considerable distance from the lines, regimental companies of stretcher-bearers were introduced, enabling surgeons and nurses to treat their wounded safe from the danger of enemy shelling. The valuable contribution of voluntary relief workers was not over-looked, their activities being carefully coordinated with those of the army medical services. In exact accordance with Article 6 of the 1863 Resolutions, voluntary medical personnel on the battlefield were strictly under military command.

Away from the theatre of operations, the Prussian aid society, under the energetic leadership of Queen Augusta, was also extremely well organised with nearly two thousand branches spread throughout the country. A royal commissioner was appointed to superintend the work of the branches and to act as intermediary between them and the military. The aid society had its own hospitals, quarantine stations and even a regular service of specially fitted-out ambulance trains carrying as many as 900 wounded men at a time away from the front to efficient hospitals within their own country. Money was no problem. Donations in cash and kind flowed in from all over the country as well as from Germans living as far afield as India, Japan, Australia and North America.

On the French side, things could hardly have been more different, or more appalling. While the Prussian soldiers slumbered comfort-ably in warm beds, the wretched French troops huddled in tents or out in the open in the heavy autumn rains and freezing winter of 1870. Unscrupulous tailors had supplied them with uniforms that fell to bits and the soles of their shoes disintegrated in the mud. Food was constantly in short supply, due entirely to shocking mismanagement. Préval, the Deputy Commissioner who had advocated mules in preference to medical volunteers at the 1863 conference, arbitrarily ordered the burning of tons of biscuits, flour, bread, coffee and sugar and huge piles of blankets, infuriating the ravenous soldiers shivering nearby. Thus, at a stroke, he inflicted more damage on the French army than could have been achieved by several brigades of Prussian troops. Hardly surprisingly, the French lost over three hundred thousand men as a result of sickness and frost-bite, three times more than those who died through enemy action. If the soldiers did not mutiny on the spot, it was probably because they did not have the strength to do so.

As for the French army's medical arrangements, they were ludicrously inadequate. Stretcher-bearers were non-existent and the few dressing stations incredibly rudimentary. There was scarcely any water to drink or dress wounds and amputations were often performed by the flickering light of candles and without chloroform. Many wounded were abandoned for days on end, eventually dying through lack of treatment or simply hunger. There was no equipment, no means of transport, no instruments, no lint and no dressings. As for the cavalry and horse artillery, they usually did not have any medical services at all, or at best one doctor with a bottle of opium pills in one pocket, a packet of emetics in the other and a small leather bag containing a handful of lint and a few bandages. Little had changed since Solferino save that there, at least, Henry Dunant had been on hand to give hope and whatever help he could.

Unfortunately, the French aid society was not much help. Although it had been in existence for six years, it lacked personnel, equipment and money and was totally unprepared for war. In a valiant attempt to make up for lost time, Count Flavigny set to work fund-raising, and relief material soon started flooding in. Within a month, seventeen field dressing units had been organised, although the calibre of their personnel was not always of the highest. For the most part ignorant, untrained and undisciplined, some of these units never reached their destinations while others, wearing no insignia, fell into enemy hands – in one instance quite justifiably because its members were carrying revolvers, thus forfeiting their right to neutrality. Those that did succeed in treating the wounded came up against the added problem of having to feed and shelter them as well. The society simply did not have the necessary resources and, communications being what they were, would often not have known where to send them if it had.

To make things worse, the Prussians closed in around Paris and the central committee feared it would soon be completely cut off from its medical units. Colonel Huber-Saladin – Dunant's erstwhile companion during his sorties into Paris society – was despatched to Brussels, heading a commission that would supervise and co-ordinate their work, while the central committee itself remained in the capital to cope with the growing demands on its services.

Busy as it was with all these activities, the French central committee had little time to devote to ensuring observance of the Convention. Even the committee itself probably failed to realise how much it was forfeiting by not doing so, depriving its own wounded of valuable benefits. Prussia, as usual, had been exemplary in this respect. Medical personnel and ambulances bore the Red Cross emblem, as did the staff provided by the central committee. Her troops had been issued with the text of the Geneva Convention and the Additional Articles, as well as a booklet explaining them. The French military medical personnel, on the other hand, had no Red Cross emblem and their army knew nothing about the Convention. The few officers who had heard of it pooh-poohed it as 'a piece of humanitarian nonsense'. Even the doctors attached to the aid society had only the vaguest idea of what it meant.

As a result, the French invariably evacuated their field hospitals at the approach of the Prussians, bundling the wounded into any carts they could find where they received no treatment, suffered tortures during transit and often died on the way. On other occasions, the Prussians came upon French ambulances unexpectedly and were astonished to see the French surgeons and nurses not wearing distinctive emblems. Unable to believe they would voluntarily deprive themselves of the advantages of the Convention, the

Prussians became highly suspicious and insisted that they attach strips of white cloths around their arms and paint them with the red cross by dipping fingers in the all too readily available blood.

During the Seven Weeks' War, the Geneva Convention was not properly applied because, although Prussia had signed it, Austria had refused. This time, even though both belligerents had agreed to abide by it, the Geneva Convention was still only partially operative. This shows how right Moynier had been when he said in Berlin that the Convention would only be properly applied if all ranks knew about it and understood the benefits. It was not, however, Moynier who was to take the lead in trying to spread this awareness throughout the French army but someone equally well versed in the subject and conveniently on the spot in Paris – none other than Henry Dunant.

A little thinner and more threadbare than he used to be, perhaps, he nevertheless still had that strange air of innocence about him, still seemed consumed with an inner fire of passionate conviction in his current cause. Dunant had in fact been busily campaigning on behalf of the Convention since the day war was declared. He had started by getting Baron Brénier, the Honorary Vice-President of the French central committee, to raise the matter in the Senate. But the Baron's speech was so woolly and the Senators' reception so unsympathetic that his voice was drowned out by the impatient drumming of paper knives on desks and the general hubbub of the assembly. He was obliged to sit down again without having achieved anything. Exactly why the Senators should have been armed with so many paper knives is not quite clear, but the prudent application of the tip of such a weapon by a kindly colleague to the posterior of Baron Brénier might have prevented him from falling asleep in mid-speech.

Dunant then wrote to Empress Eugénie who was acting as Regent in Napoleon's absence, stressing the importance of the Geneva Convention and proposing that he himself negotiate with the Prussians with a view to neutralising certain towns where the wounded could be cared for. He was informed that his letter would be forwarded to the Ministry of the Interior, but he heard nothing more. An appeal to General Trochu, the Governor of Paris, was equally unsuccessful. 'I am snowed under with work at the moment,' he was told, 'but the matter you mention will not be forgotten.' Plainly, the French military authorities had convinced the entire establishment that the Geneva Convention was just one of the Emperor's whims, and was in fact a complete waste of time.

All Dunant's efforts seemed to meet with indifference or unwillingness as he gloomily watched the inexorable Prussian advance and the steady French retreat. He heard about the mutinies at the camp in Châlons where the soldiers angrily rebelled against their incompetent leaders and the appalling conditions in which they were expected to fight. Then came the battle of Sedan and the same bloody scenes as at Solferino. The French were vastly outnumbered and encircled, General MacMahon seriously wounded, Napoleon himself almost demented with pain. Recognising the hopelessness of the situation, he commanded the white flag to be hoisted, but it was torn down by his own troops as they struggled on. Finally, driven into a frenzy of despair by the senseless slaughter and ceaseless pounding of the artillery, he sent a messenger to the Prussian King with his personal surrender, preferring to shoulder the responsibility for capitulating rather than submit his army to dishonour. But his noble gesture was to no avail. The Prussian general demanded unconditional surrender. Some eighty-three thousand Frenchmen, officers included, laid down their arms and were herded into a field to await the march to Germany. There was no shelter of any kind against the beating rain, and no food. They had no choice but to kill and eat their horses.

News of Napoleon's surrender and the defeat at Sedan reached Paris on 3 September. Seized with revolutionary fury, the citizens stormed the Chamber of Deputies and the Tuileries from which the Empress, heavily disguised, just managed to escape, being accompanied out of Paris to Deauville and thence to England. The Third Republic was proclaimed in Paris and the Government of National Defence set up with General Trochu, Jules Favre and Gambetta in charge.

For Dunant, it was not only the end of the Second Empire, but the end of an era. It was the end of the line for all his old dreams of Napoleonic glory and his 'restoration of the Holy Roman Empire'. It was time to wake up, to take up the challenge of a new government to win over to the Geneva Convention. In any case, the essentially monarchist aid society would have nothing to do with the republican government; everything was up to him. On 11 September, a week after the proclamation of the Republic, he was received by Jules Favre, the Minister for Foreign Affairs, who promised to place the matter before the government. A few days later, he was informed that a notice had been published in the *Journal Officiel* concerning Article 5 of the Convention: the article promising any inhabitant giving shelter to the wounded in his home protection and exemption from the quartering of troops and from part of any war contributions that might be levied.

Suddenly, houses all over France blossomed with white flags bearing hastily contrived red crosses. Moynier's worst fears had come to pass. Never mind if the house contained only one bed and that was the owner's, here was a heaven-sent way to safeguard oneself and one's property. In the eleventh issue of the *Bulletin*, Théodore Vernes reported that when the Germans arrived in Dijon, the main streets were literally bedecked with an astonishing display of white flags with red crosses which were not taken seriously by the enemy; the houses were ruthlessly occupied and the bogus sick-rooms invaded. The victims of such acts naturally orchestrated an outcry of indignant accusations of 'violations' of the Geneva Convention.

Like the flag, the armband gave rise to innumerable abuses, sometimes far worse. Although specifically intended to designate medical personnel, it was handed out by military and civilian authorities to all and sundry: butchers, bakers, farmers and virtually anyone producing a plausible pretext. Countless civilians simply stitched one together themselves in order to avoid active service.

The worst misuse of the armband was by those who plundered the dead and wounded on the battlefield. One horrifying eyewitness account was recorded by a captain in the Prussian Hussars who, when just regaining consciousness, saw a man dressed as an army chaplain, accompanied by two 'ambulance personnel' wearing the Red Cross armband, calmly going the rounds of the battlefield at dawn, killing off the wounded and collecting any jewellery and valuables on their bodies, usually cutting off the fingers to get the rings. Fortunately for him, he managed to muster enough strength to fire his revolver and they made off before he became their next victim.

The armband was also sometimes used as a disguise by spies, although the practice was not nearly so widespread as most people supposed. The unfortunate Colonel Huber-Saladin, returning to Paris after his mission in Brussels, was arrested as a Prussian spy in Saint-Germain and had the greatest difficulty extricating himself simply because his carriage bore the 'Prussian' flag – white with a red cross.

Such was the ignorance of the Geneva Convention, and there was not a great deal that Dunant or anyone else could do to improve matters in the difficult circumstances at the time. Nevertheless, the pleas from the International Committee and the national aid societies had stirred the world's humanitarian conscience into life and Moynier and his colleagues worked day and night organising and coordinating the response. There was an extraordinary surge of generosity from the most unlikely quarters with people everywhere, even in remote Russian villages, joining together to raise money for the sick and wounded. Foremost among them were the aid societies in neutral countries. Switzerland gave refuge to 4,000 women and children from beleaguered Strasbourg and opened its frontier to 90,000 ragged, exhausted and starving men from General Bourbaki's 'forgotten' army. Arriving in freezing temperatures, mostly barefoot in the snow, the sound of their marching was drowned out by a loud and non-stop chorus of hacking coughs.

Aid societies in other countries despatched complete medical teams to both armies. Some of these were well disciplined and highly efficient, such as eleven Dutch units, one of which was led by Captain Van de Velde who had finally thawed out after his unfortunate experience with the Danes! Others were rather less helpful. The Irish medical team was so overcome with sympathy for the French that they forgot all about medicine and joined whole-heartedly in the fighting instead. In nearly every case, these teams met with a hostile reception from the French military authorities and had the greatest difficulty getting anything useful done. One Russian unit followed MacMahon's army corps for days without managing to treat a single man.

If the French army authorities behaved in this way towards highly qualified medical practitioners, their astonished reaction to an unqualified American lady who suddenly appeared on the scene, confidently expecting to collect the wounded straight from the battlefield, scarcely bears describing. Yet this amazing and intrepid woman, the future first President of the American Red Cross, was not exactly a newcomer to the field of voluntary relief work. In fact, the reason Clara Barton was in Europe was to recuperate from her exertions on behalf of the wounded and missing during the American Civil War. Like Dunant, Clara Barton was a visionary, another dreamer. Frail in health and tending to relapse into neurosis when she did not get her own way, she overcame her nervous illnesses to fight a tireless campaign to create an American Red Cross Society and to push the United States into ratifying the Geneva Convention.

Throughout her life, Clara Barton was pursued by Florence Nightingale's reputation, complaining that she was often referred to as the Florence Nightingale of America, whereas nobody ever spoke of the Lady of the Lamp as the Clara Barton of Britain. Yet the two women were curiously alike: insecure, dogmatic, touchy, impatient with bureaucracy, both using work as an escape from depression before retiring to their beds. They never met and never seemed to want to.

The daughter of a soldier who regaled her with war stories and involved her in his strategic studies, Clara Barton had grown up with her brothers in a small town in Massachusetts with little taste for feminine pursuits. Trying to establish herself as an 'honorary' man, as she put it, she became a schoolteacher and fought for equal pay, then moved to Washington and became one of the first female clerks in the United States Patent Office. But her desire to do something significant and worthwhile was only truly satisfied during the Civil War when the Angel of the Battlefield, as the soldiers dubbed her, displayed extraordinary courage as well as formidable administrative and fund-raising skills. Exhausted she may have been at the end of it but, for Clara Barton, peace came as something of an anti-climax.

After spending some time in Geneva where she met Moynier and Appia and had several discussions with them concerning American adhesion to the Convention, Clara Barton went on to Berne and was there when war was declared. The convalescent immediately left for the front, but everywhere she went she was amazed to find herself escorted smartly off the battlefield. It was not until she reached Karlsruhe and met up with the Grand Duchess of Baden that her experience and ability were appreciated to the full. After the fall of Strasbourg, it was Clara Barton who took in relief supplies from the International Committee and organised help for the thousands of civilians who had lost everything and were homeless as a result of the bombardment.

Fresh from her experience with the super-efficient United States Sanitary Commission, Clara Barton must have wondered whether her new friends' International Committee matched up. Any doubts she may have had were rapidly dispelled when Moynier and Appia asked her to help in the depot they had just set up in Basle for the collection and distribution of relief for the wounded. She was amazed to find warehouses larger than any she had seen during the American Civil War and bursting at the seams; trains loaded with boxes and barrels pouring in from every city, town and hamlet in Switzerland and even from Austria and northern Italy, and trained nurses standing waiting, each with their badge, and every box and barrel bearing a broad, bright scarlet cross.

The International Committee's original intention had actually been merely to set up a liaison and information office in Basle to act as an intermediary between the aid societies of countries at war. But it soon found itself involved in all kinds of other, more pressing activities. It distributed food and clothing, received donations in cash or kind and sent them on to wounded soldiers and sailors, forwarded letters between wounded men and their families, printed and circulated lists of the sick and wounded on both sides, organised the liberation and repatriation of disabled or incurably wounded French through Switzerland, even set up a separate committee for the relief of able-bodied prisoners of war. For Moynier maintained that, not being mentioned in the 1863 Resolutions, prisoners of war did not come within the scope of the Convention.

Nearly all the many and varied activities conducted by the International Committee of the Red Cross today were initiated during this highly productive period of the Franco-Prussian War. But as far as observance of the Convention was concerned, the situation was far from satisfactory. At the outbreak of hostilities, both sides had magnanimously declared they would not only observe the Convention but also the Additional Clauses, despite the fact that these had not yet been ratified and were therefore not legally binding. As it turned out, the French ignored their promise while the Prussians scrupulously honoured theirs. As a result, both sides constantly accused each other of real or imagined violations throughout the war and the recriminations continued long afterwards.

In fact, even the Prussians were not irreproachable in this respect. Article 5 of the Additional Articles laid down that, with the exception of officers, wounded men falling into enemy hands, even if *not* incapable of further service, should be repatriated when cured, on condition they did not take up arms again during the war. But reports reaching the committee proved that the vast majority of French wounded fit to be moved were not repatriated. The Prussians, understandably sceptical about their enemies' observance of their part of the bargain, preferred to keep potentially reactivated soldiers in captivity. Perhaps they were also aware that, thanks to their own excellent care, this vast army of soldiers they would be returning would now be far fitter and more formidable as enemies than if they had never been wounded.

In the meantime, yet another gallant French army gave up the losing fight. In October 1870, Marshal Bazaine surrendered with

170,000 men at Metz – probably the largest military capitulation in history. The Prussians surrounded Paris. That autumn and winter, the world's glittering capital of fashion, culture, luxury and splendour was made to suffer the misery and privation of 131 long, lean days of siege.

ELEVEN

They Seek Him Here, They Seek Him There!

The menu written with a flourish on the blackboard in the window of the Restaurant des Deux Magots proposed Grilled Rat for 2 fr. 70, Sauté Poodle at 3 fr. 50 or, for those feeling really flush, Mules Marinière for 4 francs. Passing by, Dunant could not help drooling slightly at the thought of such delicacies, thinking sadly of the curling slice of cat pâté and black bean bread awaiting him at home.

With his state of finances, it was just as well that he attached little importance to the pleasures of the table, deriving his greatest joy and satisfaction from noble and lofty achievements – or, at least, endeavours – to improve the world for his fellow men. Sometimes he seems almost too good to be true, until one catches a glimpse of a fairly carefully concealed streak of vanity. He did love to bask in the warmth of praise and approval; and the higher the stratum of society it came from the better. For he was also a frightful snob. Even in his most down-and-out days, he would never have dreamed of hobnobbing with other unfortunates in similar straits to himself. He could never forget he was an aristocrat, someone of noble birth and illustrious forebears.

Luckily for him, his philanthropy was always flexible enough to allow for a little commercial speculation to creep in on the side and in Paris that July, when war seemed imminent, many of his days were spent eagerly promoting a special new kind of lint that was claimed to prevent inflammation of wounds. Dunant and a doctor friend of his planned to market this antiseptic lint and make a healthy profit in the process. For a time, the venture was fairly successful with Dunant busily negotiating with various local administrative bodies, but once the German armies arrived outside Paris in September 1870 and the siege of the capital began, he found many more pressing matters on which to attend.

The French aid society, which had cold-shouldered Dunant ever since the scandal and the judgment against him by the Geneva court, set up makeshift hospitals in many of the main public buildings in Paris, including the Grand Hôtel and even the palace of the Tuileries, and there was no shortage of devoted helpers including many society ladies. But surgical techniques seemed even worse than they had been ten years ago, gangrene was rife and a sickly, nauseating stench drifted down the fashionable boulevards. One of the most famous French surgeons proudly practised an incredibly barbarous method of amputation which culminated in the bare and conical stump of a limb being exposed to suppurate freely in the air. Four-fifths of amputees failed to survive such treatment. An American medical unit set up by a Dr Swinburn, on the other hand, achieved strikingly better results, chiefly due to insistence on a surprisingly simple but seemingly novel ingredient: scrupulous cleanliness.

It was not only the sick and wounded soldiers who suffered from the siege but the hungry and demoralised civilians as well. Together with Baron Dutilh de la Tuque, Dunant started the French Welfare Society to provide the same kind of help to civilians as the aid society gave wounded soldiers. A few weeks later, when winter began to bite, he also organised a Committee for Warm Clothing and had soon collected such vast quantities of material that he had to obtain storage space in a large building where he hoisted the Red Cross flag, since the Committee for Warm Clothing could be considered an extension of the aid society. All this activity was good for his morale and some of his old bounce and enthusiasm returned. He set about arranging entertainments for the troops on the forti-fications, ENSA style, and even laid on parties for the wounded in the centre of Paris and shows at the Comédie Française, enlisting the services of professional actors. Letters bubbling over with cheerfulness floated off to his family in Geneva via the new postal balloons.

Although Queen Augusta and the Crown Prince had prevailed on King William and the Prussian commander-in-chief to delay shelling innocent civilians – much to the annoyance of Bismarck who grudged this waste of time – the Parisians' long drawn-out resistance finally left the general little choice. Two days after Christmas, the Prussians started bombarding the city's fortifications with the same Krupp cannon that the Parisians had admired at their own Universal Exhibition three years before. A few days later, shells were bursting in the city itself, wounding and killing numerous citizens. For two weeks more, the Parisians gallantly held out, but with news of the defeat of one after the other of the remaining French armies, and only a few days' provisions left, the Government of National Defence took the decision to capitulate and an armistice was signed. Large stocks of food were immediately sent into the city by Queen Augusta. London despatched £80,000 worth of provisions to the starving citizens and New York contributed US$10,000.

One day about this time, Dunant was surprised and gratified to receive a visit from Count Flavigny, Chairman of the aid society, who asked him to act as neutral intermediary on their behalf and intercede with the Prussians to save the lives of two wounded snipers who had been taken prisoner and were due to be shot. Dunant hardly liked to mention to his old friend the Count that he did not even have enough money to get to the Prussian headquarters at Versailles. For the past three and a half years, the French central committee had studiously feigned ignorance of his plight and failed to offer him even the humblest job in the society's busy and crowded offices. Fortunately, he had not had to pay any rent for his accommodation throughout this period, a fine room on the first floor being placed at his disposal free of charge by a hotelier who saw in Dunant a splendid way to protect his premises, merely asking him in return to hoist a Red Cross flag at one end of his balcony and a Swiss flag at the other.

During the siege, he had also happened to meet a rich shoe manufacturer from Lausanne who now kindly lent him a few hundred francs with which he could pay part of his account at Miss Morton's little restaurant where he took all his meals, as well as his fare to

127

Versailles. After an eventful journey, during which he had to row himself across the Seine, he arrived at the Prussian staff headquarters and secured a promise that the snipers' lives would be spared.

Delighted with the successful outcome of his mission, but unable to return to Paris the same day, Dunant stayed the night at the Hôtel des Réservoirs where he bumped into a member of the Prussian aid society whom he had first met in Berlin during the Statistical Congress in 1863. This gentleman, who happened at that time to be acting as first secretary to Bismarck, invited Dunant to have coffee with him and some other high-flown Prussians in a small salon adjoining a hall crowded with German officers. Having as usual gone without dinner to save money, Dunant gladly accepted this invitation which had the unfortunate repercussion of his being immediately assumed to be a Prussian spy.

These suspicions were undoubtedly reinforced by an incident that had occurred in a barber's shop several weeks earlier, when the proprietor and his customers were ferociously discussing suitably bloodthirsty ways of dealing with the 'German swine' outside the city walls. Invited to give his views, the strangely silent figure in the corner replied that the days when men fought like savages were gone, and that a recent treaty made the methods they suggested unlawful. The barber and his clients were stunned, and lost no time in warning the police who immediately issued details of a Prussian spy seen in the barber's shop, a man who had said the French fought like savages, a dangerous customer indeed.

Meanwhile, peace terms were being thrashed out between Bismarck and the Government of National Defence. Jules Favre, who had recently been elected to the National Assembly, together with Thiers, Gambetta and Victor Hugo, was responsible for negotiating the treaty of Frankfurt whereby the French had to sign away Alsace and Lorraine and promise to pay an indemnity of 5,000 million francs. They were also forced to agree to a victory march of the German army through Paris.

On 1 March, 30,000 German soldiers triumphantly marched through the Porte Maillot and paraded along the Champs Elysées. The streets were silent and deserted as they passed. But behind their shuttered windows and closed doors, the citizens of Paris were seething. Months of hunger and hardship and suffering were now being crowned with this final humiliation. Their suppressed fury was directed not so much against the German victors, who marched out of the city again in two days time without incident, but against the men who had capitulated and were now in power after the recent elections which, to make matters worse, had returned a conservative majority. Paris was in revolt and refused to be ruled by the national government. The National Guard sided with the revolutionary leaders and events moved fast. Two generals sent at the head of their brigades to restore order were shot in front of the angry mob. Violence and lawlessness overtook Paris. The National Assembly was hastily transferred to Versailles and the Commune, a revolutionary council, set up in the city on 26 March. The red flag flew once again over Paris and massed thousands chanted 'La Marseillaise'.

The Communards promised Dunant that the Geneva Convention would be observed in the event of civil war. But unfortunately, only a few days later, their forces shot an army doctor by mistake, resulting in 10,000 government troops mounting a ferocious attack and massacring every prisoner they seized. From then on, every rule in the book was scrapped. Violence, summary shootings, reprisals and counter-reprisals escalated at a horrifying rate. The National Guard and the Commune revenged a particularly ruthless round of shootings by taking hostages, arresting among others the Arch-bishop of Paris, several Jesuit priests and *abbé* Déguerry, a friend of Dunant. He rushed round to the headquarters of the Commune in the Hôtel de Ville to plead for the *abbé*'s release, but all his efforts were to no avail and he only just managed to avoid being arrested himself by a drunken guard. He was also observed, although unrecognised, by spies of the Versailles government who later denounced him as one of the leaders of the 'International'. Everything and everyone was under suspicion. It was the Reign of Terror all over again; only the tumbrils rolling towards the guillotine were missing. Even the aid society was blacklisted and several of its members arrested and thrown into prison.

The French central committee, due to its close association with the International Committee, was often referred to locally as the 'International'. This caused it to be confused with the Workers' International which had also, by a curious coincidence, been inaugurated in Geneva in 1863 by Karl Marx and had recently assumed a revolutionary character with dangerous overtones.

Dunant found himself in an invidious position. Not only was he suspected by the Versailles government of being a leading revolutionary, but he was also regarded with deep suspicion by the Commune itself because of his attempts to help friends in the aid society, and others, to escape its clutches. This would have been enough to make any lesser man pack his bags and head for the Alps. Not so Dunant. With his usual sublime disregard for his own safety and with an almost naive serenity of mind, he calmly went about his business of saving the innocent.

Early one morning, Dunant was surprised to open his door to a flustered and dishevelled Count Flavigny who told him, in a state of great agitation, that he had almost been arrested at his home that morning. The head of the medical unit set up by the aid society in the Champs Elysées, a certain Dr Chenu, had been arrested by the Communards and it seemed that the Count was next on the list. He had immediately rushed round to take refuge in the sanctuary of Dunant's lodging. Completely ignoring the fact that he had done nothing to help Dunant in his troubles, he now blamed him for getting him into the aid society and demanded that he save him from the consequences. Dunant assured the Count that he was welcome to his room, but that the best thing would be to leave Paris forthwith. With the help of an influential friend, he managed to get Italian passports for Signor and Signora Flavigni and hurried them both to the Gare du Nord, the only station from which it was still possible to leave Paris.

The waiting room at the station was packed to overflowing with society ladies and old men, all desperate to leave Paris before it was too late, and all trying to conceal their fear and anxiety while awaiting the train's departure in a strained and ghostly hush. Dunant was quietly saying goodbye to the Flavignys when suddenly, pushing his way through the crowd, Count Sérurier, Vice-President of the French aid society, appeared. Pale and distraught, he rushed up to Dunant and in a strangled voice which nevertheless resounded terrifyingly in the midst of the deathly silence shouted, 'You didn't get me a passport!' Then, in a state of feverish excitement, he cried out: 'Tell Cluseret that I'll come back to Paris if necessary. Tell him. . . .' But his words were cut short by the opening of the waiting room doors. Everyone scrambled forward to climb into the train, Count Sérurier first among them. Dunant had not the slightest idea what he was talking about, for he had never even met this Cluseret, one of the Communard generals. He had always kept well clear of the political scene and could only hope that the Count's rash and compromising words would not jeopardise them both. For there were spies and informers everywhere.

Several days later, Dunant managed to rescue a priest who had defiantly continued to wear his cassock and been arrested by Communards on the hunt for clerical victims. Pushing his way through the frenzied crowds and fearlessly challenging the heavily armed National Guard, Dunant declared himself founder of the Organisation for Relief of the Wounded and claimed and obtained the priest's release.

Many other innocent and helpless people in danger of imprisonment or death were helped to escape by Dunant who assumed the role of a sort of Swiss Scarlet Pimpernel, regardless of his own safety. As well as the French papers he had acquired some years before, he still had his Swiss passport. Now, with the help of a cooperative and courageous railway inspector, this passport was constantly in transit between the Gare du Nord and Saint-Denis – the one gate from Paris kept open by the Prussians – where it was retrieved by the inspector and brought back for use by the next escaping citizen. Nobody on guard seemed to notice that the same passport was making an extraordinary number of sorties from Paris and everything went without a hitch, despite the numerous spies of the Commune constantly lurking around the station. The only difficulty in the whole procedure was experienced by Dunant in scraping together enough sous to pay for coffees at the bistro where he had to hang about in order to meet the railway inspector and have his passport returned.

Meanwhile, Dr Chenu had been released and the French aid society continued its work with commendable neutrality, nursing Communards and government troops alike, despite the Communards' attempt to take over its hospital and instal their own director. Dr Chenu refused to be ousted, or to haul down the Red Cross flag, and the Communards gradually drifted away. The central committee nevertheless moved out to Versailles where it worked together with the local aid society.

By this time, the government troops under the command of Marshal MacMahon had advanced within shelling distance of the Arc de Triomphe where Dunant was aghast one day to come across a crowd of people gleefully revelling in the excitement of the scene, cheering when shells exploded, scattering death and destruction. How futile all his efforts to relieve the suffering of war seemed in the face of such blind and bloodthirsty behaviour. Horrified by the callousness of the citizens, as well as by the violence and ruthlessness of the struggle between the army and the Communards which gave every sign of getting worse, he made an expedition out of Paris to the German lines and talked to the Crown Prince of Saxony at Compiègne about the possibility of evacuating women and children out of Paris if the situation deteriorated still further. The Crown Prince promised to help and also assured Dunant that the German army of occupation would observe the terms of the Geneva Convention.

Back in Paris, he found there had been a reshuffle within the council of the Commune. One of the former leaders, Cluseret, he whom Count Sérurier had seemed so anxious to mollify on his frantic departure from the Gare du Nord, had been imprisoned and a Committee of Public Safety set up. Movements in and out of Paris were tightened to a stranglehold and the atmosphere of panic and terror intensified by the hour as the fighting moved closer and closer to the city gates. In a desperate attempt to avert the coming bloodbath, Dunant and his ally in the French welfare society, Baron Dutilh, held secret meetings with the three chief 'generals' of the

Commune to try and break the deadlock, despite the fact that all previous attempts at mediation had failed. An appointment was made for Dunant and the Baron to have an audience with Thiers on 11 May to discuss the conclusions reached. By an unfortunate coincidence, the Committee of Public Safety chose that very day to raze to the ground Thiers' beautiful house and seize all his furniture and belongings. A move hardly calculated to put the great man in a conciliatory mood, especially in view of the fact that, having no children, his priceless collection of paintings and works of art was his pride and joy.

Sneaking quietly out of Paris early in the morning, the Baron and Dunant were completely unaware of this turn of events. Arriving at Versailles after a tortuous and perilous journey through the lines, they found Thiers holding court. Notified of their presence, he moved forward to take a good look at them, then raising his voice and addressing the gallery, he cried out: 'They burden me with all sorts of troubles, and they choose the very day when I am stricken with a great family misfortune to talk to me about conciliation!' Then, raising his voice even higher, he shouted that he was not prepared to make any compromise whatever. And, with that, Thiers withdrew and the audience was at an end.

The next day, Dunant and the Baron returned to Paris where they talked again to the three 'generals' who genuinely wanted a peace settlement and were trying to persuade the revolutionary council to accept mediation. But with the government forces at the city gates, time was running out. Dutilh determined to make one last desperate appeal to Thiers at Versailles. While he was away, the three generals were accused of being agents of the Versailles government and arrested. The man who had lent his house for the secret meetings was shot and it was learned that the Committee of Public Safety intended to shoot the Baron himself when he arrived back in town. Dunant at once set out to waylay him before he entered the city. After endless inspections by suspicious Communards he reached Saint-Denis and waited by the Seine for the Baron to appear. After only a few minutes, he came by in his carriage and Dunant stopped him and told him to turn around immediately and head back to

133

Versailles. On hearing the story, Thiers this time publicly praised the Baron's brave efforts to bring about conciliation, as well as the part Dunant had played in the attempt.

By now it was clear that Paris was in the hands of hard-line revolutionaries and there was no chance at all of a peaceful resolution to the conflict. Three days later, on 21 May, government troops entered the city during the afternoon and what became known as 'the infernal week' began. By the following day, barricades were being erected and proclamations plastered over the walls of Paris, calling the citizens to arms.

There were 80,000 regular troops within the walls, clambering up on the rooftops in their red trousers, congregating in the squares, slowly but remorselessly overrunning the hastily erected barricades of paving stones, bags of earth and mattresses. Dunant advised the housekeeper in his hotel to cover all the magnificent mirrors in the bedrooms and public rooms with criss-crossing strips of paper to prevent them shattering in the cannon blasts. Then he settled down on his balcony with Wilkie Collins's novel, *The Woman in White*, and a grand-stand view of the exchange of musket fire below.

On 23 May, Montmartre fell to the government troops and a group of fifty men, women and children were executed to avenge the two Versaillais generals who had been shot on the same spot two months before. Dr Chenu's hospital came under fire. Despite all attempts made by Dunant and the American Minister to save them, some of the hostages – the Archbishop of Paris, Dunant's friend the *abbé* Déguerry and three Jesuit priests, one of them wearing the Red Cross armband – were brought from their cells and shot. In the boulevards, the fighting turned into a massacre as the revolutionaries were driven back.

By dusk on the 24th, the desperate defenders had set fire to many buildings, including the Tuileries, and the flames spread rapidly, halted only by the crimson Seine. After one of the Communards' last defences in the place de la République had been stormed, there was wholesale slaughter by the government forces, no quarter given, no prisoners taken, captives simply being herded into public buildings and shot *en masse* with machine guns. The Gare de Lyon was set on fire and the flames devoured the barricades along the boulevards Voltaire and Philippe-Auguste, together with the heaps of corpses piled beside them. After hours of vicious fighting, the Bastille was finally taken and thousands of men, women and children herded together and forced to march long miles to Versailles. This gruesome week ended most appropriately in a last desperate struggle among the tombstones in a cemetery, and on Sunday the last barricade defended by a solitary rebel was taken and the guns at last fell silent.

Over twenty thousand rebels had been butchered – three times more dead than at the battle of Solferino. Over thirty thousand prisoners were packed into the barracks in Versailles and elsewhere, exhibited to the jeering crowds and subjected to abominable cruelties. Those who survived were deported in appallingly crowded conditions to the remote Pacific islands of New Caledonia.

Clara Barton went briefly to Paris while it was in the hands of the Commune. Horrified by what she witnessed, she wrote that Paris had plumbed the depths of folly and depravity. As for Dunant, try as he might to avert the catastrophe, he had been compelled to witness his beloved Paris being well and truly raped.

TWELVE

Moynier Heaves a Sigh of Relief

Paris that springtime was nothing to sing about. Charred and blackened rubble littered the once beautiful boulevards, burnt-out skeletons of buildings gaped obscenely, bullet-riddled walls and trees were constant reminders of what had probably been the most hellish week in the city's history. Not only had the Parisians suffered months of siege and starvation, the bitter humiliation of defeat first by the Prussians and then by their own country-men, the loss of family and friends and often the destruction of their homes, but they were now hounded by the police, ruth-lessly rounding up all those suspected of having sympathised with the Commune and imprisoning them to stop them fomenting mischief.

Dunant himself tried to remain as inconspicuous as possible, aware that he was already regarded with deep suspicion by the police for his activities during the Commune. As always, he was only minimally concerned with his own comfort and security, deploying all his energies in helping those in need of protection. He had been appalled by the events he had recently witnessed, for sheer callous inhumanity worse than anything he had seen even at Solferino. During that week, it had been killing for the sake of killing by frenzied, desperate men beyond the reach of reason. The laws of war had little hold at times like these and the events of the past week had made a mockery of the Geneva Convention.

But instead of giving way to despair, he began to think along new lines. In place of alleviating the cruelties and suffering of war and civil strife – which were, in any case, the concern of the aid societies – he envisaged forestalling them by creating a community where differences were settled by arbitration rather than recourse to arms. His detractors could sneer at such seemingly utopian dreams, but he had many friends and acquaintances who sympathised with his aims and were ready to help him – eminent and enlightened men like the pacifist, Frédéric Passy, Baron Dutilh de la Tuque, General de Beaufort, Monseigneur Dupanloup, the great pioneer of education, and Ferdinand de Lesseps, who had only completed his Suez Canal two years before in the teeth of enormous opposition and who, as an active and ardent humanitarian, had felt an affinity with Dunant ever since reading *Un Souvenir de Solferino*.

And despite all the recent horrors, Dunant could not help feeling a certain buoyancy and renewed zest for life resulting from all his frequently successful activities and adventures during the siege and the Commune. In a way, this period had almost been a replay of the time leading up to the first Geneva Conference, when his own particular talents for diplomacy and negotiation came into play. Little wonder that abler but greyer, less imaginative men felt envious of this man-of-the-world's ability to carry off such glamorous and stirring exploits that made their own achievements seem somehow narrow, plodding and pedestrian in comparison, worthy as they were.

The Franco-Prussian War had left its scars in Geneva too. The fighting may have been over but the bitterness and mutual hatred remained. All the good things that had been achieved by the International Committee and the aid societies were forgotten and from every side came criticisms and accusations of violations and abuses of the Convention. Many people even resented the committee's failure to intervene and enforce the Convention, and Moynier was constantly having to point out that they had no legal control over the conduct of troops in the field – this was a matter for the injured party to take up with its adversary. An eminent French doctor wrote in the *Revue des Deux Mondes* that the experiment conducted by the International Committee had been a complete failure, and the press predicted that the Geneva Convention would soon fade into oblivion. As for the army authorities, who had only ever tolerated such an incursion into their preserves on sufferance, they rubbed their hands with undisguised glee.

Split down the middle, misunderstood by the majority of people, disillusioned by its lack of acceptance and in danger of collapse, the movement was in deep trouble. Without the capable and clear-headed Moynier at the helm to steer it through the storm, it would surely never have survived. In December 1870, preparing itself for a long and difficult passage, the committee took on two new members: Alphonse Favre, a former professor in Geneva, and Gustave Ador, an able young barrister who acted as Secretary and soon became indispensable to his uncle, Gustave Moynier.

Back in Berlin in 1869, it had been planned to hold the next international conference of aid societies in Vienna. But after sending out a few feelers, the Viennese central committee soon realised that such a conference would be nothing more than a post mortem on the recent conflict and wisely opted out of hosting such a tricky and unproductive meeting, passing the buck back to the International Committee.

Moynier then wrote to the national societies, assuring them that the conference would not – indeed, legally could not – involve itself with violations of the Convention or recriminations on the conduct of the belligerents. Then he tried to get representatives of the principal central committees together. But it soon became clear that feeling between the erstwhile enemies still ran too high to make this possible. The conference was shelved indefinitely.

Unless some miracle could be found to bring the national societies together, the divisions between them, already deep, would widen and the whole movement would fall apart. Diplomacy had failed, logic had failed, what hope was there of survival? Moynier hit on a brilliant idea.

During an exhibition of medical equipment in The Hague in 1869, he had noticed that the Dutch committee simply referred to themselves as 'the Red Cross'. It now occurred to him that if all national societies, which hitherto had adopted a wide variety of long and often cumbersome names, were to do the same, it would eliminate endless confusion for everyone concerned as well as give them a real identity and much needed sense of unity. It is a mark of Moynier's genius that a man of his background and leanings could appreciate the power of a symbol to draw people together when all else had failed.

He strongly recommended to the national societies that they adopt the Red Cross as their name and symbol, pointing out that although governments had appropriated it to designate their military medical services, it had originally been devised for the societies and they alone had the exclusive right to this valuable prerogative.

The national societies seemed to think this was a good idea. In quick succession, they changed their statutes and became known as the national Red Cross societies, the same names they use today. Members of the French aid society had an even stronger incentive to change their indentity in this way, to prevent themselves from being mistaken for the Workers' International, a title which had caused such frequent misunderstandings and dangerous confusion during the Commune.

Curiously enough, Britain was among the slowest and most reluctant of the major powers to press ahead with an active Red Cross society. There seemed to be a certain wariness on the part of the Foreign Office towards embracing the Geneva Convention and the International Committee. As Thomas Gibson Bowles, the Conservative candidate for Dartington put it: 'It is a scheme for rendering war more easy, not less easy.' Nor was he the only Member of Parliament to mistrust something which they believed would help people slaughter each other with less sense of guilt. Finally, however, in January 1899, a permanent central Red Cross Committee for the British Empire was officially reorganised and approved.

The Universal Exhibition to be held in Vienna in 1873 seemed to promise another opportunity to bring the national societies together since they were invited, as they had been in Paris in 1867, to exhibit their medical equipment. Plans were accordingly revived to convene an international conference at the same time. But, hearing of this, the Austrian government abruptly withdrew its invitations and threatened that if there was any question of discussing the Geneva Convention, it would refuse the conference all official representation and assistance.

Although the reason for the Austrian attitude was ostensibly to avoid the risk of stormy debates that would mar the peaceful ambiance of the Universal Exhibition, the Viennese central committee confided to Moynier that the real reason lay in a plan, hatched in collusion with other governments, to modify the Geneva Convention at the very least, if not to get rid of it altogether, thus releasing themselves from the commitments undertaken in 1864.

This same year of 1873, during which the Red Cross seemed in real danger of total disintegration, also marked the tenth year of its existence. Moynier drew attention to the event by devoting the whole July issue of the *Bulletin* to 'The First Ten Years of the Red Cross' in which he traced the history of the movement from its inception. This was a remarkable piece of work in that it managed to avoid mentioning the name of Henry Dunant even once. It was as if he had never existed. Whether Moynier was really still afraid of tainting the image of the International Committee by admitting its former association with a man of 'doubtful repute', or whether he quite simply wanted to claim all the credit as his own and be recognised as the founder of the Red Cross himself, is a matter for speculation.

Another point raised by Moynier in this work was that the Red Cross, to which no fewer than twenty-two countries now belonged, should expand still further but only he thought, to those parts of the world that were civilised in the Western meaning of the word. In his view, it would be useless to attempt to enrol races with a different cultural framework because the principles and philosophy of the Red Cross would be quite alien to them and they would find such concepts as pity for the enemy wounded and associations for helping the victims quite incomprehensible or absurd. Hungary, Serbia, Rumania and Greece were about as far as the committee wanted to go in terms of expansion at this stage, although Moynier was all in favour of gradually preparing the ground in more distant countries

141

by 'spreading abroad the philanthropic notions of which Europe prides itself on having been the birthplace'.

The Red Cross had actually already expanded beyond Europe, Turkey having signed up to the Convention in 1865. In 1872, with the Viceroy's help, Appia founded an aid society in Egypt and put a young Genevan doctor in charge of running it. Brazil and China had been bombarded with literature about the Red Cross and the Convention. And a Japanese delegation visiting Switzerland was also won over to the cause. Then came the news that the Shah of Persia was about to arrive in Geneva. What a coup it would be if he could be persuaded to accede to the Geneva Convention, and what a surprise it was to hear that he already had. Only a few days before in London, the Shah had apparently received the ubiquitous Mr Henry Dunant who had had no difficulty in persuading him to give his agreement on the spot.

Moynier was not pleased. Dunant had pipped him to the post yet again. In a letter to the Federal Council concerning Persia's formal accession, he stressed that the International Committee was very anxious to avoid any misunderstanding about the capacity of Mr Dunant, who was not acting as its official representative. And he added: 'For the honour of the Red Cross, we ourselves feel very strongly that it should not be served by individuals with tarnished reputations.' The words he chose clearly indicate that Moynier was influenced by the rumours spread by the directors of the now defunct Crédit Genevois and was anxious to protect the image of the Red Cross from any association with Dunant because of 'shady dealings' rather than ineptitude or bankruptcy.

But it was somewhat risky to be making new conquests when the ground was crumbling beneath their very feet. The credibility as well as the cohesion of the movement had been badly shaken in the recent conflict when misunderstandings or ignorance about the Convention had led to recriminations, followed by retaliations, counter-retaliations and ever more appalling atrocities. Moynier quite rightly maintained that the Convention itself was not to blame but rather the negligence of the public administrations of the countries involved.

But his voice was one against many. After the Franco-Prussian War, there was a general consensus that if two such highly civilised powers could not make it work, the Convention was obviously unworkable and should be scrapped. Even governments agreed with these views, for different but understandable reasons. Before the Convention came into being, nobody had much cared if troops failed to abide by a few vague, unwritten rules. But now it was necessary to ensure that the military authorities took the necessary measures or else, at the slightest infringement, there was an outcry and the country whose soldiers had committed the violation stood arraigned in the dock of public opinion, accused of breaking the law and fighting unfairly. The old way of going about things was so much easier to handle, and less hazardous for their reputations.

As for the relief societies, they considered the Convention was not only unworkable but downright dangerous by providing unscrupulous individuals with a convenient cover – the Red Cross insignia – for spying, stealing from corpses and stirring up disorder. Everyone agreed that medical personnel ought to have neutral status but nobody wanted it at the price of the Convention.

In the end, the Convention was nearly undermined, with the best if not the wisest of intentions, by the Austrian government which proposed that each country introduce the necessary provisions into its own regulations. There would then be no need for an international convention. The French and English central committees approved. Pressure was then applied to the International Committee to conduct the necessary negotiations. Moynier flatly refused, maintaining that it was wishful thinking to suppose that countries would modify their internal legislation at this stage when they had always neglected or refused to do so before. In any case, he argued, all was not yet lost. The King of Prussia was still a staunch supporter of the Convention, and from the Russian central committee came the assurance that influential circles in that country regarded the treaty as sacrosanct.

Cutting through all the fuss and foliage, Moynier clearly recognised that the key to the problem was to ensure that the

Convention was correctly applied. Earlier that year, in January 1872, he had shown how this might be achieved in a paper entitled *Note on the Creation of an International Judicial Institution Designed to Prevent and Repress Infringements of the Geneva Convention* which might have formed the basis for the International Military Tribunal of Nuremberg set up in 1945.

The nub of his proposal was as follows. At the outbreak of war, a five-member court would be instituted, consisting of an arbitrator from each of the belligerent countries and three from neutral ones. It would be convened by the nation claiming itself the injured party, examine the case and pass sentence, which would be carried out by the national authorities holding the offender.

From all over Europe and even America came the reactions of the top legal brains to Moynier's publication, for lawyers love a document with a good long title. They generally agreed with the idea of an international court but suggested that its powers should be limited to conducting inquiries and, at the most, passing censure. Under no circumstances, in their view, should it ever pass judgment.

However, apart from provoking a great deal of intellectual and literary mileage at the time, this 'milestone in the history of international law' passed virtually unheeded by governments and central committees, and even the International Committee gradually lost interest in the whole idea.

Had it been totally unrealistic to try and draw up a code of the rules of war at such a seemingly unpropitious juncture? Not really. In spite of the apparent failure of Moynier's attempt – or, perhaps, partly because of it – there was now an unprecedented revival of interest in the subject among legal experts everywhere. Professor Bluntschli of Heidelberg University published the *Codification of International Law*, an enormous undertaking representing a comprehensive international civil code and naturally devoting considerable attention to war. After his own experience at the head of a medical unit during the recent hostilities, Bluntschli did not think much of the Geneva Convention, but he did advocate regulations of a more general kind as a means of keeping violence within reasonable bounds.

Henry Dunant in 1863, at the time of the foundation of the Red Cross. *(© Photothèque CICR (DR)/Frédéric Boissonnas)*

Henry Dunant age sixty-seven. *(© Photothèque CICR (DR)/Otto Rirtjann)*

Hospice, Heiden, where Henry Dunant died on 30 October 1910. *(© Photothèque CICR (DR)/Danemark)*

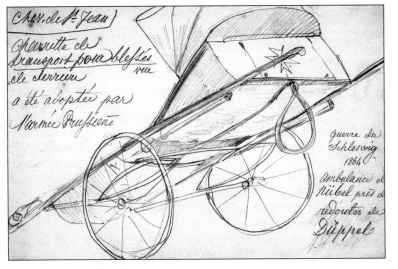

The Schleswig war. A stretcher on wheels (possibly Dr Appia's invention) for collecting the wounded, adopted by the Prussian army. *(© Photothèque CICR (DR))*

The Schleswig war. Knights of the Order of St John of Jerusalem transporting the wounded, and the Rauhen-Haus Brothers. *(© Photothèque CICR (DR)/ Danemark)*

Battle of Solferino, June 1859. An Austrian ambulance being attacked by a French patrol as it headed towards Palestro. *(© Photothèque CICR (DR)/ Danemark)*

The Committee of Five that founded the Red Cross: Louis Appia, Guillaume-Henri Dufour, Henry Dunant, Théodore Maunoir, Gustave Moynier. (© CICR)

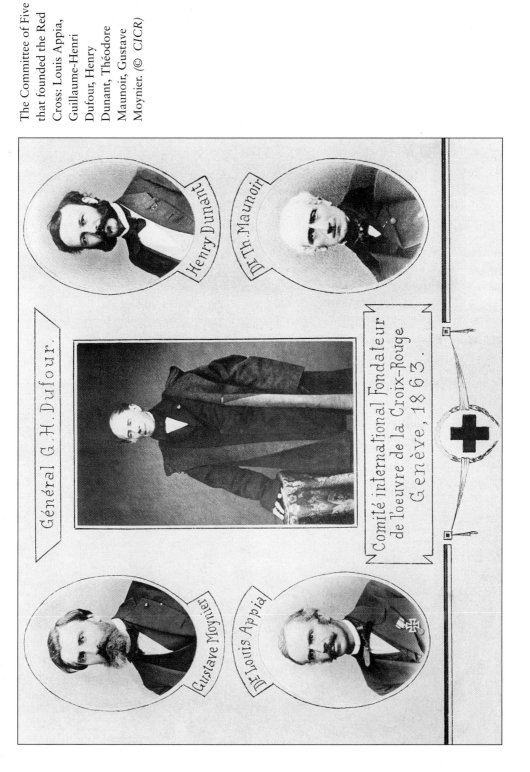

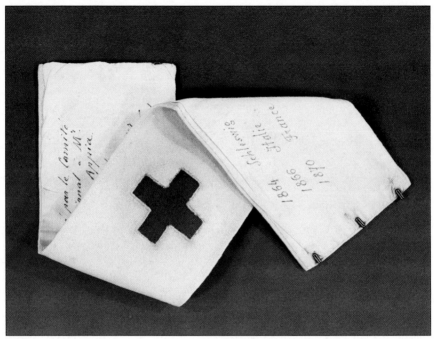

Dr Louis Appia's Red Cross armband. *(© Photothèque CICR (DR))*

Gustave Moynier at the time of the signing of the Geneva Convention. *(© CICR/A. Pfister)*

Gustave Moynier (1826–1910), President of the International Committee of the Red Cross from 1864 to 1910. *(© Photothèque CICR (DR)/Jean Arlaud)*

Clara Barton, first President of the American Red Cross. Born in Massachusetts in 1821, she rose from a small farm background to become a schoolteacher, government worker, Civil War nurse, women's prison superintendent and dedicated humanitarian. Although not a religious woman, late in life she endorsed the Christian Science movement and dabbled in spriritualism, consulting mediums and astrologers on occasion. *(© Photothèque CICR (DR))*

Geneva, Sécheron. The Villa Moynier, headquarters of the ICRC from 1933 to 1946. *(© Photothèque CICR (DR))*

Page one of a letter from Henry Dunant to Gustave Moynier.
(© Photothèque CICR (DR))

Page two of the same letter. *(© Photothèque CICR (DR))*

Napoleon III, French emperor
from 1852 to 1870.
(© Photothèque CICR)

Gustave Moynier wearing some of
the medals and decorations which
he took such pride and pleasure in
displaying. *(© CICR)*

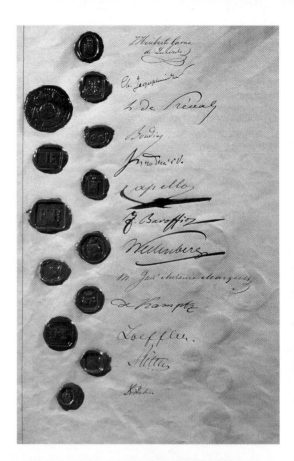

The last page of the Geneva Convention
of 22 August 1864. *(© CICR)*

Signing the Geneva Convention, 22 August 1864, in a painting by Armand Dumaresq.
(© Photothèque CICR (DR))

In reaction to Moynier's proposal of international jurisdiction, Francis Lieber, who had been commissioned by President Lincoln during the American Civil War to draw up a code of conduct for armies in conflict, advocated that a council of leading jurists be convened who would settle between themselves some of the major questions that still remained unresolved.

Moynier was more concerned with the need to codify international law, to establish clearly defined regulations that would enable a tribunal to state the legal position, whereas Lieber wanted the council to study particular issues out of which the law would be clarified. However, deciding to capitalise on Lieber and Bluntschli's interest and ideas, he worked with them on plans to set up a council of jurists who would then decide how best to proceed. In September 1873, the Institute of International Law was founded in Ghent and, from that time on, Moynier took the keenest interest in its work, which he regarded as of equal importance to that of the Red Cross.

Six months later, his attention was wrenched back to deal full-time with another crisis affecting more immediately the Geneva Convention. A formal invitation to a conference in Brussels was sent to all states by the Imperial Russian government, which claimed to have also been working on codification of the laws of war. A *Draft International Convention Regarding the Laws and Customs of Warfare*, which Russia had prepared as a basis for the work of the conference, was enclosed in which it was proposed to replace the Geneva Convention by seven articles which were less favourable to the wounded. And there was no guarantee that these provisions would not be watered down still further during discussions. There also seemed a danger that the activities of the aid societies might be restricted and that they would no longer be allowed on to the battlefield, or even into the theatre of operations.

This was an emergency and the International Committee immediately went into action. The central committees were asked to put pressure on their governments to get them to agree that provisions covering the wounded were already codified, and to instruct their delegates to the conference to ensure that the Geneva Convention was incorporated as it stood in the future treaty. The results were not encouraging, most of the central committees holding out little hope of success.

Now thoroughly rattled, the International Committee sent out an urgent circular to the central committees, stressing how dangerous it would be to attack the Geneva Convention at this stage, and how damaging it would be to their own interests. But the truth of the matter was that the national societies had become so divided and alienated from one another as a result of the war that they had failed to make the necessary revisions to the Convention themselves and had therefore placed themselves in an extremely vulnerable position.

As it turned out, the Brussels Conference, as is the nature of international conferences, became involved in much wider issues, particularly in defining which categories of combatants the states should be entitled to deploy. The necessity for this had become apparent in the recent war, during which some French units could scarcely be distinguished from civilians, and snipers not at all, which had given rise to horrifying reprisals against innocent civilians.

This complex problem provoked long and heated discussion, compared to which the matter of the treatment of the wounded seemed relatively unimportant and straightforward. Several delegates announced that their governments wished to preserve the Convention in its present form and, on the request of the Russian government itself, the circular from the International Committee was read out and created an excellent impression. Alerted to the risks of tampering with the Convention, the conference replaced the Russian proposal relating to the wounded with a clause which stated that the obligations of belligerents regarding the treatment of the sick and wounded were governed by the Geneva Convention of 22 August 1864.

But the Convention was not left entirely alone. The conference stressed the need for urgent revisions and even appointed a subcommittee which drew up a draft of a revised treaty, retaining all the main provisions of the 1864 text and even incorporating several welcome new ones. The Convention was safe, at least for the time being. As he sat back in his chair that evening, having tidied all his papers away, Moynier heaved a sigh of relief.

Someone else who had been keeping a close and anxious eye on the proceedings in Brussels was Henry Dunant. For he also was acutely concerned about the conference, although for quite a different reason. Once again, the paths of their destinies were unwittingly but inexorably interlinked.

THIRTEEN

Dunant Provokes the Russian Bear

In convening the Brussels Conference, the Tsar had not only jeopardised the survival of the Geneva Convention but also ruined the plans of Henry Dunant and his friends to hold their own diplomatic conference in order to draw up a convention for the improvement of the conditions of prisoners of war.

Since the end of the Franco-Prussian conflict, Dunant's schemes to save the world from its own excesses had crystallised. In reaction to their horror and revulsion at the anarchy and cruelty of the Commune, he and his friends started a movement called the Universal Alliance for Order and Civilisation. Its aims were to reduce the incidence of armed conflict, the cruelty of civil oppression and the violence of social disturbances by raising the moral and cultural standards of the ordinary citizen through programmes of education and training, libraries and temperance societies.

The movement's most urgent task was to defend workers against ruthless and exploitative employers and, above all, against the perceived corrupting and atheistic influence of the Workers' International. In the event, the Workers' International became widely accepted as the champion of the workers against ruthless exploitation by employers and Dunant failed in his objectives. It is only now, some 120 years later, that Communism, the offspring of the Workers' International, has been totally discredited and Dunant's ideas are gaining credence.

Since there was little likelihood of wars being eliminated altogether, the Alliance intended to extend their programmes to the armed forces so that soldiers would confine themselves to the business of fighting and not go on to wreak revenge on their enemy with acts of gruesome cruelty.

These ideas seemed unrealistically ambitious and high-flown at the time, as if Dunant expected to succeed where religion over the centuries had failed. In hindsight, of the causes Dunant initiated, the world YMCA movement flourishes in more than ninety countries, the Jews inhabit Israel, UNICEF promotes universal culture and the Red Cross is the most important and influential humanitarian movement the world has ever seen. It was only by an oversight that he did not found a nineteenth-century committee for the protection of the environment.

Despite being so far ahead of his time, the power of his energetic propaganda was such that *The Times* published a lengthy and favourable article on the Alliance in April 1872, and when an English branch was later formed, its members included such eminent figures as the Dukes of Norfolk, Somerset and Wellington, the Iron Duke himself.

As had become a habit with him when starting up any new undertaking, Dunant sought the Emperor's patronage for the Alliance. The fact that Napoleon III was now in exile in England worried him not a bit. From Chislehurst came the sort of reply he had received way back in Cavriana, just after the battle of Solferino, the reply that had become a kind of ritual, thanking him but declining the offer.

This letter from Napoleon may explain a curious incident that occurred during the first congress held by the Alliance in Paris in 1872. A gendarme burst in with a warrant to ascertain the source of their funds. Information had apparently been given to the police that the exiled Emperor was financing the operations of what was thought to be a Bonapartist faction. Proof to the contrary was easily provided, but who had tipped off the police? This incident reinforced Dunant's suspicions that his landlord had been bribed to intercept his mail and report back to Geneva, suspicions that had been roused ever since a lawyer representing shareholders of the Crédit Genevois had come to Paris some time before and made him sign a deed giving them a prior claim on any earnings until all his debts were cleared.

During this first congress of the Universal Alliance, discussion soon veered away from its altruistic, all-embracing aims and centred on the more immediate question of the treatment of prisoners of war. General d'Houdetot read out an excellent paper on the subject written by Dunant in 1867, which he had unsuccessfully tried to include on the agenda of the first international Red Cross conference. Now it was a different matter and the congress enthusiastically applauded the address and set up a committee with a view to convening a diplomatic conference.

A repeat of Dunant's 1863 promotional tour of the European capitals was now called for. But he was in no fit state to go. For some time he had been plagued with acute eczema which particularly affected his right hand, while long years of worry and lack of proper food were now taking their toll, racking him with troublesome indigestion. Although he tried his best to keep up appearances, his previously almost inexhaustible resources of energy were running low and had to be topped up with strong doses of dogged determination.

Some people, half believing the Geneva calumny, turned a blind eye to his plight. But other, truer friends like Count Flavigny, now safely installed in England after Dunant had rescued him from the Commune, and an English army surgeon who knew how much Dunant had accomplished during the recent war, tried to mount a rescue operation on his behalf. An appeal was published in the British medical press in June that year; it raised precisely £2.

The trouble was that Dunant was too proud to ask for help from anyone. In 1869, Marshal Canrobert, who was well aware of everything that Dunant had done, urged him to go and see the Emperor and ask his help. But, as Dunant later said, it went against the grain to look as if he was claiming a reward for the creation of the Red Cross.

Fortunately for him, at about this time his Uncle David died in Geneva and left him an annuity of 1,200 francs a year, just enough to scrape by in those days. Through all these years, he had kept in close touch with his family in Geneva, particularly with his sister Marie and his doctor brother Pierre. Now Pierre, who must have sensed that Henry was going through an especially bad patch, sent him a small loan. With this, he could afford to go to England where he hoped to win subscription-paying members and much needed funds for the Universal Alliance, as well as support for the international conference on prisoners of war.

What a sad contrast between this departure and the first time he had set out to storm the capitals of Europe, the handsome young charmer with his glossy, dark-reddish hair and luxuriant sideburns that were so fashionable under the Second Empire, a bold gold watch-chain straddling his pale lemon waistcoat. Now he was a sick man, decrepit and down at heel, his emaciated exterior curiously at odds with the eager flame still shining from his sunken eyes.

To pile on the misery, Moynier who had heard of the journey, sent the English Red Cross the text of the judgment passed against the Crédit Genevois, adding 'This affair created a great scandal in Geneva, whence Mr Dunant has since disappeared and would no longer dare to show his face.'

Arriving in London, Dunant called on a friend of his, a prominent figure in the Social Science Association, an organisation with similar aims to those of the Universal Alliance. Lord Elcho listened with interest and promised to preside if Dunant succeeded in calling a meeting to rouse public interest in prisoners of war. Over the next few days, Dunant paid visits to various other members of the Association and, after much persuasion and promises to pay the costs of the conference out of his own pocket, succeeded in getting the Association to sponsor a meeting to be held at the Society of Arts in the Adelphi on 6 August.

Already primed by Florence Nightingale on the plight of victims of war, his listeners were receptive to somebody who had plans and remedies for the problem, someone of whom most of them had already heard as the author of *Un Souvenir*. They settled back in their seats and looked up at their distinguished guest, speaking so carefully in English, although it was strange he was so shabbily dressed, they thought, and so dreadfully thin as well. But they were soon carried away by Dunant's ardour and eloquence. After painting a vivid picture of the appalling treatment to which so many prisoners of war were still exposed, he warned his audience that war was imminent and that international agreement to protect prisoners of war must be secured before it broke out. He ended by asking that delegates be sent to the international conference for which preparations were being made by the Alliance in Paris.

Dunant's speech was loudly applauded by the assembly and received flattering press coverage, *The Times* awarding it a whole column. Indeed, so impressed was the Association by its success that he was asked to go and lecture to their members in Liverpool and Manchester. Much as he would have liked to, he could not afford the fare and had to plead an overload of work as an excuse. But the compliment he appreciated most of all was a letter from Florence Nightingale, thanking him for sending her a copy of the speech and congratulating him on 'the success of your noble work, truly a work of God'. She thanked him too for linking her 'poor name' to this great work since it seemed to her to be 'a recognition of the way all Englishwomen from the poorest to the richest have worked during the last war under your auspices and those of the Cross. . . .'

Another lady who was destined to play an important part in Dunant's life was also impressed by his lecture at the Adelphi. This was Léonie Kastner, the wealthy widow of a famous musician and the daughter of an even wealthier banker, who had already met Dunant in Paris. She had been won over to the aims of the Alliance, even generously offering handsome premises in one of her Paris houses, in the rue de Clichy, for use as its headquarters.

Léonie Kastner provided exactly the kind of female companion-ship Dunant appreciated. Fitting comfortably, although only just, into the older-woman category he had always cultivated – he himself was now forty-four – she was a highly intelligent companion whose idealistic and charitable impulses almost matched his own. Moreover, she was far too sensitive and sensible a woman ever to embarrass or alarm Dunant with unwelcome sexual overtures.

Herself a fervent Bonapartist, one of Léonie Kastner's greatest ambitions was to meet Napoleon III. Dunant therefore asked for an audience for her and her son Frédéric while they were still in

England, and this was granted. The ex-Emperor graciously received mother and son and, after being handed a copy of the Adelphi lecture thoughtfully provided by its author for this purpose, benevolently enquired how he was getting on and proceeded to encourage Madame Kastner to help him in any way she could. He seemed to be unaware that he was talking to a multi-millionairess.

Napoleon's own attempts to come to Dunant's rescue had been thwarted on several occasions. When Bourcart had approached him some years before, several friends had indeed come forward with substantial contributions but Bourcart's letters and messages on the subject, together with several large sums of money, including 1,500 francs from Mr Schlumberger, had mysteriously gone astray and Dunant knew nothing about these gestures until twenty-five years later. Some time afterwards, the Emperor had asked the *duc* d'Aumale to make enquiries in Geneva, where he was told that there was no need to worry about Mr Dunant, his wealthy family made him an allowance of 3,000 francs. One does not have to look far to find whose 'worthy and respectable' hands were at work.

In the meantime, Dunant had to find some way of earning a living. He decided to approach the Peace Society whose president, Henry Richard, had been condemning war and advocating arbitration for the past twenty years. He immediately warmed to Dunant and offered him the job of Secretary of the Peace Society in its offices in Pall Mall.

Shortly afterwards, Henry Richard proposed that Dunant should speak at the forthcoming annual congress of the Social Science Association. The Peace Society was paying his fare so Dunant set off on 11 September for Plymouth where the congress was being held. His fame as the author of *Un Souvenir* and the speaker at the Adelphi had preceded him and the hall was packed. His subject was 'Arbitration considered as a means of preventing war' and he warmed to it by the minute, becoming so carried away by his own zeal that he completely drained his last dregs of energy. With some alarm, the audience noticed his voice growing fainter and anxiously watched the speaker swaying dizzily from side to side, clutching the lectern for support. Momentarily recovering, he smiled reassuringly and continued, but faintness overpowered him again and he collapsed into his seat, just finding enough strength to hand his speech to the man beside him to finish reading. At the end, there was tumultuous applause, which Dunant could only acknowledge with a smile, for with all their enthusiasm and adulation it had not occurred to anyone to offer their unfortunate speaker anything to eat.

The press were unanimous in praising his speech and the proposals it contained. On 13 September, the *Globe* printed the following:

SOCIAL SCIENCE CONGRESS AT PLYMOUTH

One of the most important papers read was by Mr. Henry Dunant (of Switzerland), founder of the Red Cross and of the Convention of Geneva. He made a proposal for introducing among the civilized Powers a High Court of International Arbitration with a view to avoid war. Mr. Dunant said: 'A new world has been discovered in our days, and every day reveals its extent: it is the world of international ideas. . . .'

True to form, Dunant made a collection of his press cuttings and had his lecture printed and circulated around the country by the Peace Society. Suddenly he was famous again and received numerous dinner invitations for which he must have been thankful, having almost starved in Plymouth. In his memoirs, he records how he suffered in secret from cold and hunger in his boarding house in Devon, eating only a breakfast of tea and cold meat every day during the fortnight he was there and nothing else; no lunch or dinner, unless he was lucky enough to be invited somewhere.

Needless to say, a copy of his lecture, which contained references to several efforts made by the ex-Emperor towards arbitration, was promptly despatched to Napoleon III who was staying at Cowes that September. And miraculously this time, for the very first time, he actually received a reply, handwritten by Napoleon himself, thanking him for his 'flattering words' in Plymouth and congratulating him on his generous efforts in this humanitarian cause. At last Dunant had tangible proof of his connection with his revered Emperor. And it was only just in time. Three months later, in January 1873, Napoleon III underwent an operation for gallstones and died.

After all this excitement, Dunant settled down to work at enlarging the membership and swelling the subscriptions to the Peace Society. But the minimal salary was scarcely enough to live on, adding to his worries and aggravating his eczema to such an extent that he was hardly able to write. Madame Kastner helped him from across the Channel, tactfully inventing good works for which she could repay him, such as the distribution of temperance tracts – no doubt a source of great consolation to the largely illiterate workers.

He also continued his campaign for a convention on prisoners of war and gave a lecture on the subject in Brighton during September 1873. The *Morning Post* was most complimentary, declaring that there was probably no man living who was worthy to be considered as great a public benefactor as Dunant, the originator of the Geneva Convention and the founder of the Red Cross. The article ended: 'We sincerely wish Mr. Dunant God-speed in this his latest effort in the cause of humanity.'

In February of the following year came news from the *comte* d'Houdetot in Paris that he had been nominated International Secretary of the new Society for the Improvement of the Condition of Prisoners of War. This had held its first international congress a few days before and had been attended by many important figures from all over Europe as well as the United States, just as had the International Committee for Relief to Wounded Soldiers, precursor of the Red Cross, in Geneva eleven years earlier. The Society was now planning a diplomatic conference for May and Dunant was asked to return to Paris to help in the preparations.

The invitations sent out by the fledgeling Society to the European and American governments had unexpected and dramatic results. Tsar Alexander II, a far-seeing, humane and enlightened man, had highly approved of the Geneva Convention, but sought to raise the sights of the civilised world to reduce the calamities of war by restricting their causes rather than merely alleviating their effects. Having taken the initiative in this direction at St Petersburg in 1868, he was reluctant to relinquish it. But now, here was Henry Dunant about to steal his thunder yet again. On hearing about his Society's invitation, he therefore swiftly instructed the Russian ambassador in Paris to forestall it by saying that for some time past the Imperial Cabinet had been contemplating a similar project, although along more general lines, and that it seemed logical to combine the two in a conference to be convened by the Tsar in Brussels. The Russian government smugly proceeded to issue formal invitations and there was nothing Dunant or his colleagues could do to compete. Only America, despite a personal plea from the Tsar to President Grant, declined to attend.

The Brussels Conference opened on 27 July 1874 and its deliberations were followed with nail-biting anxiety by Moynier and the International Committee of the Red Cross in Geneva, concerned for the fate of the Convention, but quite unaware that the crisis had been sparked off by Henry Dunant. Lengthy debates ensued on the seventy-one articles of the Draft Convention drawn up by the Russian Cabinet, during which the proposed convention on prisoners of war was swallowed up and lost in the morass of conflicting views and interests. Moynier may have heaved a sigh of relief at the end of it but Dunant was distinctly discouraged. He would have to wait another thirty-three years before his convention on prisoners of war was finally signed, in The Hague in 1907.

On returning to London, Dunant continued working for the Peace Society and promoting the Universal Alliance. Not content with this, his thoughts strayed back to one of his earlier preoccupations: slavery. The recently published works by Stanley and Livingstone had rekindled all the indignation he had felt as a young man when reading *Uncle Tom's Cabin* and, despite the activities of the Anti-Slavery Society and the treaty concluded with the Sultan of Turkey abolishing the slave trade, he was well aware that this iniquitous practice still survived in pockets of Africa and elsewhere. In November 1874, he published a paper appealing for international action to stop the cruel exploitation of African natives. This was taken up by the Universal Alliance which campaigned for an international diplomatic conference. But they met with opposition and vested interests all along the way and little was achieved.

There seemed no end to Dunant's aspirations. Undeterred by this small setback, he homed in once more on the Middle East. Persuading the Universal Alliance to take action on behalf of repressed Christian and Jewish minorities in Syria, and oscillating between the German 'Temple' settlers and the British Israelites, he formed the Syrian and Palestine Colonization Society. A prospectus was published which spoke optimistically of obtaining the Sultan's agreement and the granting of vast concessions of land, through which an extensive network of railways would be laid. Alas, this turned out to be wishful thinking, but it demonstrated once again the extraordinary facility with which Henry Dunant could found a society.

In 1876, uprisings by the Christians in the Turkish provinces of Bulgaria, Serbia and Bosnia, followed by their ferocious suppression by the Turks, put paid to any chance there might have been of negotiating with the Sultan and set in train a chain of events that culminated in Russia declaring war on Turkey the following year. All prospects of diplomatic neutrality for Palestine and Syria, or concessions for partners and colleagues evaporated, and with them Dunant's last hopes of repaying his debts and retrieving his place in the sun.

FOURTEEN

A Musical Interlude

In May 1874, shortly after he had left London to do battle for the prisoner of war convention at the Brussels Conference, the *Standard* hailed Dunant as 'The Peter the Hermit of the new Red Cross'. Doubtless this was meant as a compliment but, in any case, he was probably gratified to know that his name was still linked with this, his proudest achievement. Even his private correspondence was always headed with the Red Cross stamp and all his English circulars were signed by 'Henry Dunant, founder of the Red Cross on the Continent', a tactful acknowledgement of Florence Nightingale in his host country.

Back in London later the same year, while championing his old causes of anti-slavery and the colonisation of Palestine and struggling, with increasing difficulty, to scrape a living, Madame Kastner providentially came to the rescue with an appeal on behalf of her son. Frédéric Kastner, a physicist, who had inherited his father's fascination for the Aeolian harp and the music of the spheres, had succeeded in inventing a strange instrument which he called the pyrophone. Rather like an organ, its notes were produced by gas jets in a series of glass tubes of differing lengths and dimensions. By touching a key, the gas jet inside the tube separated like the fingers of a hand and emitted a note. When the key was released, the flames came together and the note ceased. The intervals between the notes and their pitch were regulated by the varying lengths and widths of the tubes and the adjusted height of the jets.

Madame Kastner herself had already spent close on 100,000 francs on developing and making the necessary modifications to this invention. Being a highly educated and extremely capable lady, as well as an excellent musician, she had also spent considerably more time and trouble on it over its long years of teething troubles than her son himself, who found plenty of other less strenuous pastimes to attend to in Paris with the help of the handsome allowance made by his mother, whose only extravagance was her desire to see him covered in glory.

Jean Georges Kastner having been a member of the Institut de France, his widow approached the Académie des Sciences in Paris who studied the ingenious instrument with considerable interest. Musical evenings were held at the Kastner residence and one of these was attended by *The Times* correspondent in Paris who recorded the astonishment of the audience at hearing this extra-ordinary instrument 'which played some very powerful and very moving *morceaux*'. César Franck and Berlioz, who had been friends of her husband, came and played it. Jenny Lind was said to have sung to it and Gounod considered using the singing flames in one of his operas. Frédéric himself wrote a slim volume entitled *Les Flammes chantantes* in which he explained the underlying theory and how it worked, with accompanying technical diagrams.

Léonie Kastner now thought the time was ripe to introduce the pyrophone to London, and who better for the job than Dunant. If he could achieve the same kind of publicity and impact for her Frédéric's invention as he had for the Red Cross with *Un Souvenir* and his crusade to the courts of Europe, she promised him 50,000 francs, a sum that would release him from at least a large part of his debts.

Although this endeavour was scarcely up his street, Dunant agreed to try, not so much because of the promised reward, which he probably realised he had little chance of winning, but mainly because of his gratitude for all Madame Kastner's generosity and goodness to him. In January 1875, therefore, he persuaded Professor Tyndall, an eminent physicist, to give a lecture and a demonstration of the pyrophone at the Royal Institution. A few weeks later, he followed suit as best he could himself in the Adelphi amphitheatre of the Society of Arts, where some of those among the erudite audience who had been present at his earlier lecture on prisoners of war

160

might well have been surprised at his wide-ranging interests, or perhaps envied the enforced silence of the incarcerated soldiery.

He started off by giving a very clear and precise explanation of the scientific principles behind the pyrophone and how it worked, followed by a lyrical description of its beautiful yet melancholy tone which he compared, in its sweetness and roundness, to 'a human and impassioned whisper, like an echo of the inward vibrations of the soul'. Jokingly (a new departure for him) he extolled its ancillary merits as a heating apparatus and, in the best salesman tradition, recommended the 15-jet model for luxury residences or ballrooms. Then, in the presence of many famous musical and scientific personalities, a 13-branched instrument began playing 'God Save the Queen'. There was much amusement, amazement and applause.

In the intervals between lectures and performances in private houses, Dunant deployed all his skill and waning energies in propaganda and public relations, even organising an exhibition at the Crystal Palace where the instrument was put on show and played to the general public. But although it aroused a certain amount of interest, it was nothing like enough to make Frédéric Kastner's fame or fortune. And Dunant did not have the necessary scientific knowledge or mechanical expertise to maintain the delicate instrument in perfect working order. The pyrophone broke down and the performances came to an end. A worthy home was found for it in a glass cabinet in the Science Museum in South Kensington where it can still be seen beside its accompanying inscription: 'Lent by Mr. Henry Dunant, 1876'.

Now, with his last lost cause behind him, Dunant began a nomadic existence divided between England, France, Germany, Italy and Switzerland, every stop in this sad itinerary recorded on a diary-sized scrap of paper, the only written record of his twelve years of wandering. Sometimes he stayed with Madame Kastner in Strasbourg or Paris. But his main base was Stuttgart where Pastor Wagner, who had translated *Un Souvenir* into German, now needed help with his literary work and invited Dunant to live with him. He had another friend in Stuttgart, the young Professor Rudolf Müller who found him writing assignments and translations for which he earned small sums which could be saved to pay for sorties into the outside world.

In 1877, Madame Kastner asked him to accompany her on a grand tour of Italy that took them to Venice, Florence, Livorno, Bologna and Rome. They were away almost a year. Her husband's fame as a composer of military music, operas and comic operas, her own wealth and Dunant's renown as the founder of the Red Cross opened all doors to them and they were welcomed by the cream of society. At the German Embassy in Rome, Dunant was overjoyed to see old friends from the time of the Statistical Congress in Berlin, and others he had met at the victory celebrations over ten years previously. The only thing that marred his enjoyment was the uncomfortable feeling that people were commenting on his relations with Madame Kastner and inevitably putting the worst possible interpretation on them. Was this impression the product of an understandably overwrought imagination, or were there more sinister forces once again at work?

His suspicions certainly seemed well grounded judging by several incidents that occurred on their way back north. Dunant describes in his memoirs how, at Roveredo, they overheard the hotel proprietor saying in Italian: 'He's a wicked man, he beats her.' And in their hotel in Lugano, a commotion broke out on the ground floor just after they had settled in, when policemen stormed in and advised Mr Beha, the owner, to turn his new guests out immediately. Mr Beha sent them packing but apparently not before they had found time to poison the minds of the entire hotel staff against them. Everyone from the porter to the coachman, the servants and chambermaids, the gardener and the chef had been told he was an out-and-out rascal, a cruel monster, a dangerous and unprincipled character, and Madame Kastner a martyr and his defenceless victim. The housekeeper of the hotel displayed an extraordinary degree of venom towards them throughout their stay. It was no longer a question of being a Prussian spy, for the hotel belonged to Germans. Now he was quite simply a scoundrel after Madame Kastner's money. And, for good measure, the French police added that he was one of the leading Communards who had escaped from the hulks!

Things reached such a pitch that a famous Italian poet staying at the same hotel became so indignant that he shouted for everyone to hear: 'It's outrageous, these foreigners who come all the way here to persecute someone who hasn't done them any harm!' Dunant himself was overcome with impotent fury and Madame Kastner shared his indignation. Together they started revising the notes he had written in Rome – a practice he had adopted as a kind of release valve for his frustrations – and now they even resolved to publish them. Madame Kastner offered to pay and located a printer willing to oblige. Dunant himself stayed in the hotel, his stomach tied in knots with bitterness and frustration, unable to eat for days.

Although it seems unlikely they ever discussed the subject between themselves, Dunant makes his feelings for Madame Kastner quite clear in his memoirs, as well as in letters to friends and family. He obviously had the greatest admiration for her intelligence, intellect, good humour and charm. He was also eternally grateful for all her goodness to him. But he was rather in awe of her, and especially of her colossal fortune. He states quite positively that he never lived off her. She paid generously for the work he did, perhaps especially generously since she felt herself partly responsible for the persecution he suffered, but that was all.

He also states categorically that she was never his mistress and there is no reason to disbelieve him. His feelings for her were probably summed up as well as they possibly could be by a touching and revealing note in his memoirs: 'One can experience a strange feeling for a woman, a passionate attachment which is not love yet akin to it, a kind of amorous friendship blended with profound veneration.' Had it not been for his Calvinist upbringing and, above all, for that unfortunate and traumatic incident in his youth with Louise Dubois which had left so deep a scar as to effectively paralyse and stifle all his sexual impulses, it might have been a very different story.

Undoubtedly, their ambiguous relationship gave rise to much speculation at best, and a great deal of slander and poisonous insinuations. It was all too easy to think of reasons for the way things were between them and none of them were to Dunant's credit. This situation was also a heaven-sent way for those venomous hypocrites in Geneva to prevent people helping Dunant financially. Years later, he discovered that Queen Augusta had wanted to help him but the person she spoke to in Geneva, whom she believed would be the man best placed to know, informed her that Dunant was living with a rich mistress who let him want for nothing.

Although Léonie Kastner's feelings towards Dunant are not recorded, her attachment to him was probably partly due to the humanitarian outlook they shared, a characteristic she had inherited from her father, along with 2 million francs. Dunant was also a cultivated, interesting and charming man, the ideal travelling companion in fact. Moreover, in return for her generosity to the Universal Alliance, Dunant had appointed the feckless Frédéric its assistant secretary, thereby providing his life with a pattern and purpose it would otherwise have lacked, and for this she was eternally grateful. She may also have felt drawn to him romantically, but probably realised at quite an early stage that the disparity in their fortunes made any more permanent alliance unlikely if not unwise.

From 1879 onwards, according to Dunant, police pressure applied to him and Madame Kastner by their enemies became so intolerable that they decided to stop seeing one another. From then on, they kept in touch by correspondence. She continued to give him various jobs to do and to send him small sums of money which she insisted he spent on treating his worsening eczema at various spas in Switzerland. During this period, he visited several such resorts, including a little place called Heiden which he particularly liked, and Baden where Madame Kastner visited him and they dined together.

In 1882, Frédéric Kastner died. Disappointed by the failure of the pyrophone, for which he blamed Dunant, he had been going downhill for some time and eventually took to drink. He also became involved with a scheming and spiteful young woman who, in order to safeguard her interests, managed to turn both mother and son against Dunant. Madame Kastner was influenced despite her better judgement. After the death of Frédéric, she gradually severed links with him.

During his last visit to England between 1885 and 1887, she nevertheless asked Dunant to enter the pyrophone in the forthcoming International Exhibition of Inventions in South Kensington. In a letter to his niece Andrienne later that year, he described what a terrible time he had protecting it from his enemies, who did everything in their power to hamper his efforts and damage the pyrophone. In the end things got so bad, he told her, that he had to pay the policemen at the exhibition to guard the fragile and delicate instrument.

While he was in London, Madame Kastner also sent him a considerable sum of money, asking him to divide it between whichever charities he thought fit, a generous gesture which Dunant appreciated all the more because she knew how much he was suffering from the systematic harassment of his enemies, who went out of their way to prevent him obtaining any kind of occupation or paid employment. Nevertheless he did work for a short time with an anti-vivisection society and drafted a brochure for them. She also urged him to take plenty of exercise in the countryside around London while performing his charitable activities. Faithfully he followed her instructions, subscribing anonymously to various good causes in England and buying yet more bundles of temperance tracts which he religiously distributed as he went his rounds.

From then on, Dunant's tracks grow increasingly faint. In September 1886, he spent some time in the Isle of Wight. The following year saw him at Weston-super-Mare; his activities there remain a mystery but probably did not include going for a donkey ride along the beach. At all events, it is the last entry in his 'log'.

Some time later, his brother Pierre in Geneva, by now a successful doctor, received a letter from Stuttgart. Pastor Wagner had died and Henry was at the end of his resources. His family put their heads together. In spite of everything, they decided, they could not let him starve or abandon him to his fate. They elected to make him an allowance of 1,200 francs a year, and thankfully this time it did not get 'lost in the post'!

FIFTEEN

Exit Moynier, Centre Stage

So relieved was everyone concerned that the Geneva Convention had emerged intact from the Brussels Conference in 1874 that nobody dared lift a pen to it for another thirty years. Nobody, that is, except for Moynier and even he did not get very far. His excellent *New Version of the Geneva Convention*, based on the protocol prepared by the Brussels subcommittee, retained all the main principles of the 1864 text but, with lessons learnt from the Franco-Prussian War, included several important and evidently indispensable provisions, notably protecting the Red Cross emblem against abuse and ensuring that troops and civilians complied with the Convention. But national Red Cross societies and governments alike wanted nothing to do with the proposed revision, judging it inopportune, and they were probably right.

Sacrosanct the Geneva Convention may have been but it was not the only weapon in Moynier's arsenal. He also had an excellent outlet for expression and action in the Institute of International Law in Ghent where he was regarded with the greatest admiration and esteem. He decided to approach the problem from an entirely different angle, indeed from an almost opposite one. Instead of trying to persuade governments to produce a convention effectively implementing the laws of war, he aimed to achieve the same results by approaching the 'users' – the troops themselves – and providing them with clear and precise instructions on the ways of war.

The Institute, fully aware of the inadequacy of existing military regulations on this score, welcomed Moynier's idea of a kind of instruction manual for officers and soldiers which, laying down the guidelines for better laws, might prompt the states to improve their

167

own internal legislation and thus eventually have the same effect as an international convention. At least it was worth a try.

Within a few months, Moynier had written the *Manuel des lois de la guerre sur terre* single-handed. It was an admirable piece of work, skilfully steering a middle course between military and humane imperatives, clearly and precisely summarising in a few pages all the written and unwritten laws of warfare on land, setting out not only the rules but also the reasons for them, and all expressed in such a way as to be easily assimilated by the rank and file.

Presented to the plenary assembly meeting in Oxford in 1880 and unanimously approved by the Institute, the *Oxford Manual*, as it came to be known, was sent to all European governments and to America and was soon translated into many languages, even Chinese. It had far-reaching effects, several states incorporating its recommendations into their own military regulations, and aroused widespread interest in legal and military circles. Duke Nicolas de Leuchtenberg, in command of a cavalry division during the recent Russo-Turkish War, expressed his regret that the manual had not existed earlier and deplored the crimes resulting from unjust and unnecessary reprisals that were still the norm.

'Crimes' was almost too mild a word to employ for the outlandish atrocities perpetrated in that Eastern war that began in 1875 with the rising of the Christian communities in the Turkish provinces of Herzegovina, Bosnia and Bulgaria and its barbarous suppression by the Turkish irregulars, the Bashi-Bazouks. A hideous tale of torture, pillage and massacre reached a horrified Europe and provoked Gladstone's famous and well-merited invective: 'Let the Turks now carry away their abuses in the only possible manner, namely by carrying off themselves. Their Zaptiehs and their Mudirs, their Bimbashis and their Yuzbashis, their Kaimakams and their Pashas, one and all, bag and baggage, shall, I hope, clear out from the province they have desolated and profaned.'

This conflict confronted the Red Cross with several entirely new and unexpected conundrums. To start with, it had to revive the Ottoman national society which had died a natural death at the same time as its founder, Dr Abdullah-Bey. Several neutral societies

168

wanted to send relief supplies if only there had been somewhere to send them, others were uncertain whether the Red Cross should become involved in a civil war at all. And what about refugees? Turkish repression had led to an enormous exodus of refugees and wounded to the adjacent countries of Montenegro, Serbia and Austria and the Viennese central committee had opted not to help them. Moynier reacted with a blast in the *Bulletin*: 'It is inadmissible that in a country having a Red Cross society, wounded combatants, whoever they may be, should remain without assistance. The fact that the wounded are insurgents is no grounds for not looking after them. The motives of the Red Cross are exclusively humanitarian and absolutely unconnected with politics. It is perfectly possible to bandage a wounded man without taking sides with him. . . .'

Another problem was whether a signatory state such as Turkey could withhold the benefits of the Geneva Convention from its rebellious subjects. Here again was an opportunity for Moynier to clarify another important point of principle. Unlike a commercial treaty or a postal convention, he argued, the Geneva Convention is not merely a reciprocal agreement between governments whose effects are limited to the contracting parties. It is a humanitarian profession of faith, a moral code which cannot be compulsory in certain cases and optional in others. Rebels should be treated as humanely as anyone else.

Unlike Austria, the tiny state of Montenegro welcomed an overwhelming influx of 50,000 refugees, Christians and Muslims alike, but rapidly realising it lacked anything like adequate resources to help them, applied to join the club of Red Cross societies. After completing the necessary formalities over its adherence to the Convention, the International Committee despatched a mission to Montenegro to create a new Red Cross society to which other societies could send relief, and to organise assistance for the sick and wounded. The three envoys had a most friendly and enthusiastic reception from Prince Nicholas who asked them to take charge of a makeshift hospital at Saint-Luka, four days' hike from the capital. This proved a daunting assignment; particularly in view of it being the custom among their Montenegrin patients to wash only once in their lives, on the day of baptism. But once the new society was set up, help came flooding in from sister societies. A Russian mobile unit arrived and quickly installed a hospital with 100 beds while, true to form, the Berlin central committee sent a gift of 5,000 francs for the new society.

Recognising the advantages of belonging to the Red Cross, Serbia followed suit, adhering to the Convention and setting up its own society. Like Montenegro, it sided with the Christian rebels and declared war on Turkey. It also did its best to respect the Geneva Convention. Unfortunately, the same could not be said of Turkey, despite all the efforts of a small and mainly Christian group who endeavoured to revive the Ottoman society for the relief of the wounded. As its leader confided in a letter to Moynier, the trouble could probably be traced to the emblem and he asked if it would be possible to replace the cross by the crescent. 'I am really loath to raise such a trifling detail,' he concluded, 'but the Muslim population is so immersed in fanaticism that we fear that this trifle may bring obstacles to the success of our work.'

He was scarcely exaggerating the danger. This 'trifling detail' had already given rise to the most appalling atrocities. Enemy wounded falling into Turkish hands were stripped, mutilated or massacred. Medical units bearing the Red Cross flag were fired upon. Before slaughtering a member of the Serbian medical service, the Turks first chopped off his arm bearing the white armband and slashed the Red Cross to pieces with their swords. Such blatant and continual violations of international law were not due simply to ignorance but to deep-rooted, centuries-old, hereditary hatred of the crimson cross that had survived from the time of the Crusades, a hatred which now flared up with renewed destructive fury at what the Muslims perceived as a Christian emblem.

Despite Moynier's reluctance to depart from the unity of the distinctive sign of medical units, there really was no alternative but to replace the cross by the crescent in this instance and diplomatic negotiations were begun to obtain governments' consent to this modification. Russia, which had just entered the war, wisely foresaw another difficulty: the adoption by the Turks of the red crescent for their own medical personnel was no guarantee that they would respect the red cross of enemy medical units and personnel. The Tsar demanded reciprocal guarantees and eventually received formal assurances from Turkey that the Red Cross would be respected.

But despite the red crescent and despite the assurances, nothing changed. After the battle of Chipka on 21 July, *The Times* correspondent witnessed nightmare scenes of mutilated Russians who had been decapitated, their feet, hands, ears, noses and genitals amputated, their contorted muscles and twisted limbs testifying to the tortures of mutilation carried out on living men. One wounded man was still lying on the stretcher where he had been placed, and nearby were the corpses of two stretcher-bearers wearing the Red Cross badge.

The Turkish Red Crescent performed extremely well, considering that it started with virtually no resources of its own, no help from the government and a non-existent official medical service. Soon it had acquired the services of sixty foreign doctors and sent nine field units and a hospital train to the armies to bring the wounded back to Constantinople. At the end of the war, representatives of the Red Crescent who were organising the repatriation of wounded Turks were struck by the scrupulous way the Russian army had observed the Geneva Convention, treating their Turkish invalids with greater care than their own.

The end of the war posed another problem for the Red Cross. Panicking at the arrival of the Russians in Adrianople, entire populations had fled to Constantinople which was overflowing with refugees, thousands of whom were dying daily from hunger and cold. The Red Crescent soon decided that it would help these victims of war in the same way as it helped sick or wounded soldiers and it appealed to the International Committee to obtain help from neutral societies. This was a precedent for the International Committee, which hesitated to mobilise the entire Red Cross movement to help civilians, but not for long. It passed on the Red Crescent's request (which met with a generous response) thereby marking an important turning point in its history: the first time the Red Cross had gone to the help of civilian victims of a conflict.

In refreshing contrast to the conduct of the Turks, both sides in the Serbo-Bulgarian War of 1885 behaved in exemplary fashion, the greatest care having been taken to ensure that officers and troops were thoroughly conversant with the Geneva Convention. The Serbian and Bulgarian Red Cross societies too were extremely efficient and mutually cooperative, treating the enemy wounded as well as their own, exchanging lists of wounded and even correspondence to and from their families. Most remarkable of all was the complete transformation that had occurred in field hospitals. Gangrene and its awful stench were now things of the past. Amputations were rare – and nearly always successful. Only 2 per cent of the wounded died. This extraordinary improvement was partly due to the neutral Red Cross societies which completely took over the care of the wounded and which now employed only highly qualified and trained medical personnel. But even more significant was Louis Pasteur's revolutionary and life-saving discovery of how to prevent infectious diseases. From then on, all Red Cross medical teams were equipped to sterilise surgical instruments and dressings.

Another factor dramatically affecting military surgery at that time was the introduction of the small-calibre bullet which inflicted wounds of a quite different and far less lethal kind. Projected at high speed and with a greater force of penetration, this new, narrower bullet did not remain in the body and left only small holes at its points of entry and exit. Treated with the new techniques, the great majority of such wounds healed so quickly that soldiers could be back in action within a matter of weeks, if not days. Under these circumstances, medical units and hospitals could be regarded as factories for recycling troops and their neutral status merely an excuse for acquiring extra combatants. Observance of the Geneva Convention assumed an entirely new military importance.

Until the end of the nineteenth century, the Red Cross had never actually been involved in naval warfare, mainly because it had not yet succeeded in getting states to ratify the nine naval clauses forming part of the series of Additional Clauses adopted by the Diplomatic Conference of 1868. The Sino-Japanese War of 1894 demonstrated how vitally necessary this had become and resulted in the Red Cross making its maiden voyage in the stormy waters of maritime warfare.

The Japanese Red Cross society, although excellently organised and highly efficient on the battlefield, lacked the necessary boats to transport its sick and wounded back to Japan. It therefore placed doctors and medical orderlies on board warships and transport ships of the Japanese fleet and learnt some new and valuable lessons in the process. Until then, it had always been assumed that naval battles would result in either a trivial loss of men, if the ship's armour plating withstood the pounding of enemy cannon or the thrust of its ram, or wholesale loss through shipwreck if it did not. Apart from collecting the shipwrecked, it was therefore thought that a small medical unit would be quite adequate to treat the few wounded.

During the naval encounters of the Sino-Japanese War, however, it was the light 10 to 15 centimetre-calibre gun rather than the cannon or ram that was the decisive weapon, showering down projectiles that demolished superstructures, exploded in the engine room and started raging fires that left the Chinese ships drifting hopelessly out of control. There were large numbers of wounded and a desperate need for hospital ships. But even if these had been available, it would have been sheer suicide for them to have ventured into the battle zone without the benefit of neutrality. It was to take another four years and another major maritime war before the need for this was brought home sufficiently strongly to result at last in the signature of a naval convention.

In 1898, America went to war with Spain over the independence of Cuba and the Philippines. The Red Cross was immediately involved for, thanks to the untiring campaigning of Clara Barton, the United States had finally acceded to the Geneva Convention. And what a battle that had been. Five years of endless correspondence, pamphlet writing and fruitless discussions with senators who expressed no interest in the matter, partly because some of their wives had set up rival organisations. There was a Ladies' National Red Star Association, a Blue Anchor, even a White Cross Society, but none of these survived for long.

It was only when President Garfield came to office in 1881 that things began to move. In May, the first American Red Cross Society was founded in Washington, with Clara Barton as its President, and almost immediately went into action in the great forest fires of Michigan. Garfield had been planning to persuade Congress to accede to the Geneva Convention in his next annual message, but an assassin's bullet decreed otherwise. Fortunately his successor, Vice-President Arthur, also supported the cause and, in March the following year, signed the Geneva Convention. Americans paid little attention to the event, but there were huge celebrations by Red Cross societies in Europe and, in Geneva, Moynier paid tribute to 'the energy and perseverance of that remarkable woman, Clara Barton'.

Recognising that the Spanish-American War was one that would be fought largely at sea, the International Committee lost no time in requesting the Swiss government to urge Spain and the United States to enforce observance of the Additional Articles as a working agreement. This move was successful and the naval commanders of both powers received instructions to respect the neutrality of hospital ships and their personnel.

In next to no time, three Red Cross hospital ships appeared on the high seas, and a proud sight they were with their white paintwork and red superstructure (as laid down in the thirteenth Additional Article), and their white flag with the red cross flying beside the American Stars and Stripes. The first of these vessels was, appropriately enough, called the *Moynier*, a tribute that delighted its namesake back in Geneva. It was soon joined by two larger hospital ships also belonging to the American Red Cross: the *Red Cross* and the *State of Texas*.

After the defeat of the Spanish fleet, Clara Barton with an American Red Cross team was on board the *State of Texas* as it steamed into Santiago de Cuba laden with provisions and relief. The city was still under siege by the American army and being bombarded relentlessly, but a little detail like that would hardly deter her. Immediately Clara and the team set to work feeding the starving population and nursing the sick and wounded. They also helped the besieging army, which was going down like flies with yellow fever, typhoid and dysentery, as it's medical service was practically non-existent.

The Spanish Red Cross, although unable to acquit itself as successfully as its American counterpart on the high seas through lack of funds, nevertheless performed valuable work in caring for the sick and wounded arriving back from Cuba. The president of the Spanish Red Cross wrote to Moynier: 'The whole country blesses the Red Cross and newspapers of every shade of opinion applaud and encourage it.'

The war between Spain and the United States came to an end in December 1898 and confronted the Red Cross with yet another problem: several thousand Spanish prisoners of war in the hands of the Filipinos. The Spanish Red Cross asked the International Committee to organise a joint campaign by Red Cross societies for their liberation. But the International Committee unanimously rejected this request. Moynier had always held that prisoners of war did not come within the mandate of the Red Cross. The other reason holding him back was that there was still no convention protecting prisoners of war. But this was in fact imminent and would materialise the following year at The Hague.

In 1859, the American doctor Thomas W. Evans visited the battle-fields of the Italian campaign and reported on what he saw in the hospitals at Turin, Brescia, Castiglione and elsewhere. 'Surgeons with neither instruments, medicines or linen, not even a pair of scissors . . . the sight of a thousand quivering forms on every side, suffering tortures to which no relief could be given. . . .' Such descriptions seem to come from a bygone age. Yet only thirty years after they were written, flourishing Red Cross societies around the world were equipped with their own hospitals, training schools, hospital trains and even hospital ships. Great progress had been made in preventive medicine and even the microscope had become a common sight in field hospitals. Gone, too, were those 'voluntary relief workers' with their smattering of medical knowledge, although they had been perfectly capable of holding patients down on an operating table while a leg was laboriously amputated with a saw already dripping with blood. In their place were highly qualified doctors and nurses, trained in peacetime by Red Cross societies which opened schools, built hospitals and organised courses for this purpose. In many countries, the army's medical services were no match for the Red Cross society in terms of either resources or efficiency.

Nor were sick and wounded soldiers any longer the only beneficiaries. The Red Cross had extended its help and protection to sailors, refugees, civilians, and soon it was to do the same for prisoners of war. As well as dispensing medical treatment, it now despatched aid, organised the exchange of lists of wounded and news to and from their families. The network of Red Cross societies had grown wider and stronger. During the recent wars, the neutral societies had played a valuable and important part. Surveying the situation with justifiable satisfaction, Moynier decided the time had come to try once more to bring them together at an international conference.

After several abortive attempts and a lapse of fifteen years since their last reunion in Berlin, he finally succeeded in convening a conference in Geneva in 1884 to which, for the first time, were invited not only delegates from the national societies but also repre-sentatives from the twenty states signatory to the Geneva Conven-tion. Various subjects were discussed but the one that provoked the most impassioned debate was the role and structure of the Inter-national Committee. Some speakers agreed with the view long held by Moynier: the need for a central body invested with a certain authority that was recognised by the governments signatory to the Geneva Convention, in order to create a legal and stable bond between the Red Cross societies. Others maintained that the moral authority of the International Committee was universally accepted and acknowledged precisely because it was completely unofficial and in no way imposed. The International Committee itself had also come round to this conclusion. Finally, despite considerable opposi-tion, the conference voted to maintain the status quo.

Moynier described this singular lack of institutional structure rather well in a lecture he gave in 1891. 'The Red Cross as a whole is something that cannot be grasped. . . . Each state has its own society which devotes itself primarily to the needs of the army and enjoys, in relation to the others, complete independence. The "international" committee . . . has never been invested with any authority and has no statutory functions to fulfil. It exists in fact but not in law and confines itself to rendering the national societies, of its own free will, various services which they very much appreciate.'

Apart from acting as the intermediary between national societies, carefully vetting the suitability of new societies and publishing the international *Bulletin*, one of the International Committee's abiding concerns in peacetime was to protect the red cross emblem which was proliferating in the most unlikely places. Orders of knighthood sprung up decorated with the red cross. Tradespeople seemed to find it good for business. In Geneva itself, a chiropodist displayed the sign of the red cross above his surgery while, on the city walls, an enormous poster advertising braces bore the red cross and even the slogan 'Convention de Genève'!

In 1890, Empress Augusta, one of the staunchest defenders of the movement and founder of the German Red Cross society, died. To commemorate her outstanding work and many generous gifts to encourage progress in the techniques of care for the wounded, the International Committee decided to set up a fund devoted to these ends. The national societies welcomed the idea and already within a year 41,000 francs had been contributed to the Augusta Fund. This started a trend. Empress Marie Feodorowna, another Red Cross patroness, donated 100,000 roubles, the interest from which was to be used to reward inventions to relieve the suffering of sick or wounded soldiers. The Empress Marie Feodorowna Fund was followed by the Florence Nightingale Foundation whose commemorative medal was to be awarded to women rendering outstanding service in the care of the sick and wounded.

By 1898 when Louis Appia died, Moynier was the sole surviving founder member still serving on the International Committee. General Dufour had died in 1875, at the age of eighty-eight, his latter years marred by toothache, depression and acute boredom, kept at bay by bouts of frenetic activity. He had never enjoyed leisure pursuits and was intimidated by women, despite being happily married and the father of four daughters. From all over Switzerland, some sixty thousand people flocked to Geneva for his funeral. Over the next ten years three other committee members followed suit. The empty chairs were taken by five newcomers, all Genevans, all Protestant, and all from the same sort of background: medical, military or legal.

By this time, Moynier himself was slowing down due to age and ill health. In a letter to a member of the Spanish Red Cross society in February that year, he wrote, 'I am going to nurse my larynx so that I shall be able to talk to you because, as you know, that is my weak point and I am usually condemned to almost complete silence. . . .' In October, he informed the International Committee of his wish to relinquish the presidency, but his colleagues suggested he offload all routine work on to a secretary and so prevailed on him to stay. Six years later, he tried again and was again talked out of it. In 1907, he made a final attempt, still without success. Sensing how irreplaceable he had become and how greatly his presence and wisdom would be missed by the entire movement, his colleagues begged him to stay on, promising to relieve him of all administrative responsibilities if only he would just remain president in name and give them the benefit of his advice.

Finally, after forty-seven years, his presidency of the International Committee only came to an end with his death in August 1910, at the venerable age of eighty-four. Moynier's disappearance made a deep impact. Everyone paid tribute to the greatness and importance of his work. The president of the French central committee recalled that it was Moynier who had transformed the diplomatic instrument of the Geneva Convention into the great humanitarian undertaking which had extended its charitable activities around the world. In Chile, the central committee lowered its flag to half mast and shrouded their arm bands in black.

And it was not only the Red Cross that would suffer from Moynier's loss. He had been one of the most constructive members of both the Public Welfare Society and the Institute of International Law. He had also crusaded on behalf of the black populations of

Africa, financing and launching a monthly periodical recording all
that had been done to help Africa and fight the scourge of slavery. He
had particularly espoused the cause of the Congo and was influential
in the decision to recognise its independence in 1885. For ten years,
he was its consul in Geneva and finally had the immense satisfaction
in 1889 of recognising the Congolese and African Red Cross
Association, the first national society set up in an African state.

Although his perseverance, dedication and administrative skills
have never been in doubt, most people fail to appreciate that the
manner in which Moynier master-minded the growth and development of the Red Cross was nothing short of brilliant. He alone
instinctively recognised the hidden, long-term dangers lurking in a
seemingly sound proposal and steered well clear of them – it was he
whose perspicacity dictated the one course of action that would
produce the desired effect, he who resisted easy solutions, convenient compromises, and never conceded defeat.

But despite all his honorary titles and orders of knighthood,
despite the universal admiration and veneration in which he was
held, despite his urbane and benevolent air, he could never quite
shake himself free from that rigid and constricting Calvinist
background that had robbed him of charm, humour and self-
confidence and obliged him to centre his life and soul on his work. It
must have been galling for him to know – and he was far too
shrewd and honest not to know – that the long rows of books he
had written would lie unsolicited and collecting dust on library
shelves while that one slim volume *Un Souvenir de Solferino* would
continue to stir men's hearts and souls for centuries to come.

One can only wonder whether Dunant ever realised how he had
haunted Moynier's life. During his years of exile, when nobody
knew where he was, Moynier must have heaved sighs of relief. After
Baumberger's article and the seemingly endless tributes to the hermit
of Heiden, all his old fears and forebodings were reawakened. When
requests for photographs of Dunant arrived, they were turned down.
When articles appeared, describing Dunant as 'founder' of the Red
Cross, and questions were raised whether something should be done
to put things right, the International Committee voted in 1904 to do

nothing. The news of Dunant's nomination for the first Nobel Peace Prize must have been the last straw.

Dunant had the dream, but without Moynier's administrative skill and his tenacity it might have stayed just that. Brilliant and highly respected for his contributions to international law, he remained painfully shy and was never lovable. He could also be very pompous. Towards the end of his life, he created a shrine to his own achievements, filling a room in his house with medals, portraits, diplomas, decorations and copies of his many written works.

Florence Nightingale died a few months after Gustave Moynier. The year 1910 had already claimed two great humanitarians. And the third?

SIXTEEN

Dunant Wins a Prize

In an idyllic setting 2,000 feet above the beautiful Lake Constance, on a golden summer's day in 1887, an old man with a long white beard and a threadbare black coat walked into the Paradiso Hotel in Heiden in the Swiss canton of Appenzell and solemnly announced that he was the founder of the Red Cross and the promoter of the Geneva Convention. One look at those smouldering eyes and nobody doubted the old man's word. Henry Dunant was given a room with full board for 3 francs a day. On a permanent basis, that would leave him about 2 francs a week pocket money out of his yearly income of 1,200 francs. Riches indeed.

After twelve years of a virtually vagabond existence, a permanent base was what he needed and Heiden had been no idle choice. It was as near to his friends in Stuttgart as it was possible to be while still remaining in Switzerland where he would have no residency problems. It was, too, as far away as possible from his enemies in Geneva while retaining a certain similarity. The shimmering waters of Lake Constance stretching across to the medieval town of Lindau on the far shore reminded him nostalgically of the Lake Geneva of his youth, a lake he was never to see again.

Moreover, Heiden was a health resort, frequented by the rich and famous, and its medical director a kindly and highly able man. Dr Altherr, taking down the details of Dunant's medical history, was surprised to find that this ancient-looking new patient was actually not yet sixty. But he was in a pitiful state, suffering from chronic cholecystitis (an inflammation of the gall bladder affecting the bile ducts), painful eczema of the right hand and almost total physical and mental exhaustion. Thanks to Dr Altherr's expert ministrations, he made a slow but steady physical improvement. And since the kindly doctor often asked him to lunch or dinner at the Hotel Freihof, where all his patients taking the cure regularly stayed, he began to come to life mentally and socially as well. One of the guests at the Freihof was the Crown Prince of Saxony, an old friend whom Dunant was delighted to see and talk to again.

Gradually, he made friends with the local inhabitants and their children and, through them, got to know William Sonderegger, the young schoolmaster, and his wife. In next to no time, the two men slipped quite naturally into a father and son relationship, Sonderegger providing a receptive and encouraging audience for the old man's colourful stories and long monologues, and reaping wise and useful advice in return. Frau Sonderegger and her children surrounded him with warmth and affection and for the first time since leaving Geneva he could enjoy a taste of family life.

Although he became a regular and welcome fixture in the Sonderegger household, he nevertheless spent a lot of time alone in his hotel room where all his old torments, bitterness and sense of injustice reared their heads with renewed force now that his physical strength was returning. The Red Cross had spread around the globe but here he was, its founder, forsaken and forgotten. He determined to vindicate himself, to prove to the world the part he had played, and started to write his memoirs.

Looking back on his years of misery, he analyses the reasons for his downfall with extraordinary lucidity: 'I was misjudged by some and censured over severely by others for errors which arose out of ill-starred and complex ventures, but I was never guilty of deception. . . . It was alleged I was a man of ability but that is quite contrary to the truth. I was the dupe of a burning imagination, of an over-impressionable temperament, of an easy disposition which made me prone to be too trusting. . . . I was taken in and have had to suffer cruelly for my ingenuousness, my incompetence. . . .'

Then he reflects bitterly that if it had not been for jealous enemies influencing the authorities at the Paris exhibition, he would certainly have received the Grand Prix that everyone agreed should rightfully be his as the founder of the Red Cross, whereupon he would have received help from all sides to clear his debts. For twenty years he had worked without respite, in hardship, penury and often hunger, to pay back what he owed. But his enemies had done all they could to frustrate his efforts, to destroy him utterly so that he could never rise again. They even spread the rumour that he was not the real Dunant to deprive him of his fame. 'These thoughts keep me sleepless for hours each night,' he wrote, 'causing a kind of nervous fever that cries out loud for vengeance. . . .'

No doubt it was as a result of such feverish thoughts fuelling his overwrought imagination that when he read about a riot that had broken out in the Tessin, he stormed upstairs to his friend Sonderegger late one night crying, 'The Apocalypse has arrived!' Poor Madame Sonderegger was scared out of her wits and wondered seriously if Dunant had taken leave of his.

From the tone of his memoirs, it seems clear that those diabolical bankers had not only convinced the whole of Geneva, including Gustave Moynier, that Dunant was entirely to blame for their crash, they had even convinced Dunant himself. However did they do it? Could it have been that at the board meeting preceding the bank's liquidation, after soundly castigating him for letting them down over the Felfela quarries, they persuaded him that the best thing for him to do was to sell any assets he possessed, pay the proceeds into the bank and leave the country till things quietened down? All that mattered was to get him out of the way before he could spill the beans in any court case that might arise. Grateful for their 'solicitude', the naively trusting Dunant never to his dying day realised that he had been framed.

In calmer moments, a new and vaguely comforting theory began to take root in his mind. Many of the great men in history had suffered for their greatness, been ridiculed, victimised and even persecuted for their genius by the blind and ignorant resentment of their contemporaries. By no means alone, he was in illustrious company and he eagerly began citing examples. From Socrates to Ibsen and Galileo, from Benjamin Franklin whose invention of the lightning conductor was greeted with gusts of laughter, to the 'public enemy' Wilberforce who abolished slavery in the English colonies, he amassed at least 340 examples and planned to publish a book on these martyrs of civilisation. Needless to say, certain parts of this history read more like his own autobiography.

The owners of the Paradiso Hotel opened a pension at Lindenbuehl in 1890 and Dunant moved with them to this new mountain retreat, a bleak and windswept place that increased his sense of isolation and vulnerability to all his unseen foes. He missed his friends at Heiden and wrote numerous letters to Sonderegger, sometimes with fatherly advice, at other times with angry tirades against the state and Church, the 'intellectual and moral sources of all slavery'. The once devoted churchgoer now declares he hates all Churches, ' . . . the Baptists, the Methodists, the Wesleyans, the Derbyists, the Congregationalists and all the other "ists" under heaven. . . . I shrink in horror from professed Christianity. I am a disciple of Christ as in the first century, simply that.' And one letter ends: 'It is my wish, then, to be carried to my grave like a dog, without any of your ceremonies which mean nothing to me.'

This sudden and somewhat surprising outburst against the Church stemmed partly from his anger at 'those abominable Protestant clericals' who claimed that he had converted to Catholicism to please the Empress Eugénie. There was not a word of truth in it. For his part he claimed that the clergy had been against him in Algeria, particularly the Jesuits with whom the infamous French admini-stration there was riddled.

As his second winter at Lindenbuehl came around, Sonderegger suggested that he return to Heiden and live with his family. Dunant was touched but hesitated to accept. Meanwhile, he heard that a Red Cross conference was to be held in Rome the following April and set his heart on Sonderegger attending on his behalf. But the wretched young schoolmaster could not possibly extricate himself from his duties, even if he could have afforded the journey. In any case, he was far more concerned with his friend's personal plight and took the initiative by sending a letter to the conference revealing Dunant's sorry situation, as well as his active and continuing concern for the affairs of the Red Cross. While this letter created a certain stir, most of the members of the assembly being astonished to learn that their movement's founder was still alive, not a great deal came of it.

Dr Altherr was concerned about his famous patient. The eczema on his right hand was still troublesome, the thumb so swollen and painful that he could scarcely write. He decided to bring Dunant back to Heiden and instal him in the hospital where he could receive professional care. Together with the considerable volume of correspondence he had already accumulated, he was settled in a suite of two rooms – a study with a view of the lake and a bedroom facing south – where he was to spend the next and last eighteen years of his life.

Unlike many other old men who are content to potter their time away, Dunant wasted not a minute. He had so many plans and projects to attend to, quite apart from his correspondence and his memoirs and his programme of self-rehabilitation. He worked feverishly to outpace his enemies, and death itself. Soon after arriving at the hospital, he started work on a new German version of *Un Souvenir de Solferino* with Sonderegger's invaluable and scholarly assistance. But Dunant was an exacting taskmaster and it was hard going every word of the way. One day, a page of the manuscript was missing. Disaster. The Sonderegger home was turned upside down and then downside up, every shelf and drawer and nook and cranny searched and double searched without success, Dunant categorically refusing to admit it might possibly be among his own leaning towers of papers. This trivial incident became magnified and distorted in his tormented mind to the scale of high treason. Sonderegger was banished from his presence and Dunant never addressed a word to him or his family ever again.

At about the same time as Sonderegger had written to the Red Cross conference in Rome, the local section of the Red Cross in Heiden sent another letter to Dunant's friend in Stuttgart, Dr Rudolf Müller, which had a far greater impact. Dr Müller published an appeal in a daily newspaper in Ulm, calling for financial help for Dunant. The local section of the Red Cross society in Winterthur heard about this and made enquiries to Dr Altherr who substantiated the rumour. 'He gets up early every day', he reported, 'and works constantly for the Red Cross, either writing letters or forming new projects. Sometimes he becomes rather over-excited and touchy, especially when talking about his bitter experiences and disappointments. We can't get him to go out; he lives like a hermit in his hospital room.'

Closely linked with the local branch of the Samaritans, the Winterthur section of the Red Cross believed in action. Under the impetus of its clerk, Johann Pfister, another schoolmaster, the section decided to undertake a comprehensive rescue programme. A 'Dunant Commission' was set up, composed of the president, a clergyman member of the section and Pfister himself. The first stage of their campaign was to provide moral support and they began by sending him the annual report of their section together with the then sensational book by the pacifist Bertha von Suttner entitled *Die Waffen Nieder*. In a dedication on the fly-leaf, Pfister paid tribute to Dunant's own achievements which were 'indelibly inscribed in the history of human civilization'.

Touched, Dunant wrote back at once to thank them and expressed the wish to be named honorary member of this longest-established Red Cross section in Switzerland. Eight days later, his wish was granted, an event of particular significance to Dunant who had not been deemed worthy of such recognition since 1876 when the section of Liège had also made him honorary member. The next part of the programme consisted of financial help and here the Winterthur section, in conjunction with those of Zurich and Aarau, opened a subscription for an annual pension for Mr Dunant and the aim of collecting 1,000 francs as a Christmas gift. The response was hesitant, surprisingly sceptical. The Dunant Commission reacted vigorously, protesting that the events of thirty years ago were past history and the need to help a sick and impoverished old man prevailed over any criticism. Eventually, on Christmas day, Pfister was able to present Dr Altherr with the sum of 900 francs for the founder of the Red Cross who had recently suffered a relapse.

The following year, Winterthur again went into action on Dunant's behalf, but this time the response was strangely lukewarm and sluggish, as it only just managed to scrape together the same sum. In 1894, the financial wells of good will dried up still further, yielding only 565 francs. Meanwhile, the Dunant Commission pressed ahead with the third part of their programme: a campaign for moral rehabilitation. To help satisfy the old man's insatiable desire to communicate his ideas through publication, they succeeded in getting a local paper to print a series of articles on the origins of the Red Cross and the Geneva Convention in their Sunday supplement. Then, towards the end of 1893, Dunant suggested that the Winterthur section publish a general review of Red Cross activities in its annual report. Winterthur agreed, little realising what it was letting itself in for. Poor Pfister was inundated with a veritable avalanche of letters, newspaper cuttings and suggestions. The hitherto modest annual report swelled to over twice its normal size. Even Dunant himself recognised the load he was imposing and wryly apologised to Pfister for 'nearly assassinating him with letters'.

Although the two men never met, the mutual affection that developed between them is plain to see in their correspondence. Dunant quickly recognised Pfister's genuine concern and kind intentions, as well as appreciating his discretion and respect, and responded with trust and gratitude. In his letter of 31 March 1894, Dunant wrote: 'I have suffered so much over the last 27 years that you can never know how grateful I am for the goodness and the persevering kindness shown to me by those at Winterthur.'

But this kindness and the exertions of the Winterthur commission were destined to have other, far-reaching consequences. In the summer of 1895, Pfister persuaded the central committee of the Swiss Red Cross society to appoint Henry Dunant an honorary member. The Society for Public Welfare followed suit (how furious Moynier must have been), as did the Alliance of the Samaritans both in Switzerland and Germany. All this generated considerable publicity and came to the notice of a journalist from Saint-Gall, a writer of some standing who had been intrigued by a recent report in a Geneva newspaper saying that Dunant was long dead. Georg Baumberger applied to Dr Altherr to see if an interview could be arranged and, on Altherr's recommendation, Dunant agreed.

The young journalist displayed just the right blend of deference, modesty and enthusiasm to open Dunant's floodgates. Out poured all the stories of long-ago royal encounters, ministerial manoeuvrings, conferences and conventions, foreign enterprises and financial disasters, wartime adventures, the miseries, the injustices and everything else. As he listened to the imposing old man with his biblical appearance, Baumberger knew that not only was this a story that had to be told, it was the scoop of a lifetime. On 6 September, the Stuttgart magazine *Über Land und Meer* (Over Land and Sea) with the largest circulation in Germany published an article full of praise for the patriarch of Heiden. The press worldwide took up the story.

As suddenly as he had been pitched from a life of fame and ease some thirty years earlier into a poverty-stricken existence in Paris, so he was now propelled back into the limelight, the dazed if grateful recipient of torrents of sympathy, recognition and acclaim. Only a matter of months after those 565 francs had been so painfully squeezed from a reluctant public, the Dunant Committee in Stuttgart alone raised 25,000 marks. The Swiss Federal Council awarded him the Binet-Fendt prize worth 1,780 francs, and the Empress Maria Feodorowna of Russia gave him a generous annual pension of 4,000 francs. Even the Swiss Red Cross sent its contribution. All this was very welcome, but Dunant could not help noting in his memoirs that England had given Florence Nightingale over a million francs. At least he could now afford to buy new underwear, pay for the laundry, and enjoy a few luxuries like fresh fruit. Apart from such petty expenses, all the money he received went straight into the local savings bank with a view to repaying his creditors.

At last the conspiracy of silence had been broken, the wall of malice, hate and jealousy came toppling down, largely due to the breach driven into it by the faithful few of Winterthur. Dunant was very conscious of all he owed them and, in a letter to Pfister at the turn of the year, expressed his immense gratitude for the great movement of honourable rehabilitation they had initiated.

On his sixty-eighth birthday in 1896, messages of good wishes came flooding in. Pope Leo XIII sent him a signed portrait. Cardinals and archbishops conveyed their greetings and tributes.

Red Cross societies throughout Europe paid homage, and the medical profession in Russia saluted his services to humanity. Switzerland laid claim to a humanitarian of genius and an ever growing public recognised him as the founder of the Red Cross.

Nevertheless, there were some thorns among the roses. Madame Basting, the widow of his old friend from the Statistical Congress, wrote to him from The Hague, admitting that in 1863 she had suspected him of using the Red Cross to further his Algerian interests. She had also heard rumours that it was not he who had written *Un Souvenir de Solferino* at all, and even that he had bought the text from a French officer and had it printed under his own name. His enemies had certainly been both skilful and assiduous.

The Baumberger article had attracted interest from many quarters, including that of Baroness Bertha von Suttner, author of the best-selling pacifist text *Die Waffen Nieder* and one-time secretary to Alfred Nobel who had invented dynamite and made a fortune from the manufacture of explosives. In Dunant, the Baroness probably saw a useful ally in her campaign against war and in 1896, a few months before Nobel's death, she came to Heiden to see him. Although Dunant was not entirely won over to her views, he was drawn a little way into her pacifist campaign and helped her cause by writing articles as well as propaganda for the forthcoming peace congress in 1897 with all his old fiery verve and inspired rhetoric:

Ah, war is not yet dead! If it has changed its form, it is only to become more terrible. Everything that makes up the pride of our civilization will be at the service of war. Your electric railways, your dirigibles, your submarines and flying bridges, your snap-shot photography, your telegraphs, telephones and other wonderful inventions, will perform splendid service for war side by side with the instruments of human murder. . . . Train your noble race-horses for battle. . . . Train your innocent doves to be messengers of destruction. Train swallows for your birds of war. Use horses, mules, oxen, elephants, camels and dromedaries for military transport and to be your fellows in the field! Use the whole creation for your slaughter. Drive all together with you to the blood bath! But be speedy so that everyone will be ready for the great day of the carnage. Spur on your ingenious inventors who perfect their destructive weapons with such joy and such enthusiasm! Heap honours on them, cram them with gold! . . .

In August 1898 with America and Spain at war and international tension running high, with people everywhere obsessed with fear of widespread conflict and filled with feelings of foreboding, the Tsar unexpectedly called for the convening of a large-scale conference to 'put an end to the incessant production of armaments and to seek ways to prevent the calamities that threaten the entire world'. Pacifists immediately became very excited and interpreted this as the fulfilment of all their hopes – mistakenly, as it transpired. When the Russian Foreign Minister toured the European capitals to sound out opinions, he found no inclination towards disarmament and told Bertha von Suttner that the most they could hope for was to halt the arms race.

Dunant busily involved himself in preparations for the conference at The Hague in May. The Baroness was to be his mouthpiece and he primed her carefully for the role:

Permit me, Madam, to insist very strongly on what I consider a capital point, namely the extreme importance of seeing the Congress pass an official diplomatic resolution on the subject of a *Permanent Diplomatic Commission on Mediation* . . . and for this, personal dealings on your part with the delegates are necessary. . . . Stand firm on the necessity, the urgency, the opportuneness and even the courtesy towards his Majesty the Tsar of a formal diplomatic decision of The Hague Conference, in a 'resolution' to be made obligatory by subsequent ratification . . . It is important to talk the delegates over, to win them one by one, to astonish them by the moderation of our desires and the definiteness of what we wish. You alone, madam, are capable of doing this. . . .

Apparently, he had lost not an iota of his persuasive powers nor budged an inch from the tactics he had adopted to create the Geneva

Convention thirty-five years before. But since then he had raised his sights, intent now on forestalling war, and the conference at The Hague went some way to achieving his aims. A Convention for the Peaceful Regulation of International Conflicts was agreed and extra safeguards for prisoners of war were incorporated in the Convention on the Laws and Usages of War.

At this point, the subject of the Nobel Peace Prize came up and there was lively debate, even controversy over possible candidates. The Norwegian parliament initially favoured Dunant, but it was argued that his efforts had been to mitigate the sufferings of war rather than to abolish it. Hans Daae, the Norwegian army doctor whom Dunant had first met at the Statistical Congress, staunchly backed his candidature, as did Princess Gabrielle Wizniewski and her International League of Women for General Disarmament, of which Dunant was honorary president. The other front-runner was Frédéric Passy, the famous French pacifist and an old friend of Dunant.

Finally, in December 1901, the Norwegian committee awarded the prize jointly to Henry Dunant and Frédéric Passy. They would each receive about 10,000 francs. Dunant was overjoyed and immediately wrote to thank Baroness Suttner who had been responsible for Nobel's decision to institute a Peace Prize, and who, incidentally, did not altogether approve of the committee's choice, reassuring her that all his life had been spent in the cause of international peace.

Dunant not being fit enough to travel to Norway in person, Dr Daae received the Peace Prize in his stead and placed the money in a special account in a Christiania bank, safely out of the clutches of his creditors. In any case, since the money had been neither inherited nor earned in the usual way, any claims they might make upon it would probably have been invalid. As trustee of the fund, Dunant was determined not to spend any of the prize money for his own affairs.

Life in Heiden continued peacefully. The only time Dunant ever left this haven in all the twenty-three years he was there was to attend the first Zionist Congress in Basle in 1897. Now that his bitterness was subsiding, he spent more time in contemplation and study of the scriptures. But his reading also had a lighter side and he often sat, gazing out over Lake Constance, turning the pages of the *Fortnightly* or chuckling over *Punch*. Meanwhile, he continued working on a book that was never published in his lifetime *L'Avenir sanglant*, a dire warning to the world of sure disaster if there was no halt in the arms race. Apart from the historian Jakob Burckhardt, he was the only man in Switzerland to have predicted the First World War and all its horrors.

A new edition of *Un Souvenir de Solferino* appeared and stirred a new generation. Old friends surfaced, like Baron Dutilh de la Tuque who sent long letters from Pau, reminiscing over their adventures during the Commune. Clara Barton wrote from Maryland, predicting that in centuries to come, the name of Henry Dunant 'will be written higher on the scroll and in broader letters than today'.

In 1908, plans were made for his eightieth birthday on 8 May. A commemorative medal was struck in Stuttgart with his portrait and an inscription in Latin. His nephews Maurice and Charles came from Geneva. Wearing a white gown emblazoned with a red cross, he presided over the celebration feast, a frail and prophetic figure, receiving greetings and tributes from around the world.

Physically weaker but now at peace with the world, he made his will (see Appendix V), leaving legacies to all those who had helped and cared for him in the latter years of his life, and a sum to found a free bed for the sick and needy of Heiden. Appointing his nephew Maurice as his executor, he bequeathed him all his books, documents and letters: a substantial heritage for they were piled right up to the ceiling in his study! Shortly afterwards, on 30 October 1910, he died peacefully at the age of eighty-two, leaving instructions that he was to be cremated at Zurich 'with no ceremony whatsoever'.

The following morning, the housewives of Heiden, shaking duvets out of their bedroom windows, saw the local carpenter walking along the road leading to the church, pulling a handcart bearing a simple, unvarnished coffin. It was unaccompanied by a single friend, unadorned by a solitary flower. Henry Dunant's wishes were being observed to the letter.

EPILOGUE

The Situation Today

It's now just over 140 years since the first Geneva Convention was signed in 1864. How have things changed since then? What is the situation today?

First of all, there's been a tremendous evolution in the types of combat. Solferino, Waterloo and all the great battles of the nineteenth century and most of those of the twentieth were fought out in open countryside, away from urban centres, not of course during harvest time when the crops had to be brought in. Bayonets clashed, cannon roared, horses whinnied, but all civilians might have noticed was a faint rumbling in the distance, a few puffs of black smoke. If the civilians did suffer, it was at the hands of the victors after the battle was over.

From the First World War onwards, the introduction of aviation and in particular the airship completely changed the scenario for civilians, bringing them into the combat zone. Hitler's deliberate bombing of towns and villages during the Second World War, to clog the roads of France with refugees during the German invasion, followed by the Blitz on London, Coventry and other British cities, propelled civilians into the front line. Flying bombs nicknamed 'doodlebugs', snarling overhead and then ominously falling silent as they dropped, were specifically aimed at demoralising the civilian population. The mournful wail of air raid sirens, the rush for cover in air-raid shelters and to black out windows, the bombing, the dead, wounded and maimed, the ruined homes, the devastated towns. The culmination, of course, being the destruction of New York's Twin Towers in the World Trade Center, a tragedy from which the whole world is still reeling.

From simply protecting the wounded, sick and shipwrecked at the outset, the Geneva Conventions have had to enlarge their field of action considerably, to cover a far wider range of potential victims: prisoners of war, civilians, children, even cultural property. As methods of warfare became ever more lethal and sophisticated, means of prohibiting unnecessarily cruel weapons had also to be taken into account. Reacting to the initiatives taken at Geneva, Tsar Alexander II organised an international conference at St Petersburg with the intention of mitigating the wounds and sufferings of war by limiting the capacity of weapons to inflict pain, and in particular by prohibiting the use of the dum-dum bullet. In recent years, other Conventions have prohibited the use of bacteriological and chemical weapons, laser weapons and anti-personnel mines. As regards the impact of new technology, technological superiority alone now enables wars in which an army need never set foot on foreign soil, yet is still able to defeat its adversary.

Perhaps most important of all, two additional Protocols to the Geneva Convention, signed in 1977 and now ratified by 161 and 156 countries respectively, strengthen the protection of victims of international and non-international armed conflicts. One does not need a very long memory to think of dozens of such non-international armed conflicts in recent years, sometimes the bloodiest and most tragic of all.

Ethnic and religious differences appear to have become a permanent feature of many modern-day conflicts, although it could be argued that that has always been the case. New actors capable of engaging in violence have emerged, such as kamikaze and other suicide bombers. The overlap between political and private aims has blurred the distinction between armed conflict and criminal activities. The uncontrolled availability of large quantities and categories of weapons has also dramatically increased. Growing reliance on civilians by armed forces, farming out to civilians of tasks that were once strictly confined to the military, and the use of private security companies are also new features in the context of armed conflicts.

In addition to international and non-international armed conflicts, the world has recently been faced with a surge in acts of transnational terrorism, reopening certain dilemmas about the relationship between state security and the protection of the individual. This phenomenon has also led to a re-examination of the adequacy of international humanitarian law in a way not experienced since the addition to the Geneva Conventions of the two Additional Protocols.

International humanitarian law is an edifice, based on age-old experience, which is designed to balance the competing interests of humanity and military necessity. The Conventions lie at the heart of international humanitarian law; there have always been violations and they seem to be growing in scope and intensity all the time. The Tiananmen Square massacre when unarmed students were ruthlessly gunned down by tanks springs immediately to mind. The armed struggle in Chechnya, now in its sixth year, has taken a disastrous toll on the civilian population and is now one of the greatest threats to stability and rule of law in Russia.

Perhaps the most recent example and the one in the forefront of people's minds and in the press is Guantanamo Bay – or Gitmo as it is called by its unfortunate inmates. According to an article in the *Guardian* on 5 December 2004, this prison camp in Cuba is in breach of no fewer than 15 articles of the Third Geneva Convention (see Appendix IV). Without dwelling on the gruesome details, with which most people are now unfortunately only too familiar, the reasons for such seemingly inhuman and gratuitous maltreatment need to be examined. And there are reasons, maybe not good reasons, but then it's not a perfect world.

Be that as it may, the *New York Times* of November 2004, quoting from a leaked report, stated that the ICRC was accusing the United States of using techniques equivalent to torture on prisoners detained at the naval base of Guantanamo Bay in Cuba. In strict compliance with its policy of confidentiality, the ICRC naturally stated that its reports were addressed exclusively to the competent authorities and refused to confirm or deny the information. It did, however, admit to its preoccupation with the conditions and treatment of prisoners at Guantanamo, stating that no acceptable solution had yet been found. As for the United States, which naturally received the report, a spokesman for the Pentagon, Flex Plexico, categorically denied all allegations of torture at Guantanamo.

The alleged practices go far beyond what can reasonably be termed ill-treatment. This is a matter of war crimes. The International Criminal Court (ICC) urges that pressure be brought to bear on national courts. Failing appropriate action, the ICC can be called on. There is only one snag – three permanent members of the Security Council, China, Russia and the United States, have not ratified the competence of this court. All three states are totally opposed to the creation of a superior authority with the power to overrule their national jurisdictions. Were the matter to come before the Security Council, it would inevitably meet with a veto. So the ICC is powerless to intervene as far as these three states are concerned.

Over five hundred prisoners are detained at Guantanamo as I write. Most of them were captured in Afghanistan or in other theatres of the American war 'against terrorism'. The US government claims that prisoners in Guantanamo are not subject to the Geneva Conventions as they are not 'prisoners of war' but 'unlawful combatants'. Article 4 of the Third Geneva Convention defines the categories of persons who may be considered 'prisoners of war'. According to Article 5, 'should any doubt arise . . . such persons shall enjoy the protection of the present Convention until such time as their status has been determined by a competent tribunal'. No competent tribunal has adjudicated this matter.

However, despite the inability of the ICC to adjudicate, there is a counter-balancing constitutional force in the United States. Against the advice of the Ministry of Justice, and the new Attorney General, Alberto Gonzales, the American Supreme Court recently decided that detainees at Guantanamo should have access to American courts of justice. Even within the American administration, opinions are very divided. While the State Department and many within the military are in favour of applying international humanitarian law, the Ministry of Justice, President George W. Bush and the legal advisers to the White House claim that this is an exceptional case because they are engaged in a new kind of war.

Epilogue

This new kind of war is what the ICRC terms 'asymmetrical warfare', a form of conflict in which the two belligerent parties have at their disposal means and weapons that are completely disproportionate. In a war of national liberation, for instance, the state has all the military might, tanks, sophisticated aircraft and other weapons whereas the 'rebels' have to use rudimentary means and have to hide and not wear uniform so as not to be too easily seen.

This is one of the arguments used by the United States administration in Iraq and especially in Afghanistan. It claimed that members of the Taliban did not have the status of prisoners of war because they didn't wear occidental-style uniforms. America is very opposed to Protocol 1, indeed it has never ratified it, because it allows people not to wear uniforms for the reasons cited above. The articles have been adapted to enable such people to fight while still complying with the rules. Articles 43 and 44 of Protocol 1, for instance, stipulate that combatants must bear arms openly while fighting but, once they stop fighting, they do not need to wear uniforms in certain situations. This is what lies behind the oft-repeated excuse of 'unlawful combatant'.

The ICRC was violently criticised in the United States over the supposed leak of this report and after lengthy internal discussions decided to limit its presence in Guantanamo to regular visits, considering that its permanent presence virtually sanctioned these inadmissible practices. In any case, its meetings with top level American authorites regularly resulted in stalemate.

The sacrosanct principle of confidentiality dictates all the moves of the ICRC. It enables its representatives to enter into dialogue with both sides and report their findings to the governments concerned. On certain occasions, the ICRC has voiced its concerns at the treatment of prisoners under US detention and sometimes, but not often, their concerns are taken seriously. Confidentiality usually works well, but it has its limits and sometimes the ICRC is obliged to depart from its dictates and take a public stand. President Kellenberg has issued declarations to the press on several occasions, criticising the US government's treatment of prisoners. Violations have to be serious and repeated for such a course of action to be taken. In an ICRC press release dated 16 January 2004, for instance, President Kellenberg, 'while appreciating the frankness of the dialogue with the US authorities, lamented the fact that two years after the first detainees arrived at Guantanamo, and despite repeated pleas, they are still facing seemingly indefinite detention beyond the reach of the law. He also noted the ICRC's concerns regarding certain aspects of the conditions and treatment in Guantanamo that have not yet been adequately addressed.'

Modern warfare, and particularly what is colloquially called the global 'war against terrorism' makes matters increasingly complex. Given that terrorism is primarily a criminal phenomenon – like drug trafficking, against which 'wars' have also been declared by states – is the 'war against terrorism' really a war in the legal sense? Certainly, 11 September 2001 and ensuing events confirmed the emergence of a new phenomenon of transnational networks capable of inflicting deadly violence on targets in geographically distant states. The transnational, rather than international, nature of such networks is evidenced by the fact that their activities are not as a rule attributable to a specific state.

It would be less confusing to use the term 'fight against terrorism' since most of the activities undertaken to prevent or suppress terrorist acts do not involve armed conflict. The anti-terrorism campaign is being waged by a multitude of means such as intelligence gathering, police and judicial cooperation, extradition, criminal sanctions, economic pressure, the freezing of assets that do not involve the use of armed force.

As already publicly stated by the ICRC on several occasions, it believes that international humanitarian law is applicable when the 'fight against terrorism' involves armed conflict, as was the case in Afghanistan, a situation that was clearly governed by the rules of international humanitarian law applicable in international armed conflicts. But it is doubtful whether the totality of the violence taking place between states and transnational networks can be deemed to be armed conflict in the legal sense.

The problems faced by the ICRC in the twenty-first century are formidable. How can you enforce compliance with the Geneva

Convention by a reluctant state when the major powers refuse to contemplate the existence of a superior international body with the authority to override their national legislatures? How can you enforce compliance in 'asymetrical warfare' when the state has the means to fight with powerful conventional weapons, and is in a position to comply with the Convention, while the other party, with pitifully inadequate resources, is virtually obliged to flout it?

How does a state under attack by ruthless terrorists gather the intelligence it needs to fight them off and defend its people without recourse to psychological and other methods of interrogation that are unacceptable according to the Convention?

When does a freedom fighter become a terrorist? And is terrorism justified to topple an oppressive tyrannical regime? Yoweri Museveni, President of Uganda, was one of the few if not the only leader in history to have fought a guerrilla war against a tyrannical regime and won without inflicting a single civilian casualty.

If Gustave Moynier were alive today, he would not be intimidated by the enormity of the task. If amending existing Conventions and devising new laws were not enough, the man who drafted a substantial part of international law would be capable of challenging the very way we look at the law itself. After all, the Geneva Convention has been accepted and respected by almost every nation on earth for nearly 150 years without any punitive measures to back it up.

Whatever would Henry Dunant have made of all this? He would probably have burst into one of his eloquent and sometimes completely incomprehensible tirades, finally coming to a halt partly as a result of forgetting what he was actually talking about, and partly from sheer exhaustion. He would not have had much patience with the evangelical style of politics now pursued by the United States. You will remember that in his old age, he had turned violently anti-Church. He would also quite likely have produced some highly creative and original ideas to solve some of our modern-day difficulties. But he probably would not have set out on a world tour to canvass Bin Laden and other eminent characters on today's world scene, as he did so successfully back in 1863. On the other hand, taking into account his totally unpredictable and sometimes wildly unrealistic temperament, he might well have paid Bin Laden a visit, that is, if he could have found him.

Dunant would certainly have been delighted to see the Convention he devoted so much of his life and energies into creating and promoting doing so well, and in so many diverse spheres, now protecting civilians, children and cultural assets (remember it was Dunant who more or less sowed the seeds of UNESCO), and of course prisoners of war whose cause he was the first to champion, even to the extent of borrowing a few shillings to buy a train ticket to Plymouth to speak in their support.

APPENDIX I

A Day in the Life of a Delegate of the ICRC

When it first occurred to me that it would be interesting to talk to a delegate about work in the field, and how he or she goes about trying to ensure that the Geneva Convention is enforced, I didn't for a moment imagine I would get to meet such an important, high-powered and charming young woman as Susanna Swann, Head of Operations for the Near East. Based in Geneva where she spends most of her time, she only goes out into the field for short visits. She has also worked in Liberia, Rwanda, Georgia, Israel and the Occupied Territories, Serbia and Kosovo.

I started off by asking what had tempted her to become a delegate. A great many people would like the job but only a tiny élite survive the gruelling selection process. She replied that from an early age she had always been interested in current affairs, what was going on in the world, major issues, wars and conflicts and was quite keen to get involved in some way. Rather incongruously it seemed to me, she read mathematics at university. After graduating, she was still keen to get involved but had no particular qualifications. So she decided to gain some professional experience and apply for Swiss nationality in order to be able to work for the ICRC. (Marrying a Swiss might have been the easiest option but, no, you have to be unattached to join the ICRC, at least to start with.) After the lengthy procedure of applying for and obtaining Swiss nationality, she was accepted at the ICRC, and fondly imagined that she would now be off to Africa and feeding children. Which turned out to have been a slightly naive view of what the job entailed.

A.B.   Your job must be like being a CEO of a big company.

S.S.   In actual fact, work as a delegate at the ICRC, or certainly as Head of an ICRC delegation or as Head of Operations at Head-quarters, could almost be compared to that of a senior executive in a big company. It is indeed a big organisation, employing 11,000 staff. There's a lot of management involved. So you have to acquire management skills, understand about good programming, know how to network with people, learn about quality control, accountability for funds, analysing the environment. Quite unimaginable from the outset. It's a multilayered, extremely challenging and very varied job.

Diplomacy is perhaps the key factor. You meet presidents, ministers, people who have power, heads of rebel groups and suchlike. You have to try and ensure you understand their points of view. You need to take a strong stance and try to achieve what you want to achieve, to get your message across. But at the same time you have to be close to the environment you're in and the people you're with, understand their needs. You have to be able to walk around camps of displaced people and listen to what they have to say. Similarly, when you visit prisoners, you're listening to people, day in, day out. It's very diverse, multifaceted and extremely challenging. There's no end to what you can learn. There's a very strong sense of purpose and corporate culture.

A.B.   Why does the ICRC sometimes abandon ship, letting Médécins sans Frontières move in?

S.S.   When things get really tough, it may seem to the outsider like that. But actually this happens very seldom and there is always an imperative reason. At Sarajevo in Bosnia in the early 1990s, for instance, the head of the delegation was shot and it seemed very much a targeted attack. If you're attacked by design, you have to stop and think again. Security is taken very seriously. Then, in October 2003 in Iraq, there was a bomb attack on the ICRC office. That's a clear message. In such situations, it would be foolhardy to stay at all costs. But even if expatriates have to move out tempor-arily, because their presence is unwelcome, the ICRC always con-siders whether local colleagues, the delegation employees, can continue to carry on without undue risk to their security. This may allow the ICRC to continue carrying out important work, such as in Iraq, where local staff continued to carry out an extensive water programme, whereas expatriates had to temporarily leave the country. There are times when it would be very short-sighted to remain. Better to get out and then return later because if there was a very serious incident, the whole operation would have to be stopped for some time. It's sometimes better to take preventative measures.

A.B.   Which countries are your responsibility?

S.S.   As Head of Operations for the Near East, Israel, the Palestinian Occupied and Autonomous Territories, Lebanon, Syria, Jordan and Egypt are the countries I follow. Each country where the ICRC operates has its own ICRC delegation, whose head reports to the Head of Operations in Geneva. In the Near East, there are 110 expatriate delegates contracted by headquarters and, of course, in each country, we hire a lot of local staff who are absolutely key. In some situations, they have to take over, in any case they do a huge bulk of our work. So I mostly stay in Geneva and the heads of delegations talk to me and to my colleagues here on the phone and we visit each other on a regular basis. I need to go into the field from time to time, talk to people who are doing the day-to-day job, understand what's going on, the constraints they face. There's nothing like seeing it for real. It's like a refresher course. More like a reality check!

A.B.   What is a basic delegate's day really like ?

S.S.   First of all, he or she really needs to understand what is going on politically, as well as from the conflict and humanitarian points of view. For example, in the case of a delegate working in the West Bank, a day's work would include visiting villages in the area he's covering, meeting the mayor, the schoolmaster, families in need, people with relatives who have been arrested by Israeli armed forces and imprisoned in Israel. He or she will try and understand the viewpoint of all the different components of society. Based on that, he or she will come up with a picture of what life is like and this is very much helped by local colleagues who come from the area and who also sometimes act as interpreters. This will serve as a basis to define the ICRC's humanitarian response.

For example, one of the problems in the West Bank is that many families have relatives who have been arrested and imprisoned in Israel. The families are obviously very keen to go and visit them. So the ICRC has set up a big programme of visits. The delegate working in the West Bank will take part in running this programme: get the permits, organise the logistics, get buses lined up, organise the escorting, so that the security concerns of the Israelis are taken into account. This involves negotiating with the Israeli authorities. It is all done very directly. We ring them up, make an appointment and go and see them, ask if these visits are feasible. Initially, we would probably start off with the head of the penitentiary services in Tel Aviv or Jerusalem and filter down to middle management, right on down to the person on the checkpoint so that he (or she) will know that six buses are coming along with an escort and what he's supposed to do. It's better if they know us in advance and usually they do. This facilitates things.

The golden rule that delegates in the field follow in cases of problems is to go first to people in charge closest to the event, then if necessary work one's way upwards, even all the way to the Prime Minister, but it would have to be extremely important or he would become very impatient with us! But we don't only carry out programmes such as the family visit programme. One of the main reasons for the ICRC's presence in the West Bank and Gaza is to monitor how the Geneva Conventions are applied. The Conventions, and in particular the 4th Geneva Convention, define the obligations of the Israeli government as occupying power towards the population in the West Bank and Gaza. The ICRC also monitors the obligations of other parties to the conflict, the Palestinian Authority, Palestinian armed groups, and other civilians. Civilians also have a few obligations.

Appendix I

A.B. What about that famous wall. How high is it actually?

S.S. It's 8 metres high, approximately 180 kilometres long, constructed in some parts of slabs of concrete, mainly it is a wire fence you can see through. For months, the ICRC delegates monitored closely how this construction impacted on the daily lives of the population living in its vicinity. Based on these observations, the ICRC concluded early in 2004 that this barrier, insofar as it deviates from the Green Line (separating Israel from the Occupied Territories) is a violation of international humanitarian law. The ICRC fully acknowledges that the Israeli government has legitimate security concerns and an obligation towards its people to protect them from attacks.

The trouble is that this barrier sometimes does not keep to the Green Line but is constructed *within* the Palestinian territories so that some villages are cut off from each other and some villages are cut off from their land and this makes life extremely difficult for the Palestinian population living in the area. Farmers have to go from their village to their land through the gates in this barrier and that makes life complicated. Each morning you have to wait for someone to come and open the gate. Sometimes they come and sometimes they don't. A farmer may have a crop of tomatoes or apricots or olives that can't wait to be harvested. Families cannot easily access their land, get to the hospital or the school.

The ICRC considers that this barrier is illegal and contrary to international humanitarian law. What we've done consistently, ever since it was planned, has been to monitor how the barrier is affecting the population living close by. Based on our observations, we then went to the different levels of authority in the army, the Ministry of Defence, the Prime Minister's Office and we expressed our concerns regarding the humanitarian impact of this construction. We were very factual and specific. 'Here, people no longer have access to a hospital. Here, there's a village cut off from the school. A farmer who cannot access his land. What are you going to do about it?' This is how we work: a delegate talks to people, discovers their difficulties, discusses them with the team. Then we collate all the

205

complaints and make concrete recommendations to the authorities (in this specific case, the Israeli government). We generally have a good dialogue with the Israeli government. They are always ready to sit down and listen to us.

There was a time when the UN asked the International Court of Justice in The Hague to give an advisory opinion on the legality of the West Bank barrier. People were turning to us, asking what the ICRC's opinion was, as guardian of the Geneva Conventions. In February 2004, we felt we should make our position known publicly. So we published a press statement that was circulated worldwide. It wasn't a denunciation, just making our position clear. But our work doesn't stop there, it's an ongoing process. The delegates continue to monitor how the barrier affects the population, and to recommend specific changes to the Israeli government, in the routing of certain portions, for instance. But what's important is not so much the routing *per se*, but how it impacts on the lives of the people who live in the area.

Under Intifada, life has become very tough on both sides. Very dangerous, very violent and very difficult. And the situation just drags on and on. Gradually, people's sense of hope and prospects just get eaten up.

A.B.   Have you ever actually been in a situation of danger?

S.S.   Well, yes quite frankly, on several occasions. I was in Kosovo when Nato was bombing so I didn't feel completely safe! In Liberia, when rebel groups advanced on one occasion, we had to make a pretty fast getaway. There are many situations when we have to be very careful. That is why, wherever we work, we carefully analyse the security environment and take appropriate measures to avoid as much as possible delegates being exposed to dangerous situations. But not all situations can be foreseen and avoided. For example, six colleagues were killed in Chechnya in 1996, and four colleagues were killed in Iraq in 2003.

A.B.   You seem to stay pretty calm about all this.

S.S. It's fairly easy to stay calm in an office in Geneva. But it is important to stay calm. Security is something to be considered on a daily basis. We have to look after our people, we're not looking for trouble.

A.B. Is it necessary for you to safeguard your privacy for the sake of your own security?

S.S. Not in the sense of working secretly. We seek to operate openly. There are Red Cross flags flying from our offices, open offices, open hours, addresses on our cards. People have to know where to find us so that we can help and protect them. Of course, that doesn't extend to our homes. That's different.

A.B. What would you say is the part of your work that's most satisfying?

S.S. There are many satisfactions and at different levels. When you visit someone who's been detained for months and hasn't seen anyone apart from the prison staff, it's a very special, immediate and particular contact you have. You feel that that quarter or half an hour can be very precious. The main thing is the opportunity to talk in private so we sit in a corner of the cell, or possibly a courtyard, and have a chat. The whole purpose of us visiting people in detention, wherever in the world it may be, is to see whether or not they're being given appropriate conditions and to ensure they are well treated.

Sometimes, in fact quite often, conditions can be pretty rough. The source of the problem varies from place to place. For example, the prison director may want to do better but perhaps he doesn't have the funds, or perhaps he doesn't realise that his guards are ill-treating detainees. The ICRC then tries to ensure that budgets are increased, or to ensure that the guards are disciplined. Prison visits have a preventative purpose: to prevent certain things from happening. And, of course, one of the main purposes of prison visits is to allow detainees to keep in touch with their families. And to register them, so that if they're transferred, we can trace them to the next place they're detained, keep track of them so that they do not disappear.

A.B.　Do you consider that the Geneva Conventions are adapted to the situation today?

S.S.　There are some things in the twenty-first century that aren't perhaps covered by the Conventions. But the Conventions were never designed to cover everything. It's more a problem of compliance, of enforcement. There are some rules that some people prefer to ignore. We are like auditors. We go in, we look, we make our observations known. And we do it so that the governments or authorities involved can take the appropriate measures. And we base it all on good will, i.e. we think that people are in good faith and want to abide by the rules but sometimes they have to be helped to understand which rules apply in a given situation. So we try and give them very practical guidance. Often it works, and often it doesn't.

A.B.　Are all the staff at the ICRC paid or are some staff voluntary?

S.S.　No, they are all paid. They are all professionals. If we want to keep people long enough for them to be fully trained, we have to invest in people, ensure that they and their families are well cared for. And that goes for our local staff on the spot who are absolutely key. In some situations, they have to take over, and in any case, they do a huge bulk of our work.

A.B.　What about donors, all the expenses that need to be covered?

S.S.　Our main donors are governments. As signatories of the Geneva Conventions, they have mandated the ICRC to do its work. National Red Cross and Red Crescent societies also support the work of the ICRC, as do private individuals. It's again a bit like a company. We have to make sure we look for the most cost-effective way of doing things. We owe that to our donors. If they send us money, they want to make sure it's being used in the most economic way. That's led to some changes and rationalisation. The most important factor is that we're doing a good job in the field. Does it have an impact, do people feel that it's worth having us here? That's what matters, and what helps the money come in.

A.B.   How do you define a conflict?

S.S.   An *international armed conflict* involves the armed forces of at least two states. A *non-international armed conflict* is a confrontation within the territory of one state between the regular armed forces and identifiable armed groups, or between armed groups. *Internal disturbances* occur when the state uses armed force to restore and maintain order, without there being a fully fledged armed conflict. *Internal tension* occurs when, in the absence of internal disturbances, force is used as a preventive measure to maintain law and order.

APPENDIX II

The Man in White through the Eyes of Charles Dickens

Charles Dickens was not only a great novelist, famous for the humour of his characterisation and his criticism of social injustice. Under his pen name Boz, he wrote political and parliamentary reports for the *Chronicle*. He was also a prolific journalist and expert at shorthand.

Between 1850 and his death in July 1870, Dickens edited a weekly magazine called *Household Words*. Fairly dreary in design and typography, it was however decidedly superior to the 'penny dreadfuls' and was aimed at the superior end of the market. It had a weekly circulation of 38,000 and lasted nearly a year, until May 1859, four weeks after the start of Dickens's final foray into popular journalism, *All the Year Round*.

At the age of forty-six, Dickens now became a magazine publisher and proprietor in his own right, as well as embarking on a wildly successful series of tours of public readings that took him from Britain and Ireland to France and America. This involved incessant travel, a sign perhaps of Dickens's inner restlessness. He styled himself 'The Uncommercial Traveller'.

When he was back in London, Dickens was busy writing books and articles. A shorthand writer of the time reported that Dickens was an insatiable cigarette smoker who changed his shirt collar several times a day and was always combing his hair, even during dictation. Arriving at the office at 8 o'clock, he was generally tired out at 11 o'clock and went down to his club in the Strand. The major selling point of *All the Year Round* was its serialisation of *A Tale of Two Cities* in 1859. There was great excitement over each

211

new Dickens. Boys selling it in the street were pursued by an eager crowd, just as if they were carrying news of the 'latest winner'.

In the early volumes of the journal, there was also a marked increase in the number of articles on international affairs. Foreign news centred around Italy. *All the Year Round* gave full support to the movement for Italian unification, hence perhaps Dickens's interest in Dunant's book, *Un Souvenir de Solferino*, which recounts the terrible battle of Solferino. He published four articles on the subject, under the titles 'The Travelling Amateur', 'The Orgie of Blood', 'The Price of the Orgie', and 'The Amateur's Task'.

Since this material has not hitherto been published in any form other than as articles in *All the Year Round* and can only be found through research at the University of Basle, I thought it might cast interesting insights into Dickens's character and his perception of Dunant's dedication. So I have selected certain excerpts which are reproduced below.

'THE TRAVELLING AMATEUR'

A citizen of Geneva, Monsieur J. HENRY DUNANT, has lately given to the world a startling book, Un Souvenir de Solferino, in which he details what he saw and did in the Lombard campaign, and what he would fain do now. The work, not originally intended to be published, was printed for private circulation only; but in consequence of numerous applications, and as a means of serving its purpose better, it was offered for sale, and is now in its third edition. As the author waited three years before committing his recollections to paper, the horrors he relates are both softened and abridged by the delay; the reader, however, will allow that enough remain to justify M. Dunant in pressing the question both of the Aid to be given to Wounded Soldiers in Times of War, and of the Nursing to be bestowed on them Immediately After an Engagement.

M. Dunant evidently thinks that he has done, and is doing, nothing extraordinary. There is not a particle of self-glorification in his book. He writes simply, touchingly and heartily; and it will be strange if multitudes of benevolent hearts do not answer to his appeal. He witnessed the Battle of Solferino; he also witnessed its results. A simple tourist, entirely stranger to and disinterested in the mighty struggle, he had the privilege, through a concourse of particular circumstances, of being present at the stirring scenes he describes. Moreover, when the drama was played out, he did not quit the theatre at the fall of the curtain – the closing in of the night. He remained on the spot with a heroism far greater than that of the fiercest combatant, tending and consoling, to the utmost of his strength, the disabled actors in the bloody tragedy.

He went from bed to bed, from room to room, from hospital to hospital, unappalled by heartrending sufferings and loathsome stenches, doing his duty to all, irrespective of nation, as nurse of the wounded and comforter of the dying. Being clad all in white (the heat at that time was overpowering), he was known to the patients as Le Monsieur Blanc. . . .

In the course of the following year, he had the satisfaction of meeting, in Paris, and notably in the Rue de Rivoli, amputated and invalid soldiers who stopped him to express their gratitude for the care he had bestowed on them in Castiglione. All this is told without the slightest pretension, and with the only view of putting the question home, 'Cannot you also go and do likewise?'

'THE ORGIE OF BLOOD'

The cantinières (female sutlers) advance, like well-seasoned troopers, under the enemy's fire. They raise the poor wounded soldiers, who eagerly beg for water, and they are themselves wounded while administering drink and applying bandages. Perhaps these heroic women are the same afterwards burnt by the Mexicans (on the 9th of June 1862), fastened by chains to powder carts.

Horses, more humane than their riders, at every step avoid treading underfoot the victims of this furious and frenzied battle. An officer of the Foreign Legion is laid low by a bullet. His dog, warmly attached to him, whom he had brought from Algeria, and who was the favourite of the whole battalion, was by his side. Carried on by the rush of the troops, he also is struck by a bullet, a few paces further; but he summons strength enough to drag himself back again, and die upon his master's body. In another regiment, a goat, adopted by a voltigeur and petted by his comrades, mounts with impunity to the assault of Solferino through a heavy shower of grape-shot and bullets. . . .

'THE PRICE OF THE ORGIE'

Towards the close of day, when the shades of twilight were stealing over the vast field of carnage, not a few French officers and soldiers sought, here and there, a countryman, a compatriot, a friend. If they found an acquaintance, they knelt beside him, tried to revive him, pressed his hand, stanched his blood, or bound a handkerchief round his fractured limb; but no water was to be had to refresh the poor sufferer. What floods of silent tears were shed that lamentable evening, when all false self-glorification, all fear of human opinion, were put aside! . . .

All the French surgeons displayed indefatigable devotion; several did not allow themselves a moment's rest for more than four-and-twenty hours. Two of them, who were under the orders of Dr. Méry, the head surgeon of the Garde, had so many limbs to amputate and wounds to dress, that they fainted. In another hospital, one of their colleagues, worn out with fatigue, was obliged, in order to continue his duties, to get his arms sustained by a couple of soldiers. . . .

'THE AMATEUR'S TASK'

One soldier has a broken jaw, and his burning tongue protrudes from his mouth; he struggles to rise and cannot. The Man in White moistens his lips and applies lint soaked in cold water to his tongue. Another soldier has his nose and lips slashed away by a sabre-cut; unable to speak and half-blinded, he makes imploring signs with his hand. Le Monsieur Blanc gives him drink, and pours a few drops of pure water on his bloody face. A third, with his skull cleft, is expiring on the flagstones of the church; his companions in misery push him aside with their feet, because he impedes the passage. Le Monsieur Blanc protects his last moments. . . .

Immediate succour is all-important; the patient who might be saved today, cannot be saved tomorrow. Loss of time leaves the door open to gangrene; and gangrene speedily secures its prey. Consequently, there is as crying need of male and female volunteer nurses – of diligent persons, prepared and trained to the duties, and who, recognized and approved by the leaders of the militant armies, will be aided and supported in their mission. . . .

If the terrible means of destruction now at the disposal of nations have a tendency, as is supposed, to shorten the duration of future wars, individual battles, on the contrary, are only all the more murderous. And, in the present state of things, no one can tell how suddenly war may break out, in one direction or another.

APPENDIX III

Chronology of the Conventions and Codifications of the Laws of War

It would be a mistake to think that the first Geneva Convention signed in 1864 marked the starting point of international humanitarian law as we know it today. The first laws of war were declared by major civilisations several thousand years before Christ. Hammurabi, the King of Babylon, proclaimed: 'I establish these laws to prevent the strong from oppressing the weak.' Many ancient texts, such as the Mahabharata, the Bible and the Koran contain rules advocating respect for one's adversary.

Then there were unwritten rules based on customs that regulated armed conflicts. Bilateral treaties gradually came into force which belligerents often ratified once the fighting was over. There were also regulations that states issued to their troops, sometimes being valid for only one battle or conflict. The most famous of these was the Lieber Code which did not have the status of a treaty, being intended solely for soldiers fighting in the American Civil War.

By codifying and strengthening ancient, fragmentary and scattered laws and customs of war, the Geneva Convention of 1864 truly marked the beginning of *contemporary* humanitarian law. The following are the sequels, the main treaties in chronological order:

1864   Geneva Convention for the amelioration of the condition of the wounded in armies in the field

1865   Ratification of the Geneva Convention by Great Britain

1868   Declaration of St Petersburg, prohibiting the use of certain projectiles in wartime

1899   The Hague Conventions respecting the laws and customs of war on land and the adaptation to maritime warfare of the principles of the 1864 Geneva Convention

1907   Review of the Hague Conventions of 1899 and adoption of new Conventions

1925   Geneva Protocol for the prohibition of the use in war of asphyxiating, poisonous or other gases, bacteriological methods of warfare and weapons of mass destruction

1929   Geneva Convention relating to the treatment of prisoners of war

1949   Four Geneva Conventions

1. Amelioration of the condition of the wounded and sick in armed forces in the field
2. Amelioration of the condition of wounded, sick and shipwrecked members of armed forces at sea
3. Treatment of prisoners of war
4. Protection of civilian persons in time of war

1954   The Hague Convention for the protection of cultural property in armed conflict

1972   Convention on the prohibition of development, production and stockpiling of bacteriological and toxic weapons

1977   Two Protocols additional to the four in 1949 Geneva Convention, strengthening the protection of victims of international (Protocol 1) and non-international (Protocol 2) armed conflicts

1980   Convention on prohibitions or restrictions on the use of certain conventional weapons which may be deemed to be excessively injurious or to have indiscriminate effects (CCW) which includes:

- the Protocol (I) on non-detectable fragments;
- the Protocol (II) on prohibitions or restrictions on the use of mines, booby traps and other devices;
- the Protocol (III) on prohibitions or restrictions on the use of incendiary weapons

1993   Convention on the prohibition of the development, production, stockpiling and use of chemical weapons and on their destruction

1995   Protocol relating to blinding laser weapons (Protocol IV new to the 1980 Convention)

1996   Revised Protocol on prohibitions or restrictions on the use of mines, booby traps and other devices

1997   Convention on the prohibition of the use, stockpiling, production and transfer of anti-personnel mines and on their destruction

1998   Rome Statute of the International Criminal Court

1999   Protocol to the 1954 Convention on cultural property

2000   Optional Protocol to the Convention on the rights of the child, on the involvement of children in armed conflicts

2001   Amendment to Article 1 of the CCW

2003   Protocol (V) on prohibitions or restrictions on the use of explosive remnants of war

Appendix III

In 1874, a diplomatic conference, convened in Brussels on the initiative of Tsar Alexander II of Russia, adopted an International Declaration on the laws and customs of war. But the text was not ratified because some governments represented were reluctant to be bound by a treaty. Even so, the Brussels draft marked an important stage in the codification of the laws of war.

In 1934, the 15th International Conference of the Red Cross met in Tokyo and approved the text of an International Convention on the protection of civilians of enemy nationality who are on territory belonging to or occupied by a belligerent, drafted by the ICRC. No action was taken on that text either. As a result, the Tokyo draft was not applied during the Second World War, with the consequences we all know.

THE ORIGINS OF THE 1977 PROTOCOLS

The 1949 Geneva Conventions marked a major advance in the development of humanitarian law. After decolonisation, however, the new states found it difficult to be bound by a set of rules which they themselves had not helped to prepare. Furthermore, the treaty rules on the conduct of hostilities had not evolved since the Hague treaties of 1907. Since revising the Geneva Conventions might have jeopardised some of the advances made in 1949, it was decided to strengthen protection for the victims of armed conflicts by adopting new texts in the form of Protocols additional to the Geneva Conventions.

The Geneva Conventions of 1949 and their Additional Protocols of 1977 contain almost 600 articles and are the main instruments of international humanitarian law.

COMMON ARTICLE 3 : A TREATY IN MINIATURE

In the case of armed conflicts not of an international character occurring in the territory of one of the High Contracting Parties,

220

each Party to the conflict is bound to apply, as a minimum, the following provisions:

1) Persons taking no active part in the hostilities, including members of armed forces who have laid down their arms and those placed *hors de combat* by sickness, wounds, detention, or any other cause, shall in all circumstances be treated humanely, without any adverse distinction founded on race, colour, religion or faith, sex, birth or wealth, or any other similar criteria.

To this end, the following acts are prohibited at any time and any place whatever with respect to the above-mentioned persons:

   a) violence to life and person, in particular murder, mutilation, cruel treatment and torture;
   b) taking of hostages;
   c) outrages against personal dignity, in particular humiliating and degrading treatment;
   d) the passing of sentences and the carrying out of executions without previous judgement pronounced by a regularly constituted court, affording all the judicial guarantees which are recognized as indispensable by civilized peoples.

2) The wounded and sick shall be collected and cared for.

An impartial humanitarian body, such as the International Committee of the Red Cross, may offer its services to the Parties to the conflict.

The Parties to the conflict should further endeavour to bring into force, by means of special agreements, all or part of the other provisions of the present Convention.

APPENDIX IV

Summary of the Four Geneva Conventions

The First Geneva Convention, brought into being by the newly created International Committee of the Red Cross, was signed on 8 August 1864 by twenty-four delegates. Its aim was the 'Neutralization of Army Medical Personnel in the Field', as well as the 'Amelioration of the Condition of the Wounded and Sick in Armies in the Field'.

The Second Geneva Convention was signed in July 1906 by thirty-nine delegates. The theme was the 'Amelioration of the Condition of the Sick and Ship-wrecked members of the Armed Forces at Sea'. The victims of submarine warfare and hospital ships are protected, and medical installations and transportation used at sea to transport victims of naval warfare are protected in the same way as on land. Any transportation used by the Red Cross to evacuate the wounded and sick in naval warfare is protected under this convention.

The Third Geneva Convention was signed on 27 July 1929 by forty-four delegates. The theme was the 'Protection and Welfare of Prisoners-of-war'. In the First World War, POWs were held captive for a dozen or more years and it was their wretched living and working conditions and general treatment that prompted the signing of this convention. The ICRC reserves the right to check up on the conditions of the POWs and to visit them in private. POWs should be protected against violence, intimidation, insults and public curiosity. No pressure should be placed on them for any information. A prisoner cannot be condemned without trial and can be represented by a qualified lawyer in a military court. The seriously injured or ill shall be repatriated.

The Fourth Geneva Convention was signed on 12 August 1949 by sixty-one delegates. The theme was the 'Protection of Civilians in times of War' and contains rules that ensure the safety of civilians in war-occupied territory and those who happen to be in enemy territory at the time of conflict. During the Second World War, hapless masses herded into concentration camps to be tortured and massacred remained unprotected. The Red Cross attempted in vain to gain access to these torture camps of civilians. There should be safety zones for the wounded and sick civilians, old people and expectant mothers. The occupying power should also ensure the adequate supply of food and other medical supplies to the civilians. No hostages should be taken among civilians. Looting and acts of violence are strictly forbidden. Senseless destruction of private property is not allowed.

APPENDIX V

Henry Dunant's Will

I the undersigned, Jean-Henri Dunant, citizen of Geneva, born in Geneva the 8 May 1828, Founder of the universal Red Cross movement, being sound of body and spirit, hereby certify that my last Will and wishes are as follows:

I appoint Mr. Charles Cherbuliez, notary in Geneva, to be the executor of my will, immediately after my death.

I name my nephew, Mr. Maurice Dunant of Geneva, executor, and ask him to come to an understanding with Mr. Charles Cherbuliez as to the carrying out of the following clauses:

1) I bequeath to Mrs. Emma Altherr-Simond, at the Freihof at Heiden, jointly with her husband Dr. Hermann Altherr, at the Freihof at Heiden, the sum of francs: ten thousand between them both, free of all duties, in gratitude and remembrance of their affectionate care during my long stay in Heiden.

2) I bequeath to the sister Elise Bolliger, Superior at the Hospital of Heiden, the sum of francs: four thousand, free of all duties, with my thanks for her good and loyal services over so many years.

3) I bequeath to Miss Emma Kübeli, niece of sister Elise Bolliger, and cook at the Hospital of Heiden, the sum of francs: two thousand, free of all duties.

4) I bequeath to the Hospital of Heiden, in the Canton of Appenzell, in order to establish a 'Freibett', in other words a free bed, for the poor sick of Heiden and the surrounding area, the sum of francs: thirteen thousand (Fr. 13.000.-).

5) I bequeath to Professor Rudolf Müller of Stuttgart, in memory of his fine book published in 1897, the sum of one thousand marks (M.1.000.–)

6) I bequeath to Colonel Dr. Daal Cheef i Arméens Sanitet, 13 Christian August Gade Kristiana (Norway) in gratitude for the services he rendered me, the sum of one thousand marks (M.1.000.–).

7) I bequeath to Colonel Mürset, Head Doctor of the Federal Army, the sum of one thousand francs, in tribute to his publications.

8) I bequeath to Mrs. Vve Graeter in Stuttgart, as a token of gratitude for the services rendered by herself and her family, the sum of one thousand marks (M.1.000.–).

9) I bequeath to the Refuge of the Blind in Lausanne the sum of francs: two hundred.

10) I bequeath to the house called 'La Source' founded by Mr. and Mrs de Gasparin, the sum of francs: two hundred.

11) I bequeath to my nephew Mr. Maurice Dunant in Geneva, my books, brochures, documents, medals, letters, etc.

The sums mentioned above are derived from the interests accumulated from the Nobel donation and are deposited at Kristiana, Norway, together with the Prize itself.

Finally, I entrust Mr. Charles Cherbuliez, notary, to take all the steps he deems necessary for the settlement of my affairs.

These are my last wishes made and given in Heiden, on the second May, nineteen hundred and ten.

Signed: Jean-Henri Dunant.

Recorded in Geneva, the third november 1910, Vol. 187, No 2506.

Received twelve francs centimes included.

Signed: E. Rohr

After everything that I may be owing or that may have been overlooked until the day of my death has been paid, and that the legacies contained in my preceding Will have been acquitted,

I wish that any remaining money be divided, half to philanthropic works in Switzerland and half to philanthropic works in Norway, my executor to whom I give all power to decide which philanthropic works shall benefit.

I wish and intend that my succession be submitted to the legislation of the canton of Geneva, my canton of origin.

Heiden, 27 July 1910.

Signed : Jean-Henri Dunant.

Recorded in Geneva, the third November 1910, Vol. 187, No. 2507.

Received six francs centimes included.

Signed: E. Rohr

APPENDIX VI

US Disregard for the Third Geneva Convention at Guantanamo Bay

Among the provisions of the Third Geneva Convention regarding humane treatment of prisoners of war, which the US is allegedly refusing to apply at Guantanamo Bay, are:

Article 13: Protection at all times against insults and public curiosity. No reprisals allowed

Article 14: Respect for persons and honour; no gender discrimination

Article 16: No discrimination based on race, nationality, religious belief or political opinions

Article 17: No physical or mental torture; no coercion to obtain information. Prisoners who decline to provide information may not be threatened, insulted or exposed to unpleasant or disadvantageous treatment

Article 18: Clothing, articles of personal use, to remain with prisoners

Article 20: Evacuation or transfer to be under same conditions as afforded Detaining Power

Article 21: Internment in camp allowed, close confinement prohibited

Article 22: Internment in penitentiaries prohibited. Every guarantee of hygiene and healthfulness required

Article 25: Condition of quarters must be as favorable for POWs as for the forces of the Detaining Power; allowance for the habits and customs of POWs required. Protection from dampness, adequate heat and lighting required

Article 26: Food must be in sufficient quantity, quality and variety to maintain good health and weight

Article 27: Adequate clothing, underwear and footwear required

Article 28: Canteens must be installed. Fairly priced food, soap, tobacco and ordinary items must be stocked

Articles 29–32: Proper hygiene and medical attention, including monthly health inspections, required

Articles 34–7: Prisoners must be afforded complete latitude in the exercise of religion, including attendance at services, on condition they comply with disciplinary routine

Article 38: Provisions for physical, intellectual and recreational activities

Article 70: Prisoners must be allowed to write to family and to the Central Prisoners of War Agency

Bibliography

Bimpage, Serge, *Moi, Henry Dunant, j'ai rêvé le monde. Mémoires imaginaires du fondateur de la Croix-Rouge,* Paris: Albin Michel, 2003

Bossier, Pierre, *From Solferino to Tsushima: History of the International Committee of the Red Cross,* Geneva: Henry Dunant Institute, 1978 (1st edn Paris: Librairie Plon, 1963). English version: Henry Dunant Institute and ICRC, 1985

Buirette, Patricia, *Le Droit international humanitaire,* Paris: Editions La Découverte,

Dejung, Emmanuel with Siebenmann, Gustav, *Die Zweite Wende im Leben Henry Dunant 1892–1897.* His correspondence with the Winterthur section of the Red Cross. Winterthur, 1963

Deyra, Michel, *Droit international humanitaire,* Paris: Gualino, 1998

Dickens, Charles, *All the Year Round,* Volume IX, London, 26 Wellington Street and Messrs. Chapman & Hall, 193 Piccadilly, 1863

Drew, John M.L., *Dickens the Journalist,* London: Palgrave Macmillan, 2003

Dunant, J. Henry, *Un Souvenir de Solferino,* Geneva: Imprimerie J.G. Fick, 1862. English version 1959, Washington DC: the American National Red Cross

——, *Notice sur la Régence de Tunis,* Geneva: Imprimerie J.G. Fick, 1858

——, *L'Empire de Charlemagne rétabli ou le Saint-Empire romain reconstitué par Napoleon III,* Geneva: Imprimerie J.G. Fick, 1859

——, *Memoires.* Edited and compiled by Professor Bernard Gagnebin, Dean of the Faculty of Arts, University of Geneva. Lausanne: Henry Dunant Institute and Editions L'Age d'Homme 1971

Dunant Maurice, *Les Débuts de la Croix-Rouge en France avec divers détails inédits.* Extracts from memoirs with biographic note by M. Dunant. Paris: Librairie Fischbacher, 1918.

Durand, Roger H., *Henri Dunant et le rôle du grand homme dans l'histoire,* Lausanne: Editions de l'Age d'Homme, 1973

——, *De L'Utopie à la Réalité: Actes du Colloque Henry Dunant,* Geneva: Société Henry Dunant, 1988

Epstein, Beryl and Epstein, Sam, *The Story of the International Red Cross,* New York: Thomas Nelson, 1963

François, Alexis, *Les Fondateurs de la Croix-Rouge,* 1941, Geneva, ICRC, 31pps

——, *Un Grand Humanitaire: Henry Dunant. Sa vie et ses oeuvres,* Geneva: International Committee of the Red Cross, 1928

Bibliography

——, *Le Bercean de la Croix-Rouge*, Geneva: A. Jullien, 1918

——, *Aspects d'Henri Dunant: Le Bonapartiste, L'Affairiste, Le Sioniste*, Geneva: Librairie de l'Université Georg & Cie, 1948

Gagnebin, Bernard and Gazay, Marc, *Encounter with Henry Dunant*, Geneva: Librairie de l'Université Georg & Cie, 1963

Gigon, Fernand, *The Epic of the Red Cross or the Knight-Errant of Charity*, tr. Gerald Griffin. London: Jarrold, 1946

Gumpert, Martin, *Dunant: The Story of the Red Cross*, London: Eyre & Spottiswoode, 1939

Hart, Ellen, *Man Born to Live*, London: Victor Gollancz, 1953

Hashimoto, Sachiko, *Henry Dunant and Myself*, Japan: Henry Dunant Study Centre, 1978

Kastner, Frédéric, *Le Pyrophone: Flammes Chantantes*, Paris: Eugene Lacroix,

Libby, Violet Kelway, *Henry Dunant: Prophet of Peace*, New York: Pageant Press, 1964

Moorhead, Caroline, *Dunant's Dream. War, Switzerland and the History of the Red Cross*, London: Harper Collins, 1998

Moynier, Gustave, *The First Ten Years of the Red Cross*, 1873

——, *La Croix-Rouge, Son Passé et Son Avenir*, Paris: Sandoz & Thuillier, 1882

——, *Notions essentielles sur la Croix Rouge*, Basle and Lyon: Georg & Cie, 1896

——, *Mes Heures de Travail*, Geneva: The Reading Society, 1907

Moynier, Gustave and Appia, Louis, *La Guerre et La Charité*, 1866. English trs., *Help for the Sick and Wounded* by John Furley, 1883

Mutzenberg, Gabriel, *Henry Dunant le prédestiné*, Geneva: Editions Robert-Estienne, 1984

Rothkopf, Carol Z., *Jean-Henri Dunant: Father of the Red Cross*, London and New York: Franklin Watts, 1969

Sigaux, Gilbert, *D'Homme à Hommes*, Paris: Editions de Flore, 1948 (book of the film of the same name by Christian-Jacque, starring Jean-Louis Barrault and Bernard Blier).

Suttner, Bertha von, *The Records of an Eventful Life*, Boston and London: Ginn & Co., 1910

Letters and documents from the archives in the British Museum Library, London; the Boston City Library, Boston, Mass.; the University Libraries of Geneva and Lausanne; La Bibliotheque du Centre Pompidou, Paris: The ICRC, Geneva.

Index

233